ENDANGERED PEOPLES
of Oceania

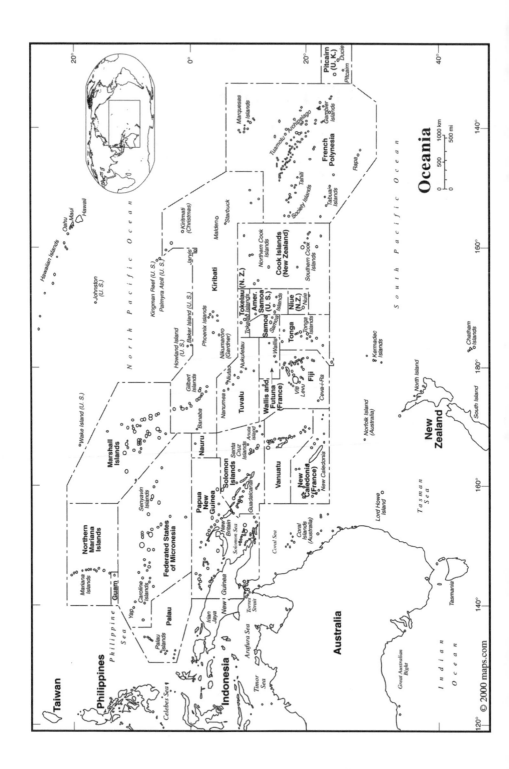

ENDANGERED PEOPLES
of Oceania

Struggles to Survive and Thrive

Edited by Judith M. Fitzpatrick

The Greenwood Press
"Endangered Peoples of the World" Series
Barbara Rose Johnston, Series Editor

GREENWOOD PRESS
Westport, Connecticut • London

Library of Congress Cataloging-in-Publication Data

Endangered peoples of Oceania : struggles to survive and thrive / edited by Judith M. Fitzpatrick.
    p. cm.—(The Greenwood Press "Endangered peoples of the world" series, ISSN 1525-1233)
    Includes bibliographical references and index.
    ISBN 0-313-30640-0 (alk. paper)
    1. Indigenous peoples—Oceania. 2. Ethnology—Oceania. 3. Oceania—Social conditions. I. Fitzpatrick, Judith M., 1948– II. Series.
GN662.E53 2001
306'.08'0995—dc21   00-020468

British Library Cataloguing in Publication Data is available.

Library of Congress Catalog Card Number: 00-020468
ISBN: 0-313-30640-0
ISSN: 1525-1233

First published in 2001

Greenwood Press, 88 Post Road West, Westport, CT 06881
An imprint of Greenwood Publishing Group, Inc.
www.greenwood.com

Printed in the United States of America

The paper used in this book complies with the
Permanent Paper Standard issued by the National
Information Standards Organization (Z39.48–1984).

10 9 8 7 6 5 4 3 2 1

Cover Photo: Kiribati dancers at the celebration of the Tenth Anniversary of Solomon Island Independence, 1988, Gizo, Western Province, Solomon Islands. Courtesy of Judith M. Fitzpatrick.

Contents

Contents

Series Foreword
Barbara Rose Johnston

Two hundred thousand years ago our human ancestors gathered plants and hunted animals in the forests and savannas of Africa. By forty thousand years ago, *Homo sapiens sapiens* had developed ways to survive and thrive in every major ecosystem on this planet. Unlike other creatures, whose response to harsh or varied conditions prompted biological change, humans generally relied upon their ingenuity to survive. They fashioned clothing from skins and plant fiber rather than growing thick coats of protective hair. They created innovative ways to live and communicate and thus passed knowledge down to their children. This knowledge, by ten thousand years ago, included the means to cultivate and store food. The ability to provide for lean times allowed humans to settle in larger numbers in villages, towns, and cities where their ideas, values, ways of living, and language grew increasingly complicated and diverse.

This cultural diversity—the multitude of ways of living and communicating knowledge—gave humans an adaptive edge. Other creatures adjusted to change in their environment through biological adaptation (a process that requires thousands of life spans to generate and reproduce a mutation to the level of the population). Humans developed analytical tools to identify and assess change in their environment, to search out or devise new strategies, and to incorporate new strategies throughout their group. Sometimes these cultural adaptations worked; people transformed their way of life, and their population thrived. Other times, these changes produced further complications.

Intensive agricultural techniques, for example, often resulted in increased salts in the soil, decreased soil fertility, and declining crop yields. Food production declined, and people starved. Survivors often moved to new regions to begin again. Throughout human history, migration became the common strategy when innovations failed. Again, in these times, culture was essential to survival.

For the human species, culture is our primary adaptive mechanism. Cultural diversity presents us with opportunities to draw from and build upon a complicated array of views, ideas, and strategies. The Endangered Peoples of the World series celebrates the rich diversity of cultural groups living on our planet and explores how cultural diversity, like biological diversity, is threatened.

Five hundred years ago, as humans entered the age of colonial expansion, there were an estimated twelve to fourteen thousand cultural groups with distinct languages, values, and ways of life. Today, cultural diversity has been reduced by half (an estimated 6,000 to 7,000 groups). This marked decline is due in part to the fact that, historically, isolated peoples had minimal immunity to introduced diseases and little time to develop immunological defenses. Colonizers brought more than ideas, religion, and new economic ways of living. They brought a host of viruses and bacteria— measles, chicken pox, small pox, the common cold. These diseases swept through "new" worlds at epidemic levels and wiped out entire nations. Imperialist expansion and war further decimated original, or "indigenous," populations.

Today's cultural diversity is further threatened by the biodegenerative conditions of nature. Our biophysical world's deterioration is evidenced by growing deserts; decreasing forests; declining fisheries; poisoned food, water, and air; and climatic extremes and weather events such as floods, hurricanes, and droughts. These degenerative conditions challenge our survival skills, often rendering customary knowledge and traditions ineffective.

Cultural diversity is also threatened by unparalleled transformations in human relations. Isolation is no longer the norm. Small groups continually interact and are subsumed by larger cultural, political, and economic groups of national and global dimensions. The rapid pace of change in population, technology, and political economy leaves little time to develop sustainable responses and adjust to changing conditions.

Across the world cultural groups are struggling to maintain a sense of unique identity while interpreting and assimilating an overwhelming flow of new ideas, ways of living, economies, values, and languages. As suggested in some chapters in this series, cultural groups confront, embrace, adapt, and transform these external forces in ways that allow them to survive and thrive. However, in far too many cases, cultural groups lack the time and means to adjust and change. Rather, they struggle to retain the right to simply exist as other, more powerful peoples seize their land and resources and "cleanse" the countryside of their presence.

Efforts to gain control of land, labor, and resources of politically and/or geographically peripheral peoples are justified and legitimized by ethnocentric notions: the beliefs that the values, traditions, and behavior of your own cultural group are superior and that other groups are biologically, culturally, and socially inferior. These notions are produced and reproduced in conversation, curriculum, public speeches, articles, television coverage, and other communication forums. Ethnocentrism is reflected in a language of debasement that serves to dehumanize (the marginal peoples are considered sub-human: primitive, backward, ignorant people that "live like animals"). The pervasiveness of this discourse in the everyday language can eventually destroy the self-esteem and sense of worth of marginal groups and reduce their motivation to control their destiny.

Thus, vulnerability to threats from the biophysical and social realms is a factor of social relations. Human action and a history of social inequity leave some people more vulnerable than others. This vulnerability results in ethnocide (loss of a way of life), ecocide (destruction of the environment), and genocide (death of an entire group of people).

The Endangered Peoples of the World series samples cultural diversity in different regions of the world, examines the varied threats to cultural survival, and explores some of the ways people are adjusting and responding to threats of ethnocide, ecocide, and genocide. Each volume in the series covers the peoples, problems, and responses characteristic of a major region of the world: the Arctic, Europe, North America and the Caribbean, Latin America, Africa and the Middle East, Central and South Asia, Southeast and East Asia, and Oceania. Each volume includes an introductory essay authored by the volume editor and fifteen or so chapters, each featuring a different cultural group whose customs, problems, and responses represent a sampling of conditions typical of the region. Chapter content is organized into five sections: Cultural Overview (people, setting, traditional subsistence strategies, social and political organization, religion and world view), Threats to Survival (demographic trends, current events and conditions, environmental crisis, sociocultural crisis), Response: Struggles to Survive Culturally (indicating the variety of efforts to respond to threats), Food for Thought (a brief summary of the issues raised by the case and some provocative questions that can be used to structure class discussion or organize a research paper), and a Resource Guide (major accessible published sources, films and videos, Internet and WWW sites, and organizations). Many chapters are authored or coauthored by members of the featured group, and all chapters include liberal use of a "local voice" to present the group's own views on its history, current problems, strategies, and thoughts of the future.

Collectively, the series contains some 120 case-specific examples of cultural groups struggling to survive and thrive in a culturally diverse world. Many of the chapters in this global sampling depict the experiences of indigenous peoples and ethnic minorities who, until recently, sustained their customary way of life in the isolated regions of the world. Threats to survival are often linked to external efforts to develop the natural resources of the previously isolated region. The development context is often one of co-optation of traditionally held lands and resources with little or no recognition of resident peoples' rights and little or no compensation for their subsequent environmental health problems. New ideas, values, technologies, economies, and languages accompany the development process and, over time, may even replace traditional ways of being.

Cultural survival, however, is not solely a concern of indigenous peoples. Indeed, in many parts of the world the term "indigenous" has little relevance, as all peoples are native to the region. Thus, in this series, we define cultural groups in the broadest of terms. We examine threats to survival and the variety of responses of ethnic minorities, as well as national cultures, whose traditions are challenged and undermined by global transformations.

The dominant theme that emerges from this sampling is that humans struggle with serious and life-threatening problems tied to larger global forces, and yet, despite huge differences in power levels between local communities and global institutions and structures, people are crafting and developing new ways of being. This series demonstrates that culture is not a static set of meanings, values, and behaviors; it is a flexible, resilient tool that has historically provided humans with the means to adapt, adjust, survive, and, at times, thrive. Thus, we see "endangered" peoples confronting and responding to threats in ways that reshape and transform their values, relationships, and behavior.

Emerging from this transformative process are new forms of cultural identity, new strategies for living, and new means and opportunities to communicate. These changes represent new threats to cultural identity and autonomy but also new challenges to the forces that dominate and endanger lives.

Introduction

Judith M. Fitzpatrick

Endangered Peoples of Oceania: Struggles to Survive and Thrive is about human populations residing in Oceania, a region that incorporates nearly thirty thousand islands and the continent of Australia. It is situated within and on the edges of the largest geographical feature in the world, the Pacific Ocean (well over sixty-three million square miles), which covers at least a third of the world's surface. Cultural identity is closely connected with place in Oceania, and almost every physical feature on the land and in the marine realm is named, telling a story about the heritage of the people. Over the generations, nearly every square inch of most islands has been transformed by cultural and subsistence activities so that the present-day cultural landscape of Oceania is a domain rich in meaning and significance. Many Pacific Islands and parts of Australia are home to newly incorporated societies struggling with multiple and conflicting economic, sociopolitical, and environmental problems. The cultural robustness of local culture groups is threatened by many facets of the larger world. Accounts of these peoples and the threats to cultural integrity and the environment are the focus of this volume. The various responses throughout Oceania described here provide illustrations of survival in the modern world.

CULTURE GROUPS

From the 1500s, early European explorers to the Pacific, including Vasco Núñez de Balboa, Ferdinand Magellan, Luiz Baez de Torres, Abel Janszoon Tasman, William Dampier, and James Cook, encountered and described the peoples of Oceania. One group in particular stood out, those now referred to as the *Polynesians*, or "people of many islands." They were the first navigators in the region traveling west across the Pacific more than two thousand years ago to the eastern archipelagos of Tahiti, including the Marquesas, and Hawaii. Later, their ancestors navigated back westward to inhabit numerous small and isolated islands throughout the Pacific, and to the large island of New Zealand, home of the Maori. All of these Polynesians have similar languages and a generally homogeneous cultural heritage. Early images of the peoples of these islands in paintings provide models for our impressions of the South Pacific even today.

Two other major cultural groups are also distinguished in the Pacific Islands: the Micronesians, or "the people of many small islands," and the Melanesians, or "the people of the dark islands," or the dark people. Distinctive from the Polynesians, both of these groups are likewise dissimilar among themselves in terms of language, sociopolitical organization, and physical attributes. For instance, on the one island of New Guinea, hundreds of distinct languages exist, in contrast to the homogeneous Polynesian vernaculars (e.g., Hawaiian, Tahitian, and Maori) spoken across an immense geographic area of the Pacific. At the time of the European contact, however, the three groups—Micronesians, Melanesians, and Polynesians—did practice similar subsistence strategies and utilized uniform gardening and fishing technology. Chapters in this volume describe societies from each of these culture groups of Oceania.

In the far west of Oceania, on the continent of Australia, there exists yet another geographically dispersed group. At contact by Europeans, the Aboriginal peoples were distinctive from island peoples in their language, political organizations, subsistence practices, and physical attributes. The Aboriginals are now believed to be the oldest peoples (forty thousand or more years) in the entire region. They have an ancient and common mythological past, popularly known as the "dreaming," that transcends thousands of miles across sparsely populated and, in places, harsh landscapes on the continent of Australia. The present-day circumstances for the Aboriginal peoples, who include hundreds of tribal identities with distinct languages and territory, are contentious. Aboriginal people have existed as an underclass on their own land since the 1800s, when outsiders, primarily from the United Kingdom, settled in Australia. British law superseded all local customary law and left the original inhabitants without land tenure. Chapters in this volume describe Aboriginal history and the recent situation, which includes legislation overturning British law (see chapters 1, 15, and 16).

DEVELOPMENT IN OCEANIA

Oceania was one of the last frontiers of European colonialism; indeed, Australia, the missing continent, was not "discovered" by Cook until 1776. Exploration and first contact with cultural groups were still taking place as recently as 1960 on the largest island in the region, New Guinea (see chapter 4). It was divided into two political entities, Irian Jaya, a province of Indonesia, and Papua New Guinea (PNG), the most populous nation state in the Pacific. Over the past thirty years there has been a rush to exploit the abundant and rich natural resources, including hardwoods, other tropical forest products, and minerals and ores (see chapter 8 and chapter 10). By the close of the twentieth century PNG was designated a bio-diversity hot spot because of the number and density of species, many still not recorded. The widespread and uncontrolled development that threatens many of these species of plants and animals has promoted intense activism by environmental groups wanting to curtail logging and mining. Local people's rights have very often been overlooked and disputes, in some cases leading to armed combat, have erupted. Details of the struggles by local owners are presented in the chapters about mining in Bougainville and Ok Tedi and those focusing on social and cultural change in small village settings (see chapters 4, 8, 10, and 14).

What comes to mind for many readers when imagining Oceania are the cultures of Hawaii and Tahiti. They have been portrayed as romantic, beautiful island paradises in history books, novels, and films. This makes these places magnets for tourists, and, as a result, much of their present-day economies depends on money generated by visitors seeking idyllic holidays. However, the economic and political situations in these island societies, as among many others in the Pacific region, are not so tranquil for the local people. Disputes over sovereignty and control of local resources dominate the political arena. Reference materials on Hawaii and Tahiti are readily available and may be used for comparison with other, less well known Polynesian societies such as the Marquesas and Anuta (see chapters 2 and 6). These islands, examined in depth in the volume, have major threats to their cultures and environments, including political power, overpopulation, migration, and isolation.

Tourism is becoming more prevalent in other parts of the Pacific too as countless development schemes emerge. In Melanesia and Micronesia eco-tourism (low impact nature tourism) is popular. Observation of local customs by tourists provides unique adventures for those visiting Vanuatu (see chapter 13). Elsewhere, in Micronesia, holidays for scuba divers have become popular near the waters polluted by nuclear tests (see chapter 5). Palau provides tourists with a diving holiday in marine sanctuaries with protected marine species and unique rock formations above and below water (see chapter 9). These chapters describe how new economic ventures influence local cultural custom and introduce new knowledge and ideas.

SURVIVAL AND IDENTITY

Understanding more about the Pacific and the ecological setting provides a perspective on how the first peoples survived in this region. The range in local plants and other species varies greatly from island to island. As one moves eastward from a rich bio-diversity zone like the large island of New Guinea across the Pacific to the western Hawaiian island chain, a drastic reduction in the number of plant and animal species is evident. Similarly, on many of the small atolls throughout the Pacific there are very few types of plants even though there appears to be lush vegetation. This pattern influenced the choice made during the first human settlement on islands and on the continent of Australia. Still, the environment continues to define whether a society today is sustainable in the modern world. Many of the cultures described in the following chapters exist in limited environmental settings and are struggling to be economically independent and autonomous while maintaining their own distinctive cultural traditions.

Migration and cultural diversity are facts in the Oceania cultural region. As a process migration has had a profound effect in defining the region since humans first inhabited the islands. Today, however, the cultural identity of migrants within adopted homelands has become a controversial issue. In this volume, there are accounts of migrants who were imported as contract laborers during the late colonial period to Fiji and Queensland, Australia (see chapters 3 and 12) and recently in Palau, where migrants arrived and threatened the maintenance of cultural patterns (see chapter 9). There are also stories of other migrants who moved from remote islands to regional cities as a result of war, natural disasters, nuclear pollution, overpopulation, or lack of services (see chapters 2, 5, 8, 11, and 15). The challenge of outside ideas is a major threat that each culture manages in its own unique manner (see chapters 9, 11, 12, and 14).

Historians suggest that the death of Captain Cook in the Hawaiian Islands, at the close of the 1700s, symbolically marked the beginning of the colonial period during which the peoples of Oceania were exposed to European culture. Disease and later firearms contributed to major population reduction among numerous culture groups. Astoundingly, some groups in the region are still today entangled in the decolonization process (see chapters 1, 7, and 14). Some of the chapters in this volume are about territories and regions that are part of large nation states or about provinces in newly emergent and struggling island states (see chapters 4, 6, 8, 10, 14, and 15). In cases like those of Bougainville and Torres Strait, contemporary political status is simply the result of lines drawn on colonial maps hundreds of years ago. Other chapters describe small island emergent nation states in Micronesia striving for autonomy in the post–World War II and nuclear-testing era (see chapters 7 and 9). Pacific scholars conclude that the contact histories and colonization period of the Pacific islands have in general many commonalities: missionaries and religious conversion, traders and resource exploitation, and a world war. As already pointed out, the islands of the Pacific are not really like the images early explorers portrayed or travel agents try to sell—a magical paradise of white sand beaches with gentle breezes rustling the coconut palms while friendly, smiling natives fish in aquamarine lagoons. Instead, the region is the most affected of all places on the planet by the nuclear arms race; it is a dumping ground for residues of mining operations; and its waters are continually fished illegally. The threats to cultural survival generated by interaction with the larger world and dependency on development schemes and the aid dollar are the focus of this volume. The cases presented here illuminate how changes modify the cultural character and environment of Oceania.

Chapter 1

The Aboriginal Peoples of Cape York Peninsula, Australia

David F. Martin

CULTURAL OVERVIEW

Cape York Peninsula is a sparsely populated region of northern Queensland, Australia, situated directly south of the Torres Strait and New Guinea. Many non-Aboriginal Australians see it as the "last frontier," a vast and remote wilderness. However, for thousands of Aboriginal people it is home, and the issues raised by increasing development pressures, intervention by government, and more general encroachment by the institutions and values of Western society pose major dilemmas for the long-term viability of their societies.

The People

Aboriginal people have lived on Cape York Peninsula for at least thirteen thousand years, their occupation predating the separation of Australia from New Guinea with rising sea levels. Although there are broad cultural similarities among the various Cape York Aboriginal groups, there is also considerable social, cultural, and linguistic diversity. The seafaring peoples of the northeast coast exploit the rich coastal and marine environment and have strong ceremonial and other links with the Melanesian peoples of the Torres Strait. Groups from the west coast and from Princess Charlotte Bay on the east coast, who exploit the complex coastal and hinterland environment, are more socially segmented, have richer ritual traditions, and speak a greater diversity of languages than those from the less ecologically diverse inland regions.

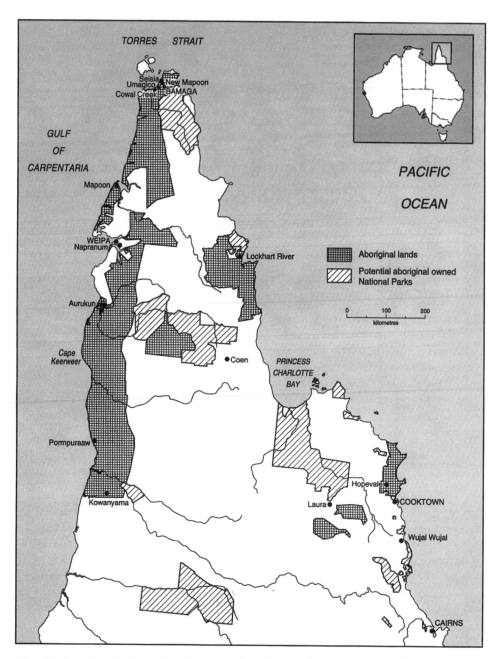

Cape York Peninsula, Australia, showing major Aboriginal communities and lands. Courtesy of David F. Martin.

The Setting

Cape York peninsula has a tropical environment with a monsoon climate characterized by distinct wet and dry seasons, and a range of diverse eco-systems that has supported a relatively large Aboriginal population. The peninsula is transected by several major river systems that flood during the annual monsoons. The east coast is characterized by reefs, islands, mangrove estuaries, extensive dune systems, beaches, and thick coastal scrubs, with dense monsoon rain forests covering parts of the ranges lying immediately inland. This contrasts with the flat western coast, where there are large rivers draining through serpentine windings into extensive mangrove estuaries, saltpans, large regions of low coastal dune systems, seasonally inundated grass plains, and lagoons. The richer and more predictable resources of the coastal regions meant that there was a higher Aboriginal population density originally here than in the less ecologically diverse central, inland areas. Most Aboriginal residents of the region now live in townships near the coast.

Traditional Subsistence Strategies

Cape York Aboriginal peoples combined hunter-gatherer technology with highly detailed environmental knowledge to sustain relatively large and sedentary populations, particularly in the coastal regions. Technology included items such as spears and spear throwers, hafted stone axes, scrapers, digging sticks, woven bags, baskets, and fishing nets. There was considerable regional diversity, in both artistic and utilitarian terms, in their construction.

For both coastal and inland peoples, vegetables formed a major food source. For coastal peoples, yams and a wide variety of edible seasonal fruits and berries provided a highly predictable and stable resource base. Such foods were less plentiful inland, with swamps, lagoons, and river and creek systems being the focal points of resource exploitation for inland peoples. Gallery forests along the river systems were significant sources of yams, fruits, and berries. Honey from stingless native bees was an important and highly prized food for inland peoples particularly.

The seafaring peoples of the northeast and eastern coasts built dugout canoes with single or double outriggers and used harpoons with detachable heads to hunt turtle and dugong (sea cow). For all coastal peoples, the estuaries were a rich source of crustaceans and shellfish, and shallow coastal waters and rivers teemed with fish, including barramundi and colonial salmon, which were speared, trapped, or netted. Breeding grounds for magpie geese and an abundant seasonal supply of their eggs were available in some coastal areas. For inland peoples, the lagoons, rivers, and creeks provided numerous varieties of freshwater fish, swamp turtle, and

3

Wuthathi elder Gordon Pablo using digging stick for yams at Shelburne Bay, eastern Cape York, Queensland, Australia. Courtesy of Kerry Trapnell, Cairns.

reptiles. Throughout the region, game animals such as various species of duck, geese, ibis, brolga, and fruit bats were hunted. They, along with reptiles and freshwater turtles, provided important, although seasonally and geographically variable, sources of food. In the late dry season, neighboring groups would cooperate to use fire in game drives for kangaroo and other marsupials such as wallabies and bandicoot.

Social and Political Organization

Features of Cape York Aboriginal societies include strongly asserted egalitarian ideals and a high value placed upon individual autonomy. Politics is nonetheless intense and is characterized by negotiability and by a strong emphasis on local factors rather than regional ones. Kinship forms a core means through which social, political, and economic relations are organized, and although there have been significant social and cultural changes since colonization last century, kinship is still central to everyday life.

The basic political units today are not communities, language groups, tribes, or clans as such, but context-dependent groupings based on such factors as kinship and marriage relationships, ritual cult affiliation, and area of origin. The basic dichotomy between inland and coastal groups also continues to provide a core dynamic to social and political life. Although there are few long-lasting hierarchies—for example, there is no

4

equivalent to a chiefly class—there is intense struggle for leadership and status centering on the control of land and ritual, other resources, and women's sexuality. Contemporary prominence, however, is increasingly based on the control of service-delivery and representative organizations, cash, and consumer goods rather than of indigenous ritual. New forms of group and corporate structures are emerging, centered around such activities as work, alcohol consumption, and the administrative and governing bodies instituted in the settlements.

Religion and World View

Religion for the Cape York peoples as for other Australian Aboriginal groups derives ultimately from the land, and mythology, songs, and dances are rich in its imagery. The landscape itself and "culture" (in its broad sense, including such features as the placing of groups in identified territories; ritual; language; principles of social, economic, and political relationships; as well as aesthetic traditions such as body paint designs) are seen as having been "left" for Aboriginal groups by heroic totemic figures in the creation period. These beings traveled the land, creating its form, naming its places and infusing them with significance, assigning areas to each clan, and leaving spiritual power in totemic centers. This period of heroic exploits is understood as being just beyond living memory, and its power can be brought into the right ordering of the present-day world through the performance of various rituals. Thus, although Cape York Aboriginal peoples are highly pragmatic and intensely political, society is not simply understood as being created by humans, and neither is landscape seen just as real estate.

Many Cape York Aboriginal people now profess Christianity, although its significance has declined in the last two generations since the missions have been replaced with secular administrations. At the same time, the centrality and relevance of the original indigenous belief systems themselves are under threat in an increasingly secular and dislocated contemporary world.

THREATS TO SURVIVAL

Cape York Aboriginal people find themselves in a situation of both great potential and serious threat. They have a significant demographic presence in the region, control large areas of environmentally and culturally significant lands, and despite severe social problems maintain distinct and vital cultures. These factors arguably provide them with major means with which to negotiate a meaningful place in the region and the wider Australian society. At the same time, the rapidly increasing penetration of the ideas, values, and institutions of the dominant society, and its deeply entrenched hostility to Aboriginal rights, pose major problems for the region's Aboriginal population.

Dispossession

The first recorded contact with Europeans in the region was with the Dutch on the west coast in the seventeenth century, and there had long been links between the northern coastal peoples and the distinct indigenous peoples of the Torres Strait. Destructive contact in the colonial period began with trepang (sea slug) and pearl shell fishermen on the northern coasts from the 1860s, and inland with the discovery of a number of gold deposits from the 1870s, which drew a major influx of both Chinese and Europeans to the southern and central areas of the Cape. The construction of a telegraph line north to Thursday Island in the 1880s facilitated the establishment of cattle stations along the center of the peninsula, and a significant sandalwood extraction industry also developed.

By the 1890s Aboriginal populations in most areas of Cape York were under severe pressure, with many groups eliminated altogether or displaced into virtual refugee camps around settlements and certain cattle stations. Around the turn of the century, public outcry in southern centers at the violence and exploitative conditions led to a more "protectionist" regime, including the establishment of mission settlements along the coasts. Aboriginal people were collected into these missions or lived in impoverished circumstances on the fringes of small inland settlements or on cattle stations. This protectionist period, which persisted essentially until the early 1970s, was characterized by paternalistic policies instituted under successive Queensland legislative bodies in which virtually every aspect of Aboriginal people's lives was subject to surveillance and control, with systematic attempts made to replace Aboriginal belief systems and practices with those of white Australians.

Large numbers of Cape York Aboriginal people were forcibly removed from their traditional lands to distant penal settlements, children were taken from their parents and raised by missionaries in dormitories, and Aboriginal settlements provided a source of cheap labor under a system in which they were allocated to employers in the region. A significant number worked on boats collecting shells in the Torres Strait, and many more lived and worked on cattle stations, where they provided the knowledge of the landscape and skilled labor crucial to the development of the pastoral industry. However, Aboriginal workers were not paid full wages, and their earnings were subject to control by local "protectors," such as missionaries and police sergeants.

Citizenship

Aboriginal people were not even counted in the Australian population census until after a 1967 national referendum gave overwhelming support to their inclusion, and not until the 1970s were equal wages and freedom of employment implemented for Aboriginal people. By the 1980s, Aboriginal people of the Cape York Peninsula, along with those of most other regions of Australia, had been largely incorporated into the cash economy, primarily through the welfare system.

Demographic Trends

The 1996 Australian census put the indigenous population of Cape York at just over fifty-six hundred, some 42 percent of the total regional population, but less than 1 percent of the total indigenous population.[1] The largest contemporary Aboriginal populations in the region live in or near the coastal Aboriginal townships that developed from the original missions. Smaller populations live in decentralized outstations on Aboriginal lands; others live in small townships such as Coen and Laura, where until recent decades they have provided the labor that was the mainstay of the Cape York cattle industry. Others have recently moved north. Most non-Aboriginal people live in the administrative and tourist center of Cooktown on the east coast and in the bauxite mining township of Weipa on the west coast, with smaller numbers in other towns and settlements and on pastoral stations.

As elsewhere in Aboriginal Australia, birth rates are much higher than those in the mainstream population, and life expectancy much lower. As a result, the Aboriginal population of the region is characterized by a comparatively large proportion of young and very young people, and by a relatively small proportion of senior people. The median age of the indigenous population in this region was twenty-three years, compared with thirty-four years for the nonindigenous population.[2] Although infant mortality rates have improved over recent decades, overall mortality rates for the adult indigenous population of the region have actually increased by more than 20 percent between 1976–94 to be 4.7 times that of the general Queensland population. Approximately two-thirds of the excess mortality rate in young adults is caused by accidents, heart disease, homicide and other violence, and suicide. Death rates through homicide and violence are eighteen times higher than for the general Queensland rate, and through alcohol related causes, over twenty-one times higher.[3]

Nearly 60 percent of the region consists of cattle stations. A number of these have been purchased in recent years by or for Aboriginal groups. Aboriginal people are major landholders in the Cape. Some 4,940,000 acres, or just less than 15 percent of the peninsula, is under direct Aboriginal control under various tenures.[4]

Political Incorporation

Official policy in Aboriginal affairs at both the federal and state levels is no longer overtly based upon discrimination, exclusion, or assimilation. The decades of the 1980s and 1990s saw a policy shift toward self-management, by which is broadly meant Aboriginal people's running their own organizations and governing bodies but within the mainstream system, and to a lesser extent self-determination, by which is meant the right to determine their own futures in accordance with their own priorities. There has been a recent policy shift away from self-determination by conservative national governments and an increasing stress on addressing socioeconomic disadvantage through achieving economic independence, even though this goal is arguably unrealistic.

However, Cape York Aboriginal societies continue to suffer from the legacy of the colonial and more recent past, and despite policy changes since the 1970s in particular, major challenges are presented by the imposition of Western economic, administrative, legal, and bureaucratic structures. The majority of Cape York's Aboriginal population now lives in former mission townships with a form of self-management under Aboriginal community councils. The original Aboriginal reserve lands in most cases were vested in the councils as Deeds of Grant in Trust, a form of community freehold. These bodies have qualified local government powers. Nonetheless, they are generally poorly resourced, have far less autonomy, and are subject to more intensive scrutiny by state government agencies in comparison with their mainstream local government counterparts.

Furthermore, the political model upon which these councils are based is that of the dominant society, not the indigenous one. The Aboriginal townships have highly complex social structures, in which family connections (especially those of kinship and marriage), language affiliations, and location of traditional lands are still of major significance. Power and authority within the Aboriginal realm are intimately related to these factors and others such as seniority and various forms of traditional knowledge. Councilors on the other hand are elected by secret ballot from the whole community for fixed terms, in a standard Western representative process that takes little or no formal account of Aboriginal values relating to who should have the authority to speak on particular issues. For example, councils are given considerable powers in areas such as law and order and justice, which severely compromise indigenous mechanisms in these arenas.

Welfare Dependence

Participation by Aboriginal people in the formal regional economy as measured by income level is very low. Over 84 percent of the Aboriginal residents of the region had individual incomes of less than $A200 (U.S. $120) per week in 1996, compared with 55 percent of indigenous Australians generally and just under 39 percent of Australians as a whole. Only some 3.5 percent of Aboriginal residents of Cape York earned more than $A600 (U.S. $360) per week, 21 percent of Australians as a whole.[5]

These figures reflect many factors, including the high reliance on government-funded work through Community Development Employment Project (CDEP) schemes; the relatively low educational and skill levels attained by Aboriginal residents of the Cape—only 4 percent aged fifteen or older had completed secondary school; and the broader characteristics of the regional formal economy including few opportunities for full-time employment or individual entrepreneurship in comparison with those of many other areas of Australia.[6]

Socioeconomic statistics do not provide an understanding of the role of the parallel Aboriginal economy. In this economy, it is typically social and cultural forms of capital that are the focus of strategic "economic" behavior, yet material forms of capital such as consumer goods and cash have become incorporated into Aboriginal value systems.

Thus, the progressive introduction of an essentially welfare-based cash economy over the past three decades has had a profound impact on Aboriginal societies, in this region as elsewhere. For instance, access to a cash income is not usually based on the social identity or status of the individual within Aboriginal society, but on his or her position in the wage market or, more generally, by categorization by the welfare system, which is predicated upon a system of rights and entitlements that are fundamentally different from those of Aboriginal societies. Individual access to cash incomes and the potential for personal autonomy have had major and generally deleterious consequences for relations between the generations, with younger people increasingly able to assert their independence from older generations. There are many other ways in which social relations have been greatly affected; for instance, men in particular are able to use their incomes for such purposes as the purchase of alcohol without reference to family and wider kin responsibilities.

The goal of moving from welfare dependence has its uncertain consequences as well. Large resource developments in the region, particularly mines, pose both threats and possibilities for Cape York's Aboriginal peoples. They carry the very real responsibility of major adverse environmental and social impacts and inevitably lead to significant sociocultural change. Maximizing economic independence through such agreements or through development of commercial enterprises almost inevitably means engaging in regional, national, and, increasingly, global markets, in which Cape York Aboriginal peoples' own social and economic mechanisms are likely to be severely uncompetitive. Emphasizing more overtly commercial goals can, in the words of one Aboriginal leader, mean "walking the razor's edge of assimilation." At the same time, properly negotiated and structured agreements with resource developers offer one of the few means for Aboriginal groups to move away from the pervasive effects of welfare dependency.

Sociocultural Crisis

The significance of food and other production within the indigenous subsistence realm continues to decline for most Aboriginal groups in the region, and there is overwhelming dependence upon government cash transfer payments of various kinds. As discussed, Aboriginal people here suffer from disastrously poor health and have a life expectancy near the lowest in the nation, particularly those in the former mission townships. Alcohol consumption is extremely high, exacerbated by ineffectual licensing laws and the common dependence of Aboriginal councils on the profits from the liquor outlets they control. Alcohol is clearly implicated in the health statistics and also in other social problems such as the very high levels of violence and other crimes in many townships, which lead to a disproportionate representation of young Aboriginal men, in particular, in the region's courts and jails. The mainstream law enforcement and judicial systems are clearly ineffectual, but there have been only a few systematic attempts in the region to incorporate Aboriginal customary law in dealing with these questions.

The high proportion of children and young adults in these Aboriginal societies has its own adverse consequences. For example, it is primarily the relatively small group of older men and women who have spent extended periods of their lives on or near their traditional lands, living and working on the reserve lands who are critical to the continuing transmission of languages, land-related knowledge, and other traditions to younger generations. However, in many Cape York communities there are a deep crisis in relations between the generations and a fundamental sundering of the mechanisms by which core Aboriginal values and concepts are transmitted.

This demographic imbalance has been exacerbated by factors such as the introduction of the welfare-based cash economy, as discussed; the availability of alcohol and more recently other drugs; and the increasing penetration of Western forms such as music, television, and videos. These not only provide alternative modes of thought and practices to those derived principally from the Aboriginal realm, but also clearly have the capacity to sustain meaning and inform mundane life for young people, in the context of the quasi-urban townships, more powerfully than do many of the indigenous ones.

Thus, for many young Aboriginal people, the systems of meaning and practices that constitute the core of "culture" are produced and reproduced through the needs, demands, and excitements of everyday life in the Aboriginal townships, with its attendant problems. This life for many of these communities is characterized by few opportunities for the realization of individual talent and creativity, whether through meaningful employment or other avenues including those of the indigenous realm.

RESPONSE: STRUGGLES TO SURVIVE CULTURALLY

The colonial frontier on Cape York was a particularly brutal one, with violence and murder in some pastoral areas extending until the 1930s. From first contact with explorers, pastoralists, and other adventurers, Aboriginal people in many areas put up spirited resistance. A number of early gold miners and pastoralists were killed by Aboriginal people, and the original relay stations on the telegraph line built in the midnineteenth century along the spine of the Cape were constructed as fortified residences because of the serious threat from Aboriginal groups. Nonetheless, the effectiveness of Aboriginal resistance here as elsewhere on the colonial frontier was reduced not only because of the superior technology of the colonists, but also because opposition was generally conducted on a local rather than a regional basis.

Through the twentieth century, Aboriginal responses in this region to the gradual imposition of an assimilationist and paternalistic policy regime could be generally characterized as ones of accommodation rather than overt resistance. However, gradually changing policy climate, broader recognition of Aboriginal rights (albeit against an underlying current of ignorance and prejudice), and emergence of a sophisticated Aboriginal leadership at national and regional levels have created new possibilities for Aboriginal people.

Legal Recognition of Aboriginal Rights and Interests

In recent decades, the Aboriginal people of Cape York have taken important steps to seek recognition of their rights in various Australian courts. The Wik peoples of western Cape York in particular have initiated a number of highly significant legal cases since the mid-1970s, including a challenge to the Queensland government over the distribution of royalties from bauxite mining proposed for their lands; in December 1996, as the result of an action they brought, the High Court ruled that native title could coexist with pastoral leases under certain circumstances.

Establishment of Regional Political and Representative Bodies

Significant steps have also been taken to overcome the limitations posed by localism by developing regional approaches to advancing Aboriginal interests. Of particular note is the formation in 1991 of the Cape York Land Council, an organization whose governing body is drawn from groups and communities across the peninsula, and whose charter is to gain recognition of Aboriginal land rights. This organization since its inception has adopted a multipronged and sophisticated approach to land and resource issues and has launched a number of significant native title claims on both subregional and regional bases.

More recently, the Aboriginal leadership of the Cape York Land Council and other regional bodies, recognizing the complexity and interrelatedness of the issues facing Cape York's Aboriginal communities, has been instrumental in establishing two other organizations—Apunipima Cape York Health Council to focus on health issues and Balkanu Cape York Development Corporation to focus on community and economic development.

Negotiated Agreements over Land and Resources

Aboriginal-controlled lands include many areas of outstanding conservation significance—for example, the monsoon rain forests in areas of the Lockhart River community lands and the wetlands in the Aurukun and Kowanyama lands. Strategic alliances between Aboriginal and conservation interests have played an important role in more recent regional politics.

From its inception the Cape York Land Council has been actively involved in negotiations over Aboriginal control and comanagement of lands and seas in the region with a variety of state and commonwealth agencies and commercial interests. There have been, for example, negotiations with the Great Barrier Reef Marine Park Authority over recognition of Aboriginal rights over the coastal waters and reefs off the east coast and with the state government over the proposed eastern Cape York conservation zone.

Negotiations have also been initiated in a number of areas with major mining companies over such matters as compensation for dispossession, return of areas of significance, and royalties and other financial benefits. Significantly, some agreements have now been reached.

Native Title and Statutory Land Claims

Queensland's Aboriginal Land Act and the federal Native Title Act provide the potential to increase Aboriginal ownership and comanagement of both land and waters significantly, and to provide access to otherwise alienated ancestral lands including for those living in the small non-Aboriginal townships of the region. The former legislation is a statutory land rights scheme, through which successful claims result in the granting of inalienable freehold title. The Native Title Act, on the other hand, was developed as a federal response to the 1992 Mabo decision in the High Court and establishes a complex administrative and legal system for the recognition and incorporation into the Australian land tenure system of Aboriginal rights and interests in their traditional lands under their own laws and customs. This regime, however, is arguably discriminatory in some of its provisions.

Aboriginal people of Cape York have recognized the importance of gaining control of, or at least access to, their lands and resources, both to ensure cultural maintenance and to assist in economic development. There are currently a number of national parks in the region for which claims under the Aboriginal Land Act have been heard or are being prepared by the Cape York Land Council, recognized as the native title representative body for the region. The result of a successful claim under this legislation is that the underlying title of the national park becomes Aboriginal freehold vested in the relevant group, but with a lease of the land back to the government as a national park, operated under a joint management board including representatives of the Aboriginal owners. There have been significant questions raised concerning the requirements for perpetual leaseback to the state of a successfully claimed park, the rights of its Aboriginal owners to live on it and use its resources, the capacity of its Aboriginal owners to have a meaningful role in joint management arrangements, and the resources available for park management. Nonetheless, completed and current claims under the Aboriginal Land Act could potentially see virtually all national parks in Cape York Aboriginal owned and under joint management regimes. There are also other, albeit smaller, areas that have been made available for claim or transferred to Aboriginal ownership under the Aboriginal Land Act, including the Quinkan Reserves near Laura, which contain numerous rock art galleries of international significance.

Several extensive native title claims have been lodged over lands in the peninsula. The ultimate import of the many claims in the region under the Native Title Act is yet to be determined. Given the extent of pastoral lands in the Cape, the unfolding political and legal responses to the High Court Wik decision and the recently amended Native Title Act will be of great significance. Even successful native title claims over pastoral lands, however, would result in negotiated, or federal court determined, coexistence regimes, not inalienable freehold title (and thus exclusive possession) as with the statutory land rights scheme.

FOOD FOR THOUGHT

Cape York's Aboriginal peoples have been subject to enormous pressures since the first incursion of Europeans into their lands in the mid-nineteenth century. The violent frontier period and the subsequent regime of governmental controls and surveillance have had profound and devastating impacts on Aboriginal societies in the region. More recent decades have seen a gradual move by governments away from the old assimilationist and discriminatory policies. In the past three decades, Cape York Aboriginal groups and organizations have successfully mounted court challenges to protect and further the recognition of their rights; have established regionally based political, advocacy, and service-delivery organizations; and have devised strategies to increase their control of lands and resources in the region through land claims and negotiated agreements.

Cape York Aboriginal societies still exhibit considerable cultural vitality. Nonetheless, alarming health, education, unemployment, and crime statistics arguably reflect the fact that they are in deep crisis. The very high levels of alcohol abuse that can be seen as both cause and symptom of this crisis, the pervasive effects of the welfare system, the alienation of younger generations, and the continuing marginalization of indigenous political mechanisms are all worrying signs for the long-term viability of these societies.

Questions

1. Access to welfare support for those people unable to find employment is a fundamental right of all Australian citizens. However, there is considerable evidence that such incomes are implicated in the breakdown of certain core Aboriginal social and family values. Are there policy options that can in part at least address this paradox?

2. In a Western, democratic country such as Australia, the rights of the individual are accorded primacy. How are such rights to be reconciled with others, such as the right of indigenous people to the maintenance of their own cultures and societies, in the context of the widespread availability of alcohol?

3. Developing Aboriginal businesses and joint ventures is seen as a crucial mechanism for moving away from the pervasive effects of welfare dependency. Yet, engagement with the commercial world in an era of global markets carries with it the potential for major social and cultural change. Are there means of maximizing the benefits from such engagement, while minimizing the deleterious consequences for Aboriginal societies? Are there other alternatives to moving away from welfare?

4. Are there alternatives to the existing essentially mainstream models of Aboriginal community government, which might draw more upon Aboriginal political and social mechanisms?

5. To deal strategically and from an equal position with the dominant society, and thus to change current political and socioeconomic disadvantage, arguably a more highly educated Aboriginal population is required. Yet, Western education necessarily involves personal and cultural change. Can this paradox be resolved,

or is change inevitable in Aboriginal cultures as in all others? What would distinguish such change from the assimilation policies of the past?

NOTES

1. Australian Bureau of Statistics (ABS), *Cooktown Statistical Summary* (Canberra: ABS, 1996).
2. Ibid.
3. Apunipima Cape York Health Council, *Annual Report* (Cairns: Apunipima, 1996).
4. David Martin, *Regional Agreements and Localism: A Case Study from Cape York Peninsula*, Discussion Paper No. 146 (Canberra: Centre for Aboriginal Economic Policy Research, Australian National University, 1997).
5. ABS, *Cooktown Statistical Summary*.
6. Ibid.

RESOURCE GUIDE

Published Literature

Chase, A. K., and P. Sutton. "Hunter-Gatherers in a Rich Environment: Aboriginal Coastal Exploitation in Cape York Peninsula." In A. Keast (ed.), *Ecological Biogeography of Australia*, pp. 1817–52. The Hague: W. Junk, 1981.

Kidd, R. *The Way We Civilise: Aboriginal Affairs—The Untold Story*. St. Lucia: University of Queensland Press, 1997.

Martin, D. F. *Regional Agreements and Localism: A Case Study from Cape York Peninsula*. Discussion Paper No. 146. Canberra: Centre for Aboriginal Economic Policy Research, Australian National University, 1997.

Newman, C. (photographs by S. Abell). "Cape York Peninsula Aborigines Assert Their Claim to the Harsh and Beautiful Northern Tip of Australia." *National Geographic* 189(6): 2–33, 1996.

Rigsby, B., and N. Williams. "Reestablishing a Home on Eastern Cape York Peninsula." *C S Quarterly* 15(2): 11–15, 1991.

Sharp, N. *Footprints along the Cape York Sandbeaches*. Canberra: Aboriginal Studies Press, 1992.

Sutton, P. J., and B. Rigsby. "People and Politricks: Management of Land and Personnel on Australia's York Peninsula." In N. M. Williams and E. S. Hunn (eds.), *Resource Managers: North American and Australian Hunter-Gatherers*, pp. 155–171. Boulder, CO: Westview Press, 1982.

Films and Videos

Familiar Places: A Film about Aboriginal Ties to Land. Canberra: Australian Institute of Aboriginal and Torres Strait Islander Studies, 1980. 53 minutes, sound, color, 16 mm. Director and camera: David MacDougall sound: Judith MacDougall. Editors: David and Judith MacDougall. Adviser and narrator: Peter Sutton.

Lockhart Festival. Canberra: Australian Institute of Aboriginal and Torres Strait Islander Studies, 1974. 35 minutes, sound, color, 16 mm. Director: Curtis Levy. Camera: Richard Tucker. Sound: Kevin Kerney. Editor: Ronda MacGregor. Advisers: John von Sturmer and Athol Chase.

WWW Sites

The Aboriginal and Torres Strait Island Commission
http://www.atsic.gov.au

Indigenous peoples and environment
http://www.altnews.com.au

Organization

Cape York Land Council
P.O. Box 2496
Cairns, Qld 4870
Australia

Chapter 2

The Anuta Islanders

Richard Feinberg

CULTURAL OVERVIEW

The People

The people of Anuta, whose language and culture are Polynesian, say that their ancestors arrived from the Polynesian heartland about four hundred years ago. According to oral traditions, the first immigrants to Anuta were from Tonga and Uvea (Wallis Island); later settlers arrived from Samoa and Rotuma—islands and archipelagoes five hundred to one thousand miles to the east. For generations, Anuta Islanders have traded and married people from Tikopia, another Polynesian culture, also located within the eastern Solomon Islands.

The Setting

Anuta is a small, isolated volcanic island, about a half mile in diameter, reaching a maximum altitude of just over two hundred feet. It is 11° 40' south of the equator, making the climate tropical. There are two seasons: During the first, from around April through October, trade winds blow steadily from the southeast; for the remainder of the year, winds are intermittent and reside predominantly in the west. The trade-wind season tends to be cool and overcast, but rain is sporadic. This is the time when Anutans, like other Polynesians, did most of their interisland voyaging. Weather during the season of the westerly "monsoons" is more volatile. At this time, the island is exposed to lengthy periods of calm weather and hot, brilliant sunshine, interspersed with torrential rains that may last for days on end.

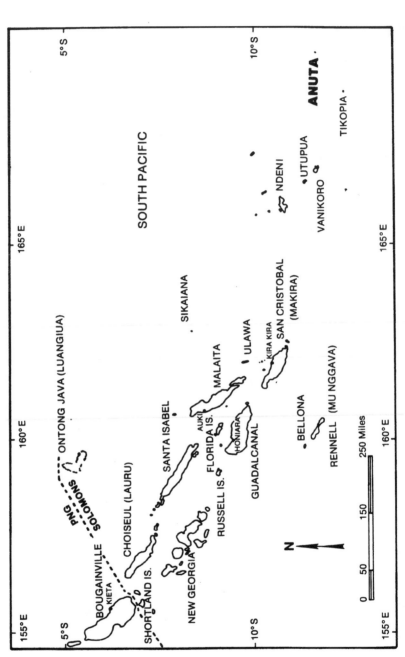

Solomon Islands. Reprinted from Richard Feinberg, *Polynesian Seafaring and Navigation: Ocean Travel in Anutan Culture and Society* (Kent, Ohio: Kent State University Press, 1988). Used with permission.

This is also the season when powerful storms occasionally devastate the island.

For the most part, Anuta is well watered and the soil sufficiently fertile to produce lush vegetation. Although most of the island looks like dense, wild jungle, in reality it is intensively cultivated. The island is surrounded by a fringing reef that, in turn, is surrounded by the open sea. There is no lagoon, and the full force of the vast Pacific Ocean continually breaks upon the island's coral perimeter. As a result, it is difficult to get out to the ocean, and when the surf is up, it may be impossible. Beyond the surf, the flat, sandy bottom, punctuated by numerous coral heads, falls off gradually for several miles.

Traditional Subsistence Strategies

Since the time of initial settlement, Anutans have supported themselves primarily through subsistence fishing and cultivation of inland garden plots. Anutans fish from outrigger canoes, either using baited, weighted hooks and hand lines on offshore reefs or trolling with a pearl shell lure or a piece of octopus tentacle. Alternatively, a large baited hook may be allowed to float at the end of several hundred feet of heavy fishing line in hopes of catching sharks or other large predatory fish. In addition, Anutans sometimes cast with a pole and a short line from the beach for small fish or cast for bonito (a type of tuna) from a canoe in the deep sea. On occasions when it is difficult to get a canoe through the surf, Anutans may spear fish either on the fringing reef or at a short distance past the surf line. Fishing in the ocean with a hand line while treading water over a nearby reef is a common procedure. Communal fish drives on the reef flat provide an often-productive alternative to individual fishing techniques.

Anutans grow a variety of crops and practice crop rotation on their terraced hillside, alternating manioc (tapioca) with the starchy root *Colocasia* taro, and tobacco. *Cyrtosperma* taro is grown in swampy depressions on the coastal flat. Sweet potato, pumpkin, and watermelon are raised largely in the village area. Large breadfruit and sago palms, along with trees for bark cloth, still used for clothing, are grown on the coastal flat. Coconut palms populate the sandy strand just inland from the beach; papaya, edible pandanus palm, and areca palm are scattered here and there around the island. The major intoxicant is betel—a mixture including the nut of the areca palm, the leaf of a kind of pepper plant (*Piper betel*), and lime, produced by heating coral until it is converted into a caustic white powder.

Religion and World View

Until the early twentieth century, the Anutans practiced a form of ancestral worship. All deceased persons became spirits, and such spirits often concerned themselves with the affairs of living descendants. The preeminent gods were the ghosts of dead chiefs, the most notable of whom was Tearakura, a man who lived nine generations ago and presided over the annihilation of virtually all of the island's male population. Other important deities were Tearakura's brothers, Pu Tepuko and Tauvakatai; their elder sister, Nau Ariki; their brother-in-law, Pu Pangatau; and their great-grandfather, Toroaki. The island has two chiefs, the higher of whom is normally the direct senior male patrilineal descendant of Tearakura. In addition to his role as political leader, the chief was expected to serve as the community's high priest.

In 1916, Anuta was converted to Christianity by the Melanesian Mission, a branch of the British Anglican church, and the entire population is said to have accepted the new religion almost immediately. Anutans are enthusiastic Christians and maintain a close connection with their church—albeit, sometimes at a reduced level of activity—even when they move to other parts of the Solomon Islands. Conversion meant that a new deity, the Christian God, was placed at the head of Anuta's pantheon and was worshiped in a Christian church, using Christian prayers, according to the Christian calendar. This, however, does not signify rejection of the old religion's truth or efficacy. Today Anutans agree that the old spirits exist, have the characteristics commonly attributed to them, and occasionally intervene in people's lives.

Social and Political Organization

Anuta is divided into four major descent groups known as *kainanga*. Each *kainanga* claims descent from one of the four great ancestors who are responsible for the island's current social organization. First in rank is the Kainanga I Mua, which claims descent from Tearakura, the former chief and premier deity. The second-ranking Kainanga I Tepuko is descended from Tearakura's younger brother, Pu Tepuko. The third-ranking Kainanga I Pangatau is descended from Tearakura's two sisters, Nau Ariki and Nau Pangatau, and their shared husband, Pu Pangatau. The lowest-ranking grouping is the Kainanga I Rotomua, which claims descent from the youngest brother, Tauvakatai. The Kainanga I Mua is headed by the senior chief, known as the *Ariki I Mua* or *Tui Anuta*, and the Kainanga I Tepuko is led by the junior chief, known as the *Ariki Tepuko* or *Tui Kainanga*. Men of the two senior *kainanga* are known as *maru*, "men of rank"; "protectors." The other two *kainanga* are chiefless, and their members are termed *pakaaropa*, which means "sympathy-producing" or "pitiable."

The chiefs' authority is based on their association with *manuu* or *mana*. This term is distributed throughout Polynesia and refers to a kind of spiritual power. It originates with the most powerful deities. Prior to conversion in the early 1900s, this meant Tearakura and his fellow spirits; currently, it is the Christian God.

Mana is transmitted across generations according to principles of primogeniture (inheritance through the first-born son) and genealogical seniority in the male line. Thus the chief has greater *mana* than anyone else in the community, and most of that is passed to his eldest son, who normally becomes the next chief. People must obey the chief and show him ritual respect because of his *mana*, and anyone who fails to do so risks divine retribution in the form of sickness, accident, or natural disaster. The chiefs' legitimacy, however, rests upon his use of his *mana* to ensure the island's health and economic welfare. In this way, he shows his *aropa*, "compassion," "generosity," toward the people, and they show *aropa* "appreciation" for him by honoring his person and obeying his commands.

Aropa is the Anutan version of a pan-Polynesian term that Americans are likely to recognize by the Hawaiian variant, *aloha*. It indicates positive feelings for another being as demonstrated by giving, sharing, or other forms of material assistance. As a central value in traditional Anutan culture, it underlies chiefly authority, and it is the basis of Anutan social structure. All Anutans constitute a single kin group and are expected to express *aropa* in their treatment of one another. The elementary unit of cooperation and support is a grouping called the *pare* ("house") or *patongia* ("food-sharing group"). It typically approximates a patrilateral extended family, but Anutans think of it as a unit that shares gardens, houses, food, and other resources and is not necessarily dependent on a genealogical connection. *Kainanga* are groups of *pare*, and adoption is by a *pare* rather than an individual, a couple, or a nuclear family. Through all of this, what differentiates Anutans from the outside world is the expectation that their conduct will be permeated with reciprocal *aropa*.

THREATS TO SURVIVAL

Demographic Trends

Because Anuta encompasses only about 0.25 square mile, a small number of people generates a remarkably high population density. During 1972–73, approximately 150 people lived on Anuta, producing a population density of 600 per square mile. Another 50 Anutans dwelt elsewhere in the Solomons. By the 1990s, Anuta's resident population was about 200, with another 50 to 100 people living away from the island.

Current Events and Conditions

Anuta is sufficiently productive that, despite the current population density, everyone is adequately fed, even in the face of periodic storms and droughts. If all those living away were to return to Anuta, however, resources would be stretched, and in time of natural disaster, famine would be a real threat. The opportunity to visit other islands, therefore, provides an important safety valve.

Although Anutans have not faced the threat of collective starvation for almost a century, their desire for imported goods and services has forced changes that now threaten the community. Anuta was first sighted by Europeans in 1791. Sporadic contact began in the middle to late nineteenth century. Since then the Anutans have viewed metal axes, adzes, knives, fish hooks, nylon fishing line, and kerosene lanterns as necessities. More recently, batteries and flashlights have been added to the list. Rice, sugar, and tinned meat are much-desired luxuries, as are the occasional tape player, radio, or Butterfly Lamp—a kind of lantern that burns kerosene under pressure, producing a bright white light similar to an incandescent bulb.

In addition to individual goals, Anutans have a number of community objectives. These include a system of piped water, availability of medicine, reliable transportation, and mosquito control. Although Anutan objectives appear modest from the perspective of North America or Australia, they have been remarkably difficult to achieve. Between 1973 and 1984 a piped water system was introduced. However, the resources to maintain the new system were very much in question. Medicines continue to be in short supply, and even now the medical orderly has minimal training. The island may still wait for several months between visits from a government ship. And since the medical department has declared Anuta to be malaria free, no attempt has been made to control the large, unpleasant mosquito population.

For Anutans to obtain the goods they covet, they need access to money. With few commercially exploitable resources, earning money requires working away from the island. Anutans recognize that education improves one's chances to find well-paying employment, so the more ambitious "houses" have made a point of sending one or more children to attend school off the island—usually in the Santa Cruz Islands (near Makira), Guadalcanal, or elsewhere in the central Solomon Islands. This, however, requires still more money to pay tuition and ship passage.

The quest for cash led several families, around 1980, to sell locally grown food to other houses that had run short. This practice was counter to the principle of *aropa*, which had been the focal point of the old social order. The senior chief ordered a halt to what he regarded as antisocial behavior, but to no avail. Eventually, a series of local tragedies convinced the chief's opponents to reform their ways, but by that time, open defiance of a chiefly edict had undermined traditional authority and challenged the political and social order.

Chiefly power was further eroded by the migration of a large number of people to the central Solomons. With Anutans scattered over many hundreds of miles, it is difficult for the chiefs and their envoys to monitor their people's behavior, and national laws preclude use of the most severe sanctions.

For Anutans living in other parts of the Solomons, money is even more essential than on Anuta, and the pressures to compromise on the kin-based collectivism demanded by *aropa* are more powerful. At the same time, Anutans have been pulled increasingly under the authority of the Solomon Islands' government.

This is particularly threatening to the Polynesian Anutans because the Solomon Islands' government is dominated by Melanesians, who constitute over 90 percent of the population of 300,000 people. Anutans identify with their putative ancestors in the Polynesian heartland to the east. They have had comparatively little contact, and virtually no intermarriage, with Melanesians, whom they perceive to be culturally very different from them. They do not trust Melanesians to be concerned about their welfare. Meanwhile, the central government is faced with the problem of creating a sense of unity in a new nation, populated by scores of culturally and linguistically distinct communities. Consequently, it has used its power to discourage local practices that might exacerbate the pervasive tendencies toward fragmentation.

These conditions make it difficult for Anutans to maintain customs that they consider distinctively their own and, thus, that are essential to their sense of cultural identity. Prominent in this regard is the Anutan chieftainship, which, regardless of people's personal feelings about their current chief, serves as a symbolic representation of the community and its special place in the cosmos. Most Anutans want to be more independent of the central government, yet they value the services the government provides—particularly shipping, medicine, and radio communication.

RESPONSE: STRUGGLES TO SURVIVE CULTURALLY

In the Anutans' view, the most pressing issues are local sovereignty on the home island and adequate housing for migrants in Honiara, the nation's capital. These issues have become deeply intertwined and are a major source of tension. Moreover, although Anutans generally agree about their principal objectives, strategies for realizing their goals have been a major object of contention.

The key to local sovereignty is widely identified as shipping. If Anutans could control their own ship, they believe they would no longer be dependent on the central government for transport to schools and places of employment. Medical treatment would become more readily available, and it would be easy to import supplies and equipment when they are needed. Much of the discussion since the 1980s, therefore, has focused on plans for the community to obtain its own ship. However, for a tiny island community with few financial resources, to purchase a ship capable of traversing hundreds of miles of open sea on a regular basis is a formidable challenge.

The housing problem for Anutans living away from the home island (primarily in Honiara on Guadalcanal and the Russell Islands) is entwined with issues of shipping and local sovereignty. In 1972, the population of Honiara, the capital of the Solomon Islands, was about twelve thousand people; over the past decades, it has approximately tripled. A few Anutans residing there have had access to their own homes, but most are not so fortunate. Those without their own homes stay with fellow Anutans, sleeping on the floor. In an attempt to increase living space, Anutans in the Honiara area purchased a plot of land in White River, a suburb just west of the city limits, where many non-Melanesian islanders from Tikopia, Rennell, Bellona, and Kiribati (formerly known as the Gilbert Islands) reside. There, they built a small house.

The building was intended to be a collective dwelling for Anutans in the area who might need a place to stay. However, one man convinced the rest of the community that, for legal purposes, the structure should be registered in his name. He then sold the house to the Honiara Town Council, pocketed the proceeds, and began a series of unsuccessful business ventures. Eventually, he left the Solomons to work for Nauru Shipping.

At that point, a man named John Tope became actively involved. Tope is a forceful, dynamic man of low genealogical rank in the island's traditional sociopolitical system. He left Anuta as a boy to attend school—first on Tikopia, later in the Russell Islands and a number of locations on Guadalcanal. For several years, he worked for the Anglican church; later, he helped to found a local grass roots, nonprofit organization, the Solomon Islands Development Trust (SIDT), and served as its first field officer, visiting rural areas on community development projects. Also, under the name of the Anuta Community Development Programme (ACDP), he initiated a variety of development projects, among the first of which was the construction of a rest house for Anutans in White River.

In an effort to accumulate the capital for this project, Tope approached governmental agencies, banks, and private individuals. However, lending agencies demanded a plan to guarantee repayment of their loans, and even would-be grantors asked to be assured that the house would have some source of income for continued maintenance. Thus, the plan began to change. No longer was the building to be a rest house to provide free lodging for Anutans; instead, the plan now was to rent the house to non-Anutans. After the loans were repaid, profits would be used to promote a variety of development projects on Anuta.

By the time the change was common knowledge, many Anutans had already come to distrust Tope's motivations, and the change of plans con-

Top, outdoor feast celebrating rite of passage for a young child on Anuta. Bottom, John Tope performs a dance inside the large White River house near Honiara. Courtesy of Richard Feinberg.

firmed their worst suspicions. Tope had a tendency to work by himself or with a small circle of confidants. Somehow, he had purchased several plots of land in the Santa Cruz islands. No one knew how he had gotten the money, the nature of the financial agreements that made these purchases possible, or what he intended to do with the land. It was widely assumed, however, that his business dealings were designed to promote his personal self-interest, and that he cared little for the overall community's well-being. This attitude violated *aropa*. The change in plans regarding the White River rest house seemed to fit the larger pattern.

Eventually Tope received a grant of twenty thousand dollars from the Canadian Diocese of the Episcopal church, to be administered by the Church of Melanesia. When the house was livable, Tope and his wife moved in, intending to oversee construction and move to different quarters when the building was completed. Immediately, other Anutans moved into the house, but with no understanding that their occupation would be temporary. Soon the building felt the effects of heavy occupancy.

While this was going on, Tope also was involved in several other projects. In partnership with a man of Kiribati ancestry, he purchased a second house—a small concrete structure a few dozen yards from the one under construction. He successfully petitioned the Honiara Town Council to return to the Anutans the house that had been sold without community authorization. And he convinced the Town Council to allot an extensive plot of undeveloped land to the Anutans for the purpose of subsistence cultivation.

Many Anutans happily availed themselves of the resources that Tope had procured. In 1988, three dozen people were living in the three White River houses, and the garden land was cultivated with manioc, sweet potato, yams, a small stand of taro, and a few fruit trees. Still, tension escalated.

Tope suggested to Anutans in White River that they build leaf houses in the garden area and vacate the large wooden building so that it might be rented out, in accordance with his agreement with the church. Most occupants believed, however, that he wished to expel them in order to convert the house into his personal business enterprise.

In the midst of all this turmoil, the man who sold the first White River house returned from Nauru and settled once again in Honiara. He claimed that he still owned the building, and he moved in, along with his Melanesian wife, a number of her kin and fellow islanders, their children, and some friends from the Polynesian island of Bellona, south of Guadalcanal. Anutans in the house were now in a minority. Other Anutans resented this turn of events, but no one wanted to precipitate a direct confrontation on the matter.

Controversy also surrounded the small concrete house. Although no one doubted that Tope had contributed to its purchase, there were many questions as to where he got the money. Suspicions turned to an earlier scheme to buy a ship.

When Tope organized the Anuta Community Development Programme, one of its major goals was to obtain a vessel. In the name of ACDP, he contacted a number of granting agencies and the governments of several foreign countries. In addition, he took up a collection from Anutans, both on the home island and throughout the Solomons, to contribute to the purchase of a vessel. From the latter sources he accumulated approximately SI $500 (approximately U.S. $70).

Eventually, the government of Singapore apparently came forward with an offer. To finalize the arrangement, Tope believed he had to travel to Singapore. The trip cost SI $6,000 (U.S. $860) for food, lodging, and air-fare. Unfortunately, the deal—if it ever existed—fell through. Tope claims to have spent his own savings on the trip. His detractors are convinced that he pocketed the community's money, used it for his trip to Singapore, and spent the remainder on the White River house. When suspicions about Tope and his activities were finally reported to the church, the diocese determined that it would hold the remainder of the grant in trust, select the carpenters, and pay the bills itself.

At this point, the house was almost finished. The contractor, however, insisted that his bills had not been fully paid and refused to complete the job until he received what he thought was his due. Since the church would not release the funds, Tope could not pay him. Some members of the An-utan community convinced the government to prosecute Tope for misuse of funds. The contractor sued Tope for his back fees. And Tope sued the church for release of the funds so that he could complete the house.

Tope's major focus had been on what he refers to as the new Anutan Settlement on a hill behind White River. By 1993, six Anutan families had laid claim to plots of land and built houses in the settlement. Each of these had at least one member working for wages somewhere in the Honiara area, and each was growing crops on the newly available land. Several other families had already laid plans to follow suit.

Although Tope was a respected leader in the eyes of many islanders, he also had some powerful detractors who minimized the settlement and its importance. His critics argued that the so-called settlement consisted of a bunch of individuals rather than a cohesive community united around a common tradition and loyalty to traditional chiefs. They emphasized the poor accommodations on the newly settled land, noting that none of the new houses had indoor plumbing and some had no ready access to water. Furthermore, the soil was hard and not particularly fertile, and it was rou-tinely compared unfavorably with that on Anuta. Tope and his family were still living in the controversial house in White River, and only a minority of Anutans in the area had moved to the settlement.

During the same period, alternative leadership was provided by Frank Kataina, the younger brother of Anuta's senior chief. Like Tope, Kataina left Anuta as a boy, and, despite only a standard three education—roughly equivalent to third grade in the United States—he worked his way up through the ranks of the Royal Solomon Islands Police, eventually serving in such prominent positions as chief prosecutor for criminal cases and superintendent of training for the national Police Training School. During the late 1970s, Kataina successfully arranged for installation of a piped water delivery system on Anuta; after he retired from the police in 1985, his interests turned to several other development projects on Anuta. The most noteworthy of these were establishing a community store, to be run as a cooperative rather than for private profit; acquiring a ship; and convincing the U.S. Peace Corps, which places hundreds of volunteers in the Solomon Islands, to post a couple of teachers on Anuta.

Progress was generally slow, and the community store proposal was as much a political statement as a plan for economic action. As the chief's brother and leading assistant, he felt compelled to guard tradition and the community's collective identity. For precisely these reasons, however, his efforts met with opposition from several families who were trying to establish their own private stores.

Since these projects had such limited success, Kataina's major contribution was to serve as "watchdog" to protect the community from schemes that might be detrimental to its interests. His long experience with government and public service made him effective in this role. The net effect of his efforts, however, was to thwart most of the projects Tope had promoted. Since Tope so infrequently delivered on his promises, his critics' suspicions were confirmed. And without community support, chances of success for his endeavors were minimal.

For a while, Kataina believed that ACDP was involved in worthwhile projects even if its actions were sometimes misguided and it was being exploited by a conniving, self-interested leader. During the late 1970s and early 1980s, he worked with Tope and the ACDP on the plan to acquire a ship, and when the deal with Singapore seemed imminent, he even considered moving there to serve as the project's office manager. When the arrangement fell apart, his first reaction was to blame not Tope but the Solomon Islands' government. The outcome, however, also raised questions in Kataina's mind about Tope and his behavior.

In the late 1980s, when the Canadian Diocese of the Episcopal (Anglican) church launched its investigation into the Anutan housing project, Kataina made a concerted effort to demonstrate the community's need for the house and attributed the problems to the unethical behavior of a single individual who was supported by a handful of his close relatives. He lobbied to have Tope and his supporters removed from the building, which Kataina now referred to as the Tearakura House, and he proposed that the house be deeded to the Anutan community at large. By 1990, Kataina had lost confidence in the ACDP and was promoting an alternative development organization.

Kataina called the new organization the Anuta Tearakura Association, for the former chief and culture hero who had created Anuta's current political and social order and had become the island's premier deity after his death. The point of this name was to emphasize that development should not be severed from tradition—from the old political, social, and religious order that made the community unique.

The Tearakura Association's major focus echoed Kataina's long-standing concerns: to improve education and develop a source of cash income on Anuta, with the ultimate objective of acquiring a ship, thereby maintaining chiefly sovereignty while protecting and building upon Anuta's distinctive historical traditions. At the same time, Kataina hoped to improve the island's water system and upgrade the school and clinic.

The Tearakura Association has met with some success, particularly on Anuta itself. Its most notable achievement has been to promote a commercial seafood business. Fresh fish is in chronic short supply in Honiara, with its large populace, but fish are abundant in and around Anuta Island. Therefore, Kataina reasoned, such an enterprise has a natural market. The problem was the unreliability of shipping and storage. The greatest immediate problem was overcome when the association had freezers installed on Anuta. In addition, Anutans have developed a profitable business catching sharks and selling dried shark fins to Asian importers, and the association has entered the business of collecting, drying, and selling bêche-de-mer (sea slug). Proceeds from these nascent enterprises have been used primarily for school supplies. Kataina attributes the venture's success largely to the involvement of an Australian business manager, David Low, who also has invested $25,000 of his own money in the operation.

The association's accomplishments in Honiara have been more limited. Despite the efforts of Kataina and his associates, Tope and his family still occupy the "Tearakura House," and the Anutan settlement is moving forward. Meanwhile, Tope objected even to the name *Tearakura Association*, suggesting that the disparity between a long-dead chief and notions of development makes the name a paradox. In the 1990s, Kataina—a man of considerable accomplishment and ability—was living in Honiara in a leaf house built on land borrowed from a non-Anutan, without plumbing or electricity.

FOOD FOR THOUGHT

The Anutan experience raises questions about the very notion of development, what it means, its viability, and even its desirability, not only on Anuta but in innumerable comparable communities.

The first, and perhaps the most obvious, question is whether Anutans can possibly achieve their objectives. They are determined to pursue development while they are equally determined to preserve their ancient customs (*nga tukutukunga tuei*). Yet, the pursuit of money necessary to attain development in the Western sense—shipping, medicine, running water, electric power, and the like—will inevitably continue to erode Anuta's ancient way of life. Some Anutans, like John Tope and his followers, consider the benefits to be well worth the cost and are prepared to sacrifice the chieftainship and the system of collective responsibility based on *aropa* and kinship. Many, on the other hand, are not prepared to make the sacrifice.

Even Kataina's strategy, however, pits the subsistence economy against market forces and commodity production. As long as two hundred Anutans were exploiting the surrounding land and sea for their personal consumption, there was a limit to environmental degradation. By contrast, capitalism imposes no upper limit to environmental exploitation, and if the seafood business is commercially successful, depletion of the ocean resources around Anuta is a real possibility. Moreover, should Kataina be successful in attracting money into the community, even through cooperative business enterprises, it will become increasingly difficult to maintain a system of social relations based on the communal ethic embodied in *aropa*.

If Anutans are successful in their quest for "development," then, will they have improved their quality of life? This question only can be answered if one has a way to measure life quality. Certain aspects of Anutan life were difficult and certainly uncomfortable back in the early 1970s. Flies, mosquitoes, ants, and cockroaches were a constant nuisance. Skin fungus, hookworm, and other unpleasant infectious disorders were endemic. For persons who became seriously ill, medical care was almost nil. The subsistence economy based on gardening and fishing was physically demanding. Formal education was all but unobtainable, and travel was, to say the least, a challenge. Yet there also were rewards deriving from Anuta's way of life. Everyone on the island was treated as family. People supported and looked after one another. A great deal of time was devoted to feasting, dancing, singing, storytelling, and general good fellowship. Almost everyone respected the two chiefs, and the chiefs took seriously their responsibility to care for their constituents' well-being. Anutans were committed Christians, and there was no denominational conflict.

Ultimately, the lure of money, travel, alcohol, and junk food is hard to resist, and expansion of the world market economy may be inexorable. The key question is whether, by the time Anutans recognize development's cost in terms of social alienation, resource depletion, and environmental degradation, it will be too late to reverse the trend.

Questions

1. How are the concepts of *aropa* and *mana* important to traditional Anutan social life? In what way do they form the basis of Anutan chiefly power and legitimacy?

2. Why are trade and travel important to Anutans despite their living on a productive island with a subsistence economy?

3. Why are Anutans suspicious of the Solomon Islands' government? How have Anutans attempted to assert their independence, and what are their chances for success?

4. Why have questions about housing become a dominant preoccupation of Anutans living on Guadalcanal, and why did their attempts to solve the housing problem become so controversial?

5. What do Anutans mean by "development," and why does it require them to become involved in the market economy? How is this inconsistent with a social system based on *aropa*?

RESOURCE GUIDE

Published Literature

Feinberg, Richard. *Anuta: Social Structure of a Polynesian Island*. Copenhagen: Institute for Polynesian Studies in cooperation with the National Museum of Denmark, 1981.

Feinberg, Richard. *Polynesian Seafaring and Navigation: Ocean Travel in Anutan Culture and Society*. Kent, OH: Kent State University Press, 1988.

Firth, Sir Raymond. *We, the Tikopia*. Boston: Beacon Press, 1967 (reprint).

Gegeo, David. "Tribes in Agony: Land, Development and Politics in Solomon Islands." *CS Quarterly* 15(2): 53–55, 1991.

White, Geoffrey. "Village Videos and Custom Chiefs: The Politics of Tradition." *CS Quarterly* 15(2): 56–60, 1991.

Yen, Douglas E., and Janet Gordon, eds. *Anuta: A Polynesian Outlier in the Solomon Islands*. Pacific Anthropological Records, Number 23. Honolulu: Bernice P. Bishop Museum Press, 1973.

WWW Sites

General information and sources on country
http://www.solomonislands.com

Solomon WWW Virtual Library
http://coombs.anu.edu.au/WWWVL–PacificStudies.html

Organization

An excellent source on issues of development and cultural preservation in the Solomon Islands is the Solomon Islands Development Trust (SIDT), which also puts out a monthly magazine called *LINK*. SIDT may be contacted at

P.O. Box 147
Honiara
Solomon Islands
Western Pacific
Phone: (677) 23409
Fax: (677) 21131

Chapter 3

The East Indians of Fiji

Brij V. Lal

CULTURAL OVERVIEW

The People

Fiji was first settled about 1600 B.C. by people of the Lapita culture from the Southwest Pacific, joined subsequently by later waves of migrants from that region. The interactions between these successive groups gave Fijian culture a distinctive character, containing elements of both Polynesian as well as Melanesian regions. The indigenous people first encountered Western explorers in the seventeenth century, beginning with Abel Janszoon Tasman (1643). Captain James Cook and Captain William Bligh visited the Fijian group in 1774 and 1792, respectively. In the nineteenth century, more Europeans came as escaped convicts from Australia, and as traders and beachcombers and missionaries. Their arrival in large numbers put pressure on local institutions and resources and complicated existing political rivalries among a dozen or so powerful chiefdoms competing for political supremacy in the islands. Internal political rivalry and the consequent inability to confront the new forces of change compelled the leading Fijian chiefs to surrender their political sovereignty to Great Britain through a Deed of Cession in 1874 when Fiji officially became a British crown colony. Five years later, the colonial government introduced Indian indentured laborers to work on Australian-owned Colonial Sugar Refining Company plantations to put the nascent economy on a firmer footing without jeopardizing the social structure of the indigenous population already reeling from the adverse effects of contact with the outside world.

Indo-Fijians are descended mainly from these immigrants, sixty thousand

33

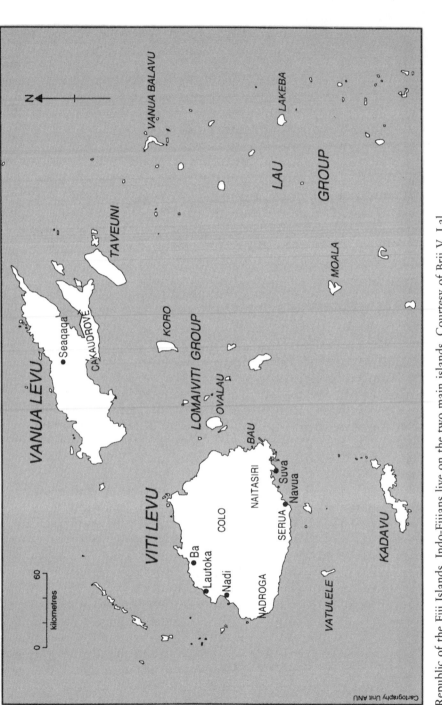

Republic of the Fiji Islands. Indo-Fijians live on the two main islands. Courtesy of Brij V. Lal.

of whom were introduced between 1879 and 1916.[1] They were joined from the 1920s onward by free migrants from India—Gujarat and the Punjab—who were artisans, petty traders, and agriculturists. The indentured immigrants had a five-year contract that provided a free return passage to India at the end of ten years of residence and labor in Fiji. Nearly a quarter of the immigrants returned, but most stayed on for a variety of reasons, including official inducement to remain in the colony to provide a dependable pool of labor to the sugar industry.

The indentured Indian migrants had a variety of social and economic backgrounds. About 75 percent of the original migrants were from the eastern districts of North India in what is today the province of Uttar Pradesh. They boarded the ships at Calcutta. The remaining 25 percent emigrated from South India after 1903. As later migrants and as minorities, the South Indians had to adapt to the dominant (North Indian) culture they encountered in Fiji. The process of adaptation resulted in the loss of language and other distinctive aspects of their traditional culture, with the result that today many people of South Indian descent do not know or speak Tamil, Telugu, and Malyalam. The cultural umbrella organization of the South Indians, then India Sanmargya Ikya Sangam, formed in 1926 and active in social and cultural affairs of the community, has attempted to maintain its ancestral culture through festivals and some language instruction. The Sangam runs a large number of primary and secondary schools in Fiji.

The Setting

The Republic of the Fiji Islands in the Southwest Pacific, 2,759 miles southwest of Hawaii and 1,692 miles northeast of Sydney, comprises three hundred islands scattered over 498,069 square miles of the Pacific Ocean. About one hundred of the islands are inhabited, with the bulk of the population—in 1996 totaling 750,000, of whom 51 percent were indigenous Fijians and 43 percent Indo-Fijians[2]—found on the two main volcanic islands of Viti Levu and Vanua Levu. Together, these two make up 87 percent of Fiji's total land area of 7,095 square miles. Like other similarly situated islands in the Pacific, Fiji has a humid tropical climate tempered by twenty-knot winds from the southeast from June to October, and directly from the east in February and March. Cyclones periodically visit the archipelago in the rainy months. The annual rainfall can range from 120 to 200 inches. Fiji's vegetation has features similar to those in the neighboring Southwest Pacific as well as in the Indo-Malayan Peninsula. Its fauna, like that of its immediate neighbors, is largely restricted to domesticated animals such as horses and dogs; land-based reptiles are nonexistent.

Social and Political Organization

Many of the social and cultural institutions of the Indo-Fijians' indentured forebears were unable to survive in the new environment in Fiji. Among them was the caste system, which had determined the social position and occupational orientation of the people in India. The plantation regime rewarded individual merit and initiative, not social status determined according to some divinely preordained criteria. The paucity of women in the immigrant population necessitated marriage across caste and religious lines. The overcrowded housing on the plantation estates caused caste and dietary taboos to be broken. Enforced interaction rather than social and physical separation became the norm in the Indo-Fijian community. There were no effective means of enforcing sanctions for violation of cultural protocol.

A part of the reason for this was the pattern of Indian settlement. In the early years, freed indentured laborers settled around the sugar mills as hired field hands or as workers in the sugar factories. A major change occurred in the 1920s when the Colonial Sugar Refining (CSR) Company, by then the sole miller of cane in Fiji, decided to break up its plantations into ten-acre blocks, which it then leased to Indo-Fijian growers. The change meant that the Indo-Fijians were no longer merely employees of the company, but independent producers of cane with personal stakes in the productivity of their farms, their work carried out under the close, watchful eye of the CSR overseers. People settled wherever land was made available by either the CSR or the indigenous Fijians, the leasing arrangements in the case of the latter made under terms and conditions specified by the government. Indian settlements in Fiji were thus dispersed, unlike the pattern of nucleated villages in India. The ten-acre farm was big enough to be economically viable, but income from it was never enough to sustain a large family. Hence many families were forced to seek some form of alternative cash employment to augment their income from cane.

In rural communities, where the Indo-Fijians first settled, and where many of their descendants still live, social institutions sprang up to regulate social behavior and relationships in the community. Until the 1960s, the system of *panchayat*, a five-person village council of respected community elders, played a vital role in adjudicating civil disputes, but its importance has declined and in many cases the institution has disappeared altogether. Its function has been taken over by religious and cultural bodies. Among the most important of these are the village Ramayan *mandalis* (religious bodies in the village), regular gatherings of devotees to recite the religious texts. For the Muslims, mosques have always been important. The cane-cutting gangs also play an important mediating role in settling minor village disputes. Since independence, government-appointed Indian Advisory

Rural Indo-Fijian group. Courtesy of Fiji Ministry of Information.

Councils have become the main channel of communication between rural Indian settlements and officialdom.

The joint family (grandparents, parents and children, and occasionally siblings) was the norm in the Indo-Fijian community in the early years. This was partly a carryover from India, but the structure also provided comfort and security to a people finding their feet in a new environment and facilitated cooperative effort in agricultural work. Today, joint families as a norm have disappeared and have been replaced by the nuclear family. In another carryover of the Indian tradition, marriages in the early years were arranged by parents and elders of the extended family. This, too, has been largely replaced by what has come to be known as love marriages. These developments have created problems of their own. Marriage breakdowns are becoming increasingly common. Domestic violence has increased. In the mid-1990s, reports of suicides appeared in the local press with depressing regularity. Care of the elderly is a pressing issue in the community. In the past, the parents could rely on their sons for support in old age, but that expectation is no longer automatic.

Religion

Most of the indentured migrants were Hindus, and about 80 percent of the Indo-Fijian population today professes that faith. Among the Hindu

Indo-Fijians, the majority belong to the Sanatani (orthodox) devotional sect, which accommodates the presence of gods, goddesses, and various local and family deities. Salvation for orthodox Hindus is attained through complete devotion, *bhakti*. Tulsidas's *Ramcharitamanas*, depicting the life and struggles of Lord Rama, is the basic religious text for Fiji's Sanatanis. Rama's story struck a particular chord with the Indo-Fijians whose forebears came from the region of Rama's kingdom. Rama was exiled for fourteen years for no fault of his own, but he did return, and good eventually triumphed over evil. His story gave people hope and consolation: One day they, too, would escape the exile of indenture. A smaller number of Indo-Fijian Hindus belong to the reformist Arya Samaj sect, started by Swami Dayananda Saraswati in 1875. The sect preaches that the word of God is revealed in the Vedas (sacred Hindu writings), which are accessible to all, and not only to the priests steeped in Sanskrit. Puritanical in approach, they decry the rituals, ceremonies, and other paraphernalia of popular religion.

Fiji's Muslim population is similarly divided into two main sects, the Sunni and the Shia. The former comprises the adherents of orthodox Islam of the type professed in Pakistan and Saudi Arabia. The Shia, the party of Ali, Mohammed's cousin and husband of his daughter Fatima, upheld the rights of the family of the Prophet to the religious and political leadership of Islam; the Sunni, literally meaning the majority community, refused to accept this claim and accorded Ali the same status as the other caliphs (Muslim political leader claiming rightful succession to office) who succeeded Mohammed. Early this century, conflicts between these two sects, and between the Sanatanis and the Arya Samajis, provoked great tension in the Indo-Fijian community as people struggled to define and assert their cultural identity in the aftermath of indenture, but they have receded into the background in recent years. A very small fraction of the Indo-Fijian community is Christian. The Christian missionaries attempted to convert Indo-Fijians to their faith but failed because Christianity was seen as the religion of the colonial officials and the plantation managers. Also, the thrust of the missionary endeavor was among the Fijians.

THREATS TO SURVIVAL

The most important threat facing the Indo-Fijian community concerns the possible nonrenewal of land leases. Nearly 83 percent of land in Fiji is owned in inalienable rights by indigenous Fijians. The rest is freehold (2 percent) and state land.[3] Yet, most of the farmers in Fiji are Indo-Fijians who grow sugar cane, rice, and other crops on land leased from the Fijian landlords through the agency of the Native Land Trust Board (NTLB). Of the approximately twenty-two thousand cane growers, thirteen thousand are on native leased land. The lease arrangement is formalized in the Agricultural Landlord and Tenant Act, which provides for thirty-year leases. These leases, first granted in the late 1960s, have begun to expire and all will have expired by the early years of the twenty-first century. The government has set up a multiparty joint parliamentary committee to investigate the problem and recommend solutions to what is clearly a thorny problem.

On one side are Indo-Fijian tenants who naturally want longer leases so that they can undertake long-term economic planning. The present arrangement does not provide much incentive for long-term investment and planning. On the other side are Fijian landlords who understandably seek greater returns from their property. Some want to repossess their land so that they themselves can enter commercial cultivation or use it for other purposes, such as housing and commercial development. Some Fijian politicians want to use land as a lever to gain political and other concessions from the Indo-Fijians. Some landlords in the western part of the island of Viti Levu want to re-lease their land on their own terms. They want to eliminate the intervention of the NLTB, which at present keeps 25 percent of the rental money to cover the cost of administration. The lease question will have to be resolved, but at the present time no solution is in sight.

Another problem that plagued the Indo-Fijian community after the military coups of 1987 was systematic discrimination in the public sector. Their absence in the higher ladders of administration has been particularly noticeable in the last decade. In the mid-1990s, for example, there were only 6 Indo-Fijian permanent secretaries compared to 22 Fijian.[4] There were only 7 Indo-Fijian deputy permanent secretaries compared to 32 Fijians, and only 33 senior government positions of 128 were held by Indo-Fijians. In 1986, the public sector comprised about 50 percent Indo-Fijians and 48 percent indigenous Fijians. By 1993, the figures were 38.5 percent and 60 percent. In the police force, there were 1,125 Fijians and 754 Indo-Fijians; a decade earlier, there was rough parity between the two groups. In the military forces, there were 3,466 Fijians and only 66 Indo-Fijians. Some of the discrimination was mandated by the 1990 constitution, whose affirmative action policies required that at least 50 percent of all positions in the civil service at all levels be staffed by Fijians; in practice, the percentage in some departments was much higher. In the allocation of scholarships, the Indo-Fijians also faced discrimination. Government policy reserved 50 percent of all scholarships for Fijians and established other special educational funds totaling $6.5 million from 1993 to promote Fijian education. For every Indo-Fijian student who received a government scholarship, 3.3 indigenous Fijians received an award.

An assumption underpinning postcoup affirmative action policies was that Indo-Fijians were generally economically better off than indigenous Fijians. Yet, many social surveys found Indo-Fijians more than well represented in the country's underclass. In the late 1980s, more than half of

Suva's squatters were Indo-Fijians. And they were well represented among those living below the poverty line. Kevin Barr, a Catholic priest, ranked the landless Indo-Fijian cane cutters, who work during the cane-harvesting season and are unemployed (and unemployable) during the rest of the year, among the poorest people in the country. The impression of Indo-Fijian prosperity is conveyed by the presence of a sizable Indo-Fijian retail class in the urban centers of Fiji, but as a representation of the entire community it is entirely misleading.

RESPONSE: STRUGGLES TO SURVIVE CULTURALLY

Indo-Fijians responded in various ways to the challenges and provocations they have faced since 1990. They adopted the strategy of passive resistance to deal with acts of violence against their property and vandalism of their places of worship. This strategy was dictated by the acute realities of power in Fiji: All the guns were on the other side. Another response has been migration. Feeling insecure and emotionally uprooted, Indo-Fijians began leaving Fiji in small numbers on the eve of independence in 1970, but the trickle turned into a stream after the coups of 1987. Estimates vary, but it is popularly believed that around eighty thousand have left the country for Australia, New Zealand, Canada, and the United States. More would leave if they could.

The emigration of Indo-Fijians has had several consequences. It has robbed the community of its best and brightest and deprived the country of much needed skills in professional fields. On the positive side, emigration has created a "remittance economy" in Fiji as people from overseas send money to help with the education of children and the payment of land rents, among other things. There is hardly a single Indo-Fijian family who does not have at least one relative overseas, so the impact of remittance on an average household is considerable. The decline in Indo-Fijian numbers has also assuaged Fijian fears about Indian domination, a fear that has distorted political discourse in Fiji for many years. Fijians are now talking much more openly about issues and concerns of their community in ways they did not in the past.

When the postcoup 1990 constitution was brought into existence by a presidential decree, the Indo-Fijian community as a whole was dismayed at its many racially discriminatory provisions and worked tirelessly for its repeal. But apart from the occasional demonstration, the main approach adopted by the Indo-Fijian leaders was negotiation with their Fijian counterparts about ways of reviewing the contested document. The negotiations were protracted, but in the end the parliament agreed to appoint an independent Constitution Review Commission, whose eight-hundred-page report, containing some 690 recommendations, completed after sixteen months of consultations with the people of Fiji, forms the basis of a new broadly acceptable constitution. All the racially discriminatory parts of the 1990 constitution have been removed; affirmative action policies have been made racially neutral; a strong and modern justiciable Bill of Rights has been incorporated into the constitution; a Human Rights Commission has been created; and generally provision has been made for effective, transparent, and accountable governance in the public sector. A unique feature of the new constitution is the formula for power sharing, which provides that any political party with more than 10 percent of seats in parliament is entitled to a place in the cabinet in proportion to its strength in the House of Representatives. With this provision, Indo-Fijians hope that their long exclusion from power will gradually end. The enactment of the constitution has been a major achievement for Fiji, and Indo-Fijians are quietly optimistic that their situation will improve in time. Removing the virus of prejudice and discrimination and stereotyping from the fabric of society will take time, patience, understanding, and tolerance, especially among those who have benefited from the culture spawned by the coups.

FOOD FOR THOUGHT

Indian presence in Fiji extends over a century, and yet many Fijians do not regard them as fully part of Fiji, with claims to equal rights and equal citizenship. They use the Melanesian concept of *taukei* and *vulagi* to express this attitude. The *taukei* is the original inhabitant, the indigenous person; the *vulagi* is the visitor, foreigner, or immigrant. The Fijian scholar Asesela Ravuvu writes that traditional protocol "requires the *vulagi* to be humble and know well his role and position in the context in which he or his ancestors have not been original settlers or *taukei*. His descendants will have little claim either, and they will continue to be *vulagi* unless they go back to where they originated." The *vulagi*, says Ravuvu, are "generally the work-horses of the physical and social settings in which they are established. They generally provide their best in order to be acceptable to the *taukei*."[5] Unless they are subservient, and know and accept their lowly position in the society, the *vulagi* will be expelled. The Indo-Fijians understandably feel distressed at this description of their community. They reply that they entered Fiji not as conquerors but as indentured workers whose labor on the Colonial Sugar Refining Company plantations built the colonial economy and enabled the government to enact policies designed to shield the indigenous society from the corrosive effects of the modern world. But this line of argument does not impress the more nationalist-minded Fijians, for whom natives will always be *taukei* and immigrants the eternal *vulagi*. The mental anguish this causes the Indo-Fijians can only be imagined.

This conflict of interests and aspirations between indigenous and immigrant communities raises the further question of what kinds of constitutional structures are appropriate for multiethnic communities. The values, understandings, and principles that inform the political systems of Western democracies may not necessarily be appropriate for non-Western societies. The Fiji Constitution Review Commission recommended alternatives that accommodate the indigenous people's concerns within a broadly based democratic framework. Most Indo-Fijians welcomed the compromises recommended by the commission even though in some respects their rights might have been curtailed. For example, as the commission recommended, and the parliament accepted, the Fijian Great Council of Chiefs play a significant role in nominating persons for the office of president; it was understood that the president would be an indigenous person.

Internally, the cultural fabric of the Indo-Fijian community is beginning to fray. Globalization is an important cause of the problem. Television, the video revolution, improved communication, and increased mobility have lessened Fiji's isolation from the rest of the world and introduced new and sometimes alien values and practices that impinge on the local life-style. Ceremonies and ritual functions that were once observed over a prescribed number of days have been abbreviated to accommodate changes brought about by modern life. Most people have generally perfunctory knowledge of the deeper philosophical and spiritual aspects of Indian culture. Schools run by Indian community organizations teach Hindi and sometimes some other vernacular languages (Tamil, Telugu, Urdu), but most people have only a passive knowledge of the language. Vernacular literature receives little public support and recognition.

The challenges facing the Indo-Fijian community are many and none is greater than the need to understand the ways in which this immigrant people, from a completely different cultural and philosophical background, adapted to the demands of the island nation—how, in short, Indian immigrants over time became transformed into Indo-Fijians. Understanding the process of cultural transformation may well be an opportunity for the next generation of Indo-Fijians to understand their struggle for representation and identity.

Questions

1. Can immigrant communities find full acceptance, with equal rights and responsibilities, in their adopted homes?
2. What should immigrant communities do to increase the chances of acceptance by the "host" communities?
3. What role may religion have in constraining assimilation by the immigrant communities?
4. What responsibility, if any, do the governments of India and Britain have to the descendants of the imported Indian laborers?
5. What factors discourage Indo-Fijians from returning to India?

NOTES

1. Brij V. Lal, *Girmitiyas: The Origins of the Fiji Indians* (Canberra: Journal of Pacific History Monograph, 1983), and K. Gillion, *Fiji's Indian Migrants: A History to the End of Indenture in 1920*, 2d ed. (Melbourne: Oxford University Press, 1973). Statistics about Indo-Fijians in this chapter are from these two sources.

2. Government of Fiji, *Provisional Census Report*, 1996.

3. Josefata Kamikamica, "Fiji Native Land: Issues and Challenges," in *Fiji in Transition*, Brij V. Lal and Tomasi R. Vakatora (eds.) (Suva: University of the South Pacific, 1997), ch. 14.

4. Brij V. Lal, *Another Way: The Politics of Constitutional Reform in Post-Coup Fiji* (Canberra: Asia Pacific Press, 1998).

5. Asesela Ravuvu, *The Façade of Democracy: Fijian Struggles for Political Control, 1830–1987* (Suva: Reader Publishing House, 1991), pp. 58–60.

RESOURCE GUIDE

Published Literature

Anderson, Grant. *Indo-Fijian Smallfarming: Profiles of a Peasantry*. Auckland: Oxford University Press, 1974.

Gillion, K. L. *Fiji's Indian Migrants: A History to the End of Indenture in 1920*, 2d ed. Melbourne: Oxford University Press, 1962.

Lal, Brij V. *Girmitiyas: The Origins of the Fiji Indians*. Canberra: Journal of Pacific History, Monograph, 1983.

Lal, Brij V., ed. *Crossing the Kala Pani: A Documentary History of Indian Indenture in Fiji*. Suva: Fiji Museum, 1997.

Mayer, Adrian C. *Peasants in the Pacific: A Study of the Fiji Indian Rural Society*, 2d ed. Berkeley: University of California Press, 1962.

Ravuvu, Asesela. *The Façade of Democracy: Fijian Struggles for Political Control, 1830–1987*. Suva: Reader Publishing House, 1991.

WWW Site

Life in Fiji with Indians
http://www.threeweb.ad.jp/~jungrog/e-index.html

Organizations

Arya Pratinidhi Sabha of Fiji
P.O. Box 4245
Suva, Fiji

Fiji History Society
P.O. Box 4694

Samabula, Suva
Fiji

Fiji Muslim League
P.O. Box 3990
Samabula, Fiji

The India Sanmarga Ikya Sangam
P.O. Box 9
Nadi, Fiji

Shri Sanatan Dharam Pratinidhi Sabha of Fiji
c/o Harish Sharma, Barrister and Solicitor
Nadi, Fiji

Sikh Gurudwara Prabandhak Committee
P.O. Box 244
Suva, Fiji

Chapter 4

The Irakia Awa of Papua New Guinea
David J. Boyd

CULTURAL OVERVIEW

The People and the Setting

The Awa, who number about fifteen hundred people, live in eight rural communities on both sides of the Lamari River in Eastern Highlands Province, Papua New Guinea. They control a rugged mountainous territory of 77 square miles that is characterized by a rather narrow grassland valley with forest confined to the mountaintops. No roads have yet penetrated into this valley, so the villages are relatively isolated and people rely on subsistence horticulture and pig husbandry for their sustenance. Although they now occasionally buy foodstuffs from stores in Okapa, a one-day walk away, they still grow nearly all the food they consume.

The ancestral homeland of the Awa is unknown, and the Awa themselves insist that they have always lived in the Lamari Valley. They are, however, most closely related genetically and linguistically to people in three other language groups (Auyana, Gadsup, and Tairora) in the Eastern Family of the Trans-New Guinea Highlands Stock. All of these similar peoples live to the north and east of the Awa, and it is assumed likely that the forebears of the Awa migrated into their current territory from those directions.

Although united by a common language (also called Awa) and various customary practices, each Awa community was politically autonomous until the imposition of political control by Australian colonial authorities in the late 1940s and 1950s. Under this new regime, intervillage warfare was outlawed, a regional governmental organization was gradually established, and local peoples were encouraged to participate in an expanding mone-

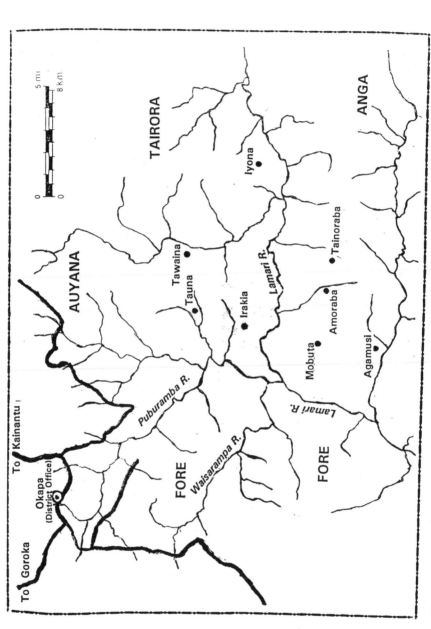

Okapa region, with Awa villages and neighboring groups. Courtesy of David J. Boyd.

tized economy by growing coffee as a cash crop and participating in labor migration. Such changes, of course, have had major effects on the lifeway of most indigenous peoples around the world, and, like that of many others, the experience of the Awa people during the last fifty years has not been one of smooth historical transition. Conflicts have erupted within and between groups, expectations of government assistance and increased prosperity have led to disappointments, and their very identity as a group has been endangered by powerful external and internal forces. Nonetheless, the Awa have persistently fought to maintain viable communities and a sense of their own uniqueness.

The experience of each of the Awa villages has differed from that of other villages somewhat over this period. To cite the most extreme examples, the community of Mobuta has had American and Australian missionaries in residence nearly continuously since 1960 and has enjoyed the benefits of, among other things, a medical aid post, a primary school, and a commercial cattle-raising project. On the other hand, the village of Lyona was nearly wiped out in a recent war with its neighbors and still struggles to reestablish a viable community. In this chapter the focus is on the village of Irakia, with a current population of about three hundred people, and their efforts to adjust to the changes of the recent past.

In the early 1990s, after several decades of rapid social change, the Irakia Awa had come to view their group survival as seriously threatened. More than half of the population was living away from their home territory seeking greater participation in the cash economy, the younger generation expressed no interest in remaining in the village, the government ignored their requests for assistance, and traditional enemies were emboldened by their seeming decline in fortune. People understood that much of the distress was related to recent regional and national changes but also accepted some responsibility for their increasingly tenuous existence. Whatever the causes of the current distress, local leaders came to the realization that they had to promote important changes that would entice members to return to the community and help reinvigorate village life. It seemed unlikely that without a concerted effort to transform local conditions the community would survive.

Traditional Subsistence Strategies

Irakians practice a complex form of shifting, or *swidden* (slash-and-burn), horticulture. Ten different garden types are recognized and are cleared in both the forest and grassland zones according to an established annual gardening cycle. This cycle commences in mid-September at the end of the dry season and the beginning of the first regular rainfall. Members of all households clear and burn plots in the forest zone and primarily plant varieties of yams and taro plus a number of subsidiary crops (e.g., maize, sugarcane, squash, beans, scallions, and various leafy greens). By mid-December, the rainy season is in full swing and households begin clearing and planting a variety of gardens. During this period, each household chooses from among the possible garden types that will fulfill their consumption needs during the next year. Although the exact kinds of garden planted differ from household to household, most families plant mixed gardens that are dominated by sweet potato or tapioca (manioc). A few families may choose to plant gardens that contain only sugarcane or gardens that are irrigated by bamboo pipelines and contain only the starch taro.

By late March, all households again engage in the preparation and planting of a single garden type, this time yam-taro gardens located in the grassland zone. This type of garden requires a high investment of labor as women turn the soil with shovels and remove all of the grass roots; however, it also produces the most highly prized food crop, yams. By mid-July, most people have finished planting these grassland gardens and again move on to select various types of gardens to round out their annual inventory. Most garden plots are planted and harvested several times before being abandoned.

The other important aspect of Irakian subsistence, until recently, was pig husbandry. Animals were obtained from the farrowing of local sows and through trade and exchange relationships. The pigs were fed daily by the women and allowed to forage freely on village lands but had to be fenced out of food gardens. Pigs were the most valuable item produced locally. They were a required part of all marriage and mortuary payments and were transferred infrequently between individuals to settle disputes. Men also were expected occasionally to give a mature pig to their wives' relatives (affines) for slaughter. Pigs were eaten only on special occasions, and people were not allowed to consume meat from animals that they themselves had raised. The Irakian herd was not large by Highlands standards, with the number of animals averaging about half the size of the human population. Also, large-scale pig exchange cycles, common in other parts of the Highlands, did not occur in this region. As will be discussed later, Irakians recently eliminated pig husbandry from their subsistence practices.

The division of labor between men and women is important, but not extensive. Men are responsible for felling trees in forest gardens and for building fences to keep pigs out of gardens. Women are solely responsible for tilling the soil in grassland yam-taro gardens and were the primary caretakers of pigs. Both men and women plant, weed, and harvest the crops. Although women's contribution of labor to gardening and pig rearing certainly is greater than that of men, few Irakian men ever entered into multiple marriages (polygyny). Today, most young people have converted to Christianity and eschew the practice.

Social and Political Organization

Kinship is the fundamental principle of Awa social organization. Membership in significant social groups is based on the recognition of shared descent relationships from male ancestors, the ideology of patrilineal descent. All children are considered members of their father's kin groups. Such kin groups are hierarchically organized: The most closely related individuals form a subclan, and several subclans unite to compose a clan. All clans control an exclusive territory and normally prohibit marriage between members (exogamy). In several Awa communities, including Irakia, the various clans are further combined into two "clan clusters" whose members view themselves as related by descent, live together in separate "hamlet clusters," and generally unite in the common defense of their clan members and territories.

Political organization is more loosely organized as no permanent leadership offices exist. Leaders attain positions of influence through their ability to convince fellow clan members to follow their lead and to support their various initiatives. Competition among the several clan leaders, called "great men" or "Big Men," often is intense at the community level as they vie with each other in public oratory, devising of warfare strategies, and promotion of personal and communal projects. Rarely is one great man able to unite the entire community. Furthermore, if a great man fails to hold sway over others or, through aging, becomes less competitive, other aspiring great men ascend and force his retirement.

Religion

Traditional Awa religious beliefs encompass complex notions of nature, human nature, and the spiritual realm. This body of beliefs involves human interaction with numerous ancestor spirits, ghosts of the recently deceased, and nature spirits. Among the Irakia Awa, an example is a married couple of elderly spirits who are said to live in the top of a tall tree in the forest. They make their presence known at all important ritual ceremonies by the sound of bamboo flute music emanating from the forest and by instruction of ritual participants in the proper conduct of the ceremonies. Such ghosts and nature spirits may reward the living with good health and plentiful food when their behavior is respectful but, when displeased, can also cause illness, misfortune, and even death. Living successfully among this array of spiritual entities requires that individuals lead culturally "proper" lives and promote the fertility, strength, and general well-being of the group.

There are no religious specialists among the Awa, but some individuals are thought to have special access to the spirit realm. For example, curers can enlist the help of spirits to heal the afflicted, and sorcerers can direct spiritual powers to achieve their own, often malevolent, ends. Since the 1980s, however, many Awa have adopted Christianity.

THREATS TO SURVIVAL

Most peoples in the Okapa region experienced periodic threats to their survival long before recent times. Local histories abound with stories of groups who were victims of intervillage warfare and ceased to be viable communities. Survivors fled their homelands and were absorbed into other communities, but the original groups were destroyed. Indeed, within the remembered past, several Irakian clans were forced off their territories during wars with neighboring villages and ceased to exist as independent groups. However, with the arrival of Australian colonial control in 1947, the threats became more subtle, but also potentially more grave.

Australian patrol officers, during their initial visits to the Awa region, stressed the importance of not fighting with one's neighbors, not allowing domestic pigs to live in people's houses, and digging pit latrines for public sanitation. Also, local men were to assist in the exploration of uncontrolled regions farther to the south by serving as carriers on foot patrols. Irakian men reluctantly complied. Later, beginning in the early 1960s, colonial officers began to promote participation in cash-earning activities. In 1963, Irakians planted their first coffee tree seedlings and, thus, began their involvement in production of a cash crop that still dominates the Highlands commercial economy. In the same year, the first Irakian men were recruited as contract laborers and transported, under the colonial government's auspices, to distant coastal plantations. Although most men remained reluctant to travel and live so far away from home, a group of fifteen men followed the government patrol back to headquarters and spent the next two years working as migrant laborers. Upon their return to Irakia, now wearing Western clothing and bearing gifts of steel tools, cooking pots, blankets, and small amounts of cash, more men decided to pursue this opportunity. By 1970, the result of the lure of money and the acquisition of manufactured goods was that more than 60 percent of Irakian males over the age of fifteen were absent from the village for extended periods. People who remained in the village complained of the hardships resulting from this loss of male labor. The preparation of food gardens increased the work load of all remaining residents, especially that of men, who had to assist in the preparation of gardens for women whose husbands were away. Many houses had fallen into a state of disrepair, and bamboo fencing that enclosed the various hamlets was dilapidated. Even more importantly, relatives and exchange partners who lived in neighboring villages were complaining that Irakians were no longer reliable partners. With so many men away from the village, pigs and other valuable items were not being transferred as frequently as exchange partners expected. In consequence, Irakians were suffering a decline in their regional prestige.

To counter this threat, Irakian great men decided, in late 1971, to prohibit additional migration by Irakian men and to demand that those men who returned to the village on completion of labor contracts remain in the community. Furthermore, they decided to stimulate the local production of pigs by adopting a pig-raising ritual practiced by the neighboring Fore people, who were acknowledged to be superior pig raisers. Assuming that the ritual would be successful in increasing the size and health of the village herd, the plan was to sponsor a regional ceremony several years hence during which they would give pork and other valuables to neighboring groups and, thereby, restore their local reputation.

About 1975, after several years of work devoted to nurturing their pigs and expanding their gardens, Irakians did sponsor a major regional feast and exchange ceremony. Relatives and exchange partners from eight nearby communities attended the event and received gifts of pork, other foods, and money. Irakians recounted the event with obvious pride and felt that they indeed had restored their good name in the region. They also noted that they never before had hosted such a large gathering.

In the same year, 1975, the flag of the Australian colonial administration was lowered and Papua New Guinea became an independent nation. Irakians expected that the change in authority would finally make them the beneficiaries of local improvements that previously had been promised them. A road would be built to the village, a school would be established, a government-sponsored medical aid post would provide health care, and a potable water system would be put in place. Unfortunately, none of these projects came to pass. In fact, contacts with government representatives actually declined and Irakians felt even more abandoned than during colonial times.

In the late 1970s, people again began to leave the village to pursue wage-earning opportunities on coastal plantations. By this time, there were accommodations at the work sites for both men and women, so whole families began to migrate, not just adult men. Initially, the number of people who left the village was small, a trickle of those who wanted more access to cash. By 1981, only twenty people were away as migrants.

In 1981, people were very alarmed by the recent unanticipated deaths of a number of male leaders. Indeed, between 1972 and 1981, there had been a decline of about 30 percent in the number of men forty years of age and older. Also, the number of independent households had fallen from seventy-three in 1972 to only sixty in 1981.[1] The communal anxiety was summarized succinctly by a woman in her fifties: "Our great men are dying and the forest is reclaiming the village."[2] This sentiment expressed the concern that, without effective leadership, humans would not be able to remain in this place. Without strong men, who had helped hack out a settlement on this ridge, the forest ultimately would seek its revenge. Although the exact causes of death remain undetermined, the recently deceased were not elderly, so people attributed their deaths to sorcery. Such unexplained deaths cause enormous fear among peoples in this region. Since sorcerers practice their treachery in secret, suspicions of who actually is responsible lead to a heightened sense of vulnerability and a willingness to suspect and accuse one's adversaries. Such feelings of hostility had already contributed to one bow-and-arrow fight with the village of Mobuta, during which one Mobuta man had been seriously, but not fatally wounded.

As the fear of sorcery grew, many families began to leave the village. A few families moved in with relatives in neighboring villages, but most migrated to coastal plantation work sites. Also, in 1985, hostilities with the village of Mobuta again flared into a year-long period of intermittent battles in which three Irakian men and two men from Mobuta were killed. Emissaries from Irakia hurriedly were sent to the coastal plantations to bring back warriors and the battle eventually ended in a stalemate.

About 1986, Irakians accused one of their own, a man in his fifties, of being an active sorcerer and the cause of the recent deaths. He is said to have confessed to these crimes and died shortly thereafter. Nonetheless, unexpected deaths continued and sorcery was again determined to be the cause. After several years of unease, villagers accused another Irakian man, who had been an influential leader of the community for some twenty years, of using sorcery to cause the deaths of others, including several of his own clan brothers. He denied the allegation and, in 1990, escaped from the village with his family and eventually went to live with relatives working in the capital city, Port Moresby. Unrest in the region, however, continued through the late 1980s and early 1990s. To the north, Fore communities battled along the road to Okapa. Police intervened but were not able to stop the fighting, and the road is now effectively closed. To the west, other Fore communities confronted each other over land boundaries, and, in the ensuing battles, several people were killed. To the south, the Awa communities of Mobuta and Amoraba took up arms and carried on a running battle for several months. A police unit finally was sent to the scene by helicopter and warned the combatants that they would return and burn down both villages if the fighting did not stop. The warning was taken to heart and a truce was declared. To the southeast, the Awa village of Tainoraba argued with its Tairora neighbors to the east over access to a road where they could market their coffee. Fighting erupted, and both sides destroyed houses, pigs, food gardens, and coffee trees. Resident missionaries finally were able to quell the fight. To the east, the Awa village of Iyona, with a population of only about seventy people, got into a fight with their Awa neighbors of Tawaina, who number over two hundred. During a hit-and-run attack, Iyona warriors killed a Tawaina woman. The Tawainans responded with a massive attack, during which a shotgun was used for the first time on Awa territory. The Iyonans were driven from their territory south across the Lamari River and nearly half of their adult men were killed.

Although the Irakian Awa never were directly threatened by the battles swirling around them, they did understand the external threat. Without a strong presence on their territory, they too could be drawn into the regional conflicts. Furthermore, they believed that they had removed the internal threat by exposing and removing suspected sorcerers from the village. Now, they had to devise a plan that would rebuild their vulnerable community.

RESPONSE: STRUGGLES TO SURVIVE CULTURALLY

The primary task of rebuilding the community was to convince members living away to return and help rebuild a viable society. At this point, in 1991, over half of community members lived away. Those at home realized that to entice members to return to live in Irakia they had to make substantial improvements in village life.

The first change instituted was the building of a church. Many of the younger generation had been converted by evangelical missionaries while living at plantations and they wanted to continue their religious observances at home. Also, local residents who had not yet adopted Christianity saw that neighboring villages who had accepted Christian missionaries seemed to be more prosperous. By 1991, weekly services were being held. Without a resident pastor, young men led the ceremonies playing hymns on guitars and reading passages from the Scriptures. Members of the congregation offered emotional testimonials of their encounters with Jesus, the Virgin Mary, and the Devil.

After this turn toward piousness, residents agreed that consumption of beer and gambling with cards should be banned. Beer drinking, which had become a part of village social gatherings in the 1980s, often led to abusive and violent behavior. And gambling, a common activity at plantations, was the cause of serious altercations in the village. Those who lost their wages tended to blame winners, and physical fights caused social disruption.

Housing construction also needed to be altered. Traditional houses were small and had low doorways that required one to stoop to enter. Such restricted entrances served to slow potential enemies, but they no longer seemed necessary. Larger, more commodious structures were needed. A major building campaign was initiated.

By 1993, these initiatives were viewed as quite successful and leaders were confident that positive changes were occurring. But more had to be done to strengthen the community and encourage people to return home. Individuals were sent to Port Moresby and to the major plantation work sites to convince migrants to return. These efforts were quite successful. In

1993 the migrants in Port Moresby and at two plantations in West New Britain agreed that they wanted to go home. One worker, who had been away from the village for more than twenty years, said, "I came to make money so my children would have a better life, but the money did not come, and now it is time to go home."[3]

Leaders in the village also decided that they had to resume male initiations for young men. Since so many young men had been living away from the village, these important rituals had not been performed for nearly a decade. Such rituals, which are physically painful, but designed to promote the health, vitality, and fertility of men, were thought to be essential to revitalizing the community. In fact, it was thought that the prior unexpected deaths of a number of male leaders had been due, in part, to a lack of ritual protection. If they now were to build a vigorous community, they had to initiate their young men to make them strong and vital members of the community. To that end, a new men's clubhouse, in which the rituals were planned and ultimately conducted, was constructed. In late 1993, the ritual took place and visitors from many neighboring communities attended, receiving gifts of pork, cash, and various commercial goods. Irakians described it as a massive social gathering and one in which they clearly demonstrated their social prowess. As a male leader stated, "Initiating our young men is the most important thing we do. It makes us who we are."[4]

In an effort to make life in the village more enjoyable to residents sports teams were organized. Men formed two soccer teams and women joined together in a basketball team. The teams occasionally compete with other villages in regional tourneys, and at home they offer their services as work groups. The women's basketball team can be hired for K4 (U.S. $3) per day to clear and till a new garden; a men's soccer team will help clear a garden or build a new house for K6 (U.S. $4.50) per day. Money earned is used to pay tournament fees and to buy uniforms. These sports have become a major focus of social life in Irakia with games played almost daily.

Understanding that people could not remain in the village without some local source of cash income, leaders promoted the planting of more coffee trees. Although coffee had been an unreliable source of cash, with prices often fluctuating widely from year to year, it still was the most lucrative cash crop. In 1995, coffee income averaged only about K150 (U.S. $113) per household, so villagers set about increasing their plots.[5] New gardens were cleared and the area devoted to coffee production increased by about 50 percent. Residents now hope that coffee production will provide for their cash requirements and that community members will not feel the need to leave the village to earn money.

The last change instituted was perhaps the most far-reaching. As early as 1991, young men had told me that they wanted to get rid of domestic pigs, but the elders would not hear of it. As the elders succumbed to old age, however, the move to do away with pig husbandry gained support.

Clockwise from left, Irakian woman pulping and washing coffee berries, men playing soccer in a grassy field, women's basketball team tilling a new garden. Courtesy of David J. Boyd.

Young women, many of whom had been raised on plantations without pigs, did not want to serve as swineherds. Also, young men, who were responsible for fencing gardens to keep pigs out, thought it an unnecessary burden. Without pigs, the village living area would be cleaner, men and women would not have to work so hard, and people would not argue over the exchange of pork when pigs were killed for distribution. With the approval of most villagers, nearly all pigs were eliminated from the village by early 1996. One elderly man refused to comply. He kept a favored sow and said that people could slaughter her for his mortuary feast. He died in August 1996, and so did his sow. Now, people purchase imported lamb ribs when ceremonial occasions require the exchange of meat.

By 1996, all of these changes had been instituted. Although compliance by villagers has not been total, conflict over the changes has been very limited. Most residents agree that they are moving in the right direction. Furthermore, large numbers of community members have returned home to live in Irakia. Only sixty-seven people (22 percent) were living away from the village in 1996, and many of those expressed their desire to return home soon.

The political opinions of returnees also have tapped into a deep local dissatisfaction with the government. After several decades of expectation that the government would sponsor development projects in the village, not one such project has been initiated. As one young leader expressed it, "Our innards are hot about this [meaning, we are angry]. If tax collectors come to steal our money, we will shoot them. We know that the police then will come and burn down our village, but we don't care."[6] In July 1996, an aspiring politician from an Auyana community, accompanied by a group of his supporters, visited Irakia on a campaign swing through the area. Irakians politely called people together to hear him out. His pitch was polished, but familiar: "It is now your time to receive something from the government. You have been ignored for too long. If you vote for me, you soon will have a road, a primary school, and a medical aid post."[7] A murmur went through the crowd. It was not friendly. Finally, a recent returnee, who had spent some twenty-five years as a migrant laborer and had returned home to stay, rose to respond: "We have heard all of this many times before. It is the same old 'garbage talk' [lies]. The government is never going to help us and neither are you. If you want to buy our votes, give us a tin roof for our church and uniforms for our soccer teams. These are things that we want."[8] Somewhat taken aback, the would-be politician admitted that he didn't have the means to provide such assistance, but he still hoped that they would vote for him. After being fed and housed for the night, the visitors disappeared over the ridge early the next morning headed for their next campaign stop.

Irakians definitely are proud of their recent accomplishments. Rather than pursuing the vain hope that outsiders—government officials, missionaries, and others—would come to their aid, they themselves have set in motion a plan to transform their lives and rescue the community.

FOOD FOR THOUGHT

Recent threats to survival for the Irakia Awa are not the result of an absolute population decline. In fact, from 242 individuals in a 1963 census, the population had grown to 299 in 1996, with only a slight decline in the late 1970s.[9] Rather, the threat has come from local depopulation due to population dispersal. As people sought to improve their lives, they left the village to seek wage employment elsewhere. Or, they sought to avoid the received local threat of sorcery.

These challenges to survival that Irakians have experienced were not precipitous events but resulted from rapid social changes taking place in the local region and beyond, and the responses of Irakians to those changes. They watched expectantly for over three decades as roads, several schools, and medical aid posts were established by outsiders to service other communities, but no such amenities were provided to Irakia. As other communities seemed to flourish, Irakia stagnated and members left the village to seek wage work and safety from sorcery. Faced with this challenge to the continued existence of their community, young leaders forged a plan of action to revive village life and defend their right to exist. With the support of most village members, the Irakia Awa have accepted the responsibility for their own future and refuse to disappear.

Questions

1. How do contemporary threats to the survival of the Irakia Awa differ from those they experienced before the colonial period?
2. Irakians seem to have gone to great lengths to respond to complaints from exchange partners that they no longer were reliable partners. Why did Irakians view such dissatisfactions as threatening, and why did they devote so much effort to making matters right?
3. Why was the exit of many men from the village as labor migrants in the late 1960s considered so threatening to the survival of the group? If it simply was a matter of the loss of labor for clearing gardens and building fences, why do you think the women did not take on these tasks?
4. Irakians claim that they now want to revitalize their community and are encouraging members to return home to live. They also have lost confidence in the government and have decided to chart their own course. At the same time, they have killed all their pigs and now have to buy meat from exchange ceremonies. They also have planted more coffee trees, the major cash crop. Although

Irakians feel that these moves give them a more independent stance, doesn't this strategy seem to tie their future even more closely to the vagaries of the monetary economy?

5. What factors seem to make the survival of the Irakians more likely or less likely?

NOTES

1. David J. Boyd and Karen L. Ito, "Culture and Contact: Reproductive Decision Making in Okapa District, Eastern Highlands Province," in Nancy McDowell (ed.), *Reproductive Decision Making and the Value of Children in Rural Papua New Guinea, IASER Monograph No. 27* (Boroko, PNG: Institute of Applied Social and Economic Research, 1998), pp. 45–79.

2. Ono, personal communication, Irakia village, Eastern Highlands Province, July 1981.

3. Waiya Oru, personal communication, Hargy Plantation, Bialla, West New Britain Province, July 1993.

4. Mote Wi, personal communication, Irakia village, July 1996.

5. Data obtained by the author during a household survey in July 1996. Sixty-two individuals representing fifty-six households reported a total income from coffee sales of K8,338 (U.S. $6,254).

6. Aiya Antabi, personal communication, Irakia village, July 1996.

7. Joe Esegi, personal communication, Irakia village, July 1996.

8. Totori, personal communication, Irakia village, July 1996.

9. K. J. Pataki-Schweizer, "A New Guinea Landscape: Community, Space, and Time in the Eastern Highlands," in *Anthropological Studies in the Eastern Highlands of New Guinea*, vol. 4, James B. Watson (ed.) (Seattle: University of Washington Press, 1980), p. 107. Additional censuses were conducted by the author in 1972, 1981, 1991, 1993, and 1996.

RESOURCE GUIDE

Published Literature

Boyd, David J. "The Commercialisation of Ritual in the Eastern Highlands of Papua New Guinea." *Man* (n.s.) 20(2): 325–340, 1985a.

Boyd, David J. "We Must Follow the Fore: Pig Husbandry Intensification and Ritual Diffusion among the Irakia Awa, Papua New Guinea." *American Ethnologist* 12(1): 119–136, 1985b.

Boyd, David J. "The Legacy of a Highlands Great Man: Sorcery and Politics among the Irakia Awa." In *Work in Progress: Essays in New Guinea Highlands Ethnography in Honor of Paula Brown Glick*, Hal Levine and Anton Ploeg (eds.), pp. 43–61. Frankfurt am Main: Peter Lang, 1996.

Hayano, David M. *Road through the Forest: Living Anthropology in Highland Papua New Guinea.* Prospect Heights, IL: Waveland Press, 1990.

Newman, Philip L., and David J. Boyd. "The Making of Men: Event and Meaning in Awa Male Initiation." In *Rituals of Manhood: Male Initiation in Papua*

New Guinea, Gilbert L. Herdt (ed.), with an introduction by Roger M. Keesing, pp. 239–85. Berkeley: University of California Press, 1982.

Videos

Several videos were made by Bob Connolly and Robin Anderson, Sydney, Arundel Productions:

First Contact 1982
Joe Leahy's Neighbors 1988
Black Harvest 1992

WWW Site

Information on culture and people
http://www.png.com

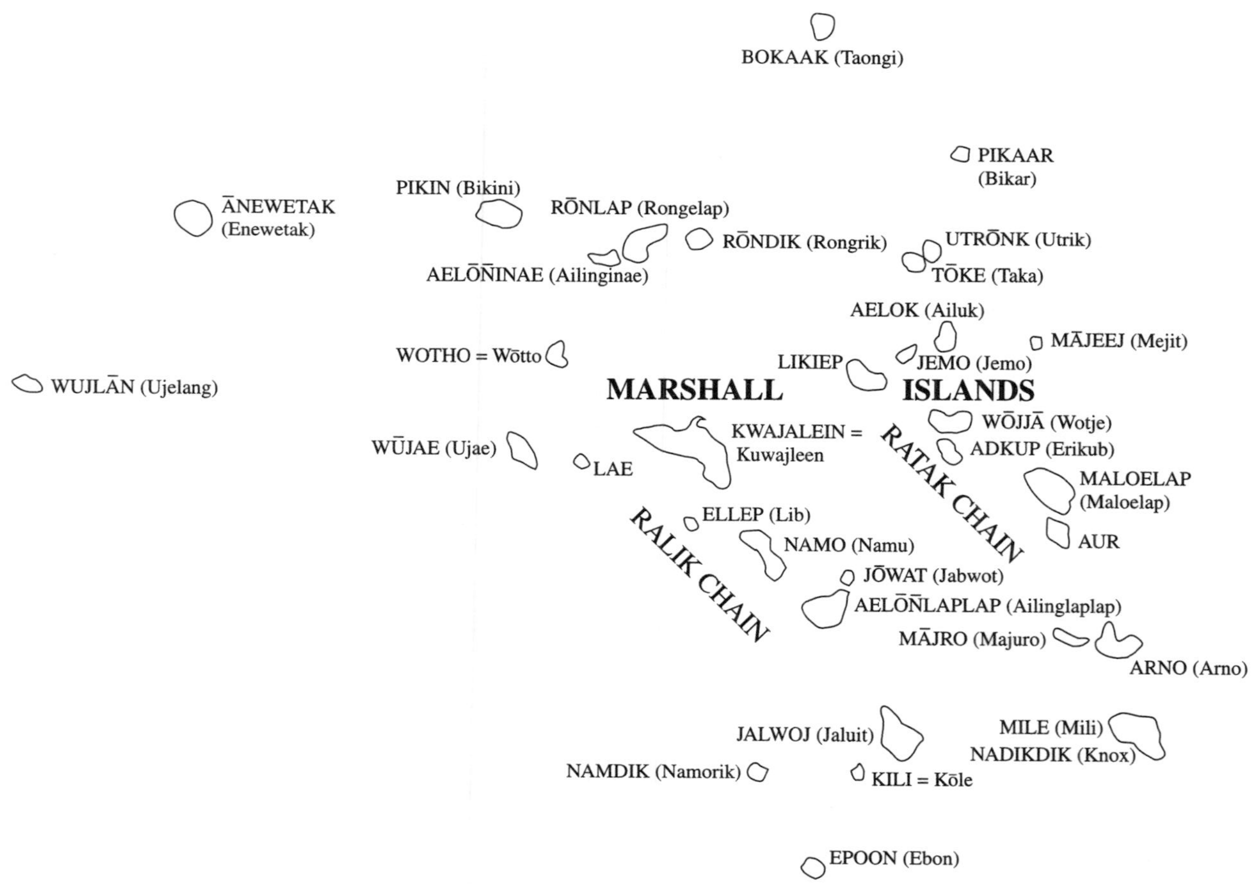

The Marshall Islands. Courtesy of Nighthawk Design.

Chapter 5

The Marshall Islanders
Nancy J. Pollock

CULTURAL OVERVIEW

The Bikini atoll in the Marshall Islands burst onto the world scene in 1954 when the United States set off an atomic bomb there as part of their initial twelve-year-long nuclear testing program. The United States was still testing military weapons there forty-five years later. The people of these islands have undergone severe disruptions to their daily life, their islands, and their ideology so that their very existence has been threatened. This chapter traces three ways in which their lives and their way of life have been threatened, first by relocation away from their home islands, second by the effects of fallout on their health, and third by the intrusions of capitalism and the cash economy that have accompanied the U.S. nuclear testing program.

The people of Bikini were removed from their home island in the northern Marshall Islands in 1946 as a precautionary measure before testing began and were relocated on an island, Kili, some four hundred miles to the south. Their neighbors on the Rongelap atoll were not removed at the time of testing, and thus suffered severe effects of fallout, but were moved subsequently when they complained of ill health. Parts of Bikini atoll were blown away, other parts became highly radioactive, and some parts remain radioactive and thus unusable today. Five ships sunk in the Bikini lagoon as part of the "experiment" attract divers today from around the world to Dive Bikini, a tourist attraction. The people of Enewetak, a neighboring atoll also used as a site for testing nuclear weapons, have also suffered severe dislocation, health, and social problems. All these people and other Marshall Islanders are seeking compensation from the United States government for their sufferings.

The People

The people of Bikini, along with the inhabitants of the other thirty-three atolls and reef islands of the Marshalls, have lived on these low-lying islands for perhaps six hundred to eight hundred years, arriving mainly from the Caroline Islands to the west. Each atoll population has established its distinct identity based on a unique heritage, though they recognize the control of the state in recent times. Thus although Bikini is part of a political state, now known as the Republic of the Marshall Islands, its people consider themselves distinct from other atoll populations.

The people of the Marshall Islands speak a language that is related to other languages of Micronesia, particularly to Pohnpeian and Truk/Chuuk. When the Congress of Micronesia was formed in the 1960s, people of individual atolls in the Marshalls did not understand the larger grouping "Micronesia," an inclusive Western term for all peoples of the Northwestern Pacific. The context varies, however. In some contexts it is used synonymously for the peoples of the United States Trust Territory of the Pacific, but that political usage excludes the people of the Gilbert Islands, who are also classified as Micronesian on the basis of their language.

People moved from large high islands such as Pohnpei and Kosrae and reached the islands we now know as the Marshall Islands through their skilled use of canoes and navigation knowledge. To cross the vast distances of the Pacific Ocean they had to be accomplished navigators. Once established, perhaps four hundred to six hundred years ago, they traveled between their atolls and the Gilberts/Kiribati atolls to the south, and also to the west to Kosrae and Pohnpei. Occasionally they were blown off course and ended up in New Britain, part of Melanesia, or other parts of Oceania. They sailed considerable distances fishing and trading. Stick charts used as maps were a mnemonic means of passing on navigation lore to succeeding generations.

The Setting

The Marshall Islands consist of twenty-nine atolls and five reef islands scattered over 750,000 square miles of the Central Pacific Ocean. The atolls form two chains running in a northwest, southeast direction between 4° and 19° north latitude, and between 160° and 175° east longitude. Los Angeles is some 5,000 miles to the east, Tokyo 3,000 miles to the northwest. The United States maintains a large military base at Kwajalein atoll, which consists of ninety islets that enclose the largest lagoon in the world with good anchorage for deep-water ships. Most of the other atolls have smaller lagoons, only some of which are navigable for large ships. Bikini was chosen for atomic bomb testing because its lagoon could accommodate large naval ships and because of its so-called remoteness and small population.

The atolls on which the people of the Marshall Islands live are fragile environments, with limited land space and an ever-threatening presence of the sea around them that can and does inundate those land spaces. Their life-style has adjusted to this fragility, but any additional threat, and specifically one so drastic as atomic bomb testing, only serves to increase the danger to those people's existence. Atolls are particularly vulnerable places for human habitation as they rise only some ten feet above sea level; have a very restricted vegetation source, because the soil is sandy, on a limestone base that is porous; and are subject to cyclones and high winds from time to time. Poor water retention is a factor that severely limits both human and other life in such places. Atolls such as the Marshalls are particularly in the spotlight today as the predictions for global warming and sea level rise will have major consequences for them. A high rate of population growth exacerbates this problem of people in relation to the resources.

There was apparently no group name for any of these islands before a European naming. The islands were named in 1788 for the English captain John Marshall, who was sailing across the Pacific in the *Charlotte*, together with Captain Thomas Gilbert in the *Scarborough* carrying the first convicts to the British colony of New South Wales, Australia. Marshall's name was given to the northernmost of the atolls of the Central Pacific, and Gilbert's to those atolls to the south of the Marshalls. Since independence in 1986, the Gilbert Islands are known as *Kiribati*.

The Marshall Islands had four successive colonial masters before becoming independent in 1986. In the 1800s the Spanish claimed the Marshall Islands along with the other atolls and high islands of the Eastern and Western Carolines and the Marianas as part of their empire. But they ceded the Marshall Islands willingly in 1888 to Germany, which was looking to establish coaling ports for its trading vessels as they crossed the Pacific Ocean. Thus, Jaluit atoll in the southern Marshalls became such a coaling port, and the first capital of the Marshalls. After Germany was defeated in World War I, her possessions in the Pacific were divided up under the Treaty of Versailles in 1919. The Marshall Islands became part of the newly formed League of Nations as mandated territories under the governance of Japan. When Japan was defeated in World War II, the Marshall Islands then became a United Nations Trust Territory under the governance of the United States. In 1986 the Marshall Islands became a self-governing republic. Yet still today under the terms of a Compact of Free Association with the United States, the United States can continue testing its missiles in return for a lease agreement that pays the Marshall Islands for the use of Kwajalein atoll for those military purposes.

The Economy

The money paid by the United States to the Republic of the Marshall Islands government for military purposes is vital to the islands' economy. Without it they would be hard pressed to maintain their nation state. They are dependent, however, on a major nation power, a point that has long been a matter of debate for the people of the Marshalls.

The coconut tree and copra, the dried meat of the coconut, have been the mainstay of the Marshall economy for over one hundred years. Family lineages own both the land and the trees on their own atolls. The sale of copra to trading ships enabled rice, flour, tea, and sugar to be purchased. Jobs and wage income are very scarce on outer islands, confined to two urban centers, one at Majuro, and another at Ebeye on Kwajalein atoll. Income from the sale of copra is dwindling, and hopes for developing the tourist industry mostly have been slow to materialize. Still, Marshalls Dive Adventures recently opened a successful tourist venture on Bikini, based on underwater remains of the nuclear testing program. Lease money for Kwajalein military base and compensation money from Washington, D.C., for the effects of the nuclear testing program are a significant input to the economy; their continuation is a matter of considerable speculation as a result of varying political pressures. United States compensation for nuclear testing ends with the compact in 2001, as does guaranteed U.S. aid, except for the rental of Kwajalein, which continues for another fifteen years.

Social and Political Organization

All people of the Marshall Islands belong to the lineage (*jowi*) of their mother. Matrilineal heritage is a very strong cultural force despite attempts by outsiders to make the people conform to aspects of Western family types whereby patrilineality and use of the father's surname are the rule. Lineages are linked to form named clans, or maxilineage, that crosses atoll boundaries. A lineage is a localized social unit, tracing back to a founding sister and mother, whereas clans are more dispersed throughout the atolls of the Marshalls. Sibling sets consist of between six and sixteen brothers and sisters, all of whom have strong ties to their mother and her sisters. Brothers maintain close ties with their sisters throughout their lives, and those ties may be stronger than ties to their wives. Formerly cross-cousin marriage was common, as a female was expected to marry her mother's brother's son. Marriages were highly endogamous (inside the group) on a particular atoll. People always maintained ties to their matrilineal atoll, even though they might move around to other atolls. Adoptions are still common but usually occur within the extended family unit.

Lineage continues to be the social unit that links people to the land. Lands inherited in the matrilineal line are known as *lamoren*. Each atoll is divided into strips of land, many running from lagoon side to ocean side of the islet. Each strip of land belongs to a named lineage that has rights to reside and to work that land, that is, to use it for collection of coconuts for copra. Some Marshallese have land rights on more than one atoll. The tie between people and their *lamoren* land on their home atoll is both materialistic and symbolic. It is a tie that is not broken by moving away.

On Bikini, where whole islets have been blown away by nuclear testing, there is a question as to how descendants of those missing pieces of land will be reestablished on the atoll once it is declared radioactively safe. When they were moved to Kili island in 1946, a new form of land division was established, but one that lacked the mythology and symbolism associated with the cultural heritage of the Bikini people's ties to land on their home atoll.

Each piece of land is controlled by a chief, an *Alab*, and workers (*rijer-bal*). The *Alab* is the head of a group of lineages closely related through female ancestors as sisters, and the workers are the members of those lineages. The *Alab* manages the lands for the chief. The chief (*Iroij*) has an inherited position that has no direct link to lineage today. A chief holds lands on more than one atoll. On Namu atoll, for example, four chiefs held supreme land rights; one of those chiefs, Lejolan Kabua, was a descendant of Kabua Kabua, a chief who was involved in the politics of the 1880s, but whose power was centered mainly in the Raiik chain of atolls. Today, all chiefs form a House of Iroij in the Marshall Islands' government.

Religion

The Congregational church has the largest congregation in the Marshalls today, followed by the Roman Catholic church, First Church of Christ, Bahai, and several other denominations. The Associated Board of Commissioners of Foreign Missions out of Hawaii arrived in the Marshalls in 1857. Local pastors were trained at Kosrae for the islands of Pohnpei, Marshall, and Gilbert.

Traditional beliefs in a panoply of gods and spirits identified with rocks and the reef held a special place in people's ties to their home atoll. For example, in Namu atoll a female goddess, Liwatoinmour, is said to have had her home on the western reef of that atoll and to have controlled the lives of the Namu people. She is still remembered today.

The Marshallese believe that their chief has a spiritual hold over them, with the ability to inflict sickness and also to heal. Displeasing a chief may cause a severe toothache or a stomach pain, which may only be assuaged by appeasing the chief. The chief was honored with gifts such as pigs, turtles, and large deep-water fish and special feasts (*kamlo*) during his presence on an atoll. In return, he was expected to look after his people, providing them with fishhooks and other implements; today, with money.

Under the copra economy a proportion of all money received in the sale of copra is turned over to the chief and a smaller proportion is given to the *Alab*. Compensation monies paid by the U.S. military government for use of Kwajalein and Enewetak were also funneled through the chief, a practice that led the Bikini people to erase their ties to a chief and to "adopt" America as their surrogate chief.

THREATS TO SURVIVAL

Nuclear testing has produced three major threats to the survival of people of the Marshall Islands. First, the population of three atolls were forcibly relocated away from their homes, which were to be used for U.S. military purposes. Second, the tests, in particular Bravo in 1954, resulted in severe health problems for the Marshallese, the extent of which was only becoming clear forty years later. Third, the tests and the continued attempts to obtain compensation money both for disruption and for the health issues have posed their own threats to the Marshallese way of life.

At the time the United States began nuclear testing in the Marshalls in 1946, the total population of the Marshall Islands was approximately 18,000.[1] The population of Bikini totaled 161 at the time of their removal to Kwajalein, a temporary base until a more permanent island home was found for them on Kili—a raised reef some two hundred miles to the south. The people of Enewetak numbered 142 when they were removed in 1947 to Ujelang, the farthest west of the Marshallese atolls. Their island of Enewetak, along with Bikini, had been declared the Pacific Proving Ground. People of the neighboring atolls in the northern Marshalls were moved off their islands only for short periods during the initial eight years of testing. However, 42,000 U.S. military and scientific personnel had moved into the area to conduct the nuclear tests.

When Bravo, the largest of the nuclear tests, was exploded in 1954, 82 Rongelap people were living on their atoll, and 400 on Ailuk and 157 on Utirik to the east of Rongelap. These people all experienced radiation fallout as a result of a wind change the night before the Bravo test was exploded. At 15 megatons (or 15,000 kilotons) Bravo was the largest of sixty-seven bombs tested between 1946 and 1958 by the United States in the Marshall Islands. The hydrogen bomb device was exploded from a barge launched into the atmosphere, producing fallout from 114,000 feet. Debris was scattered as large particles that fell directly below the explosion, while finer particles entered the upper atmosphere to be scattered over a wider area. A wind change during the explosion from the southeast to the northwest meant that fallout was carried eastward over populated islands. Rongelap, Rongerik, Ailingae, and Utirik atolls received doses of radiation measuring between 900 roentgen units and 10 roentgen units (research in

1962 showed that for any person receiving more than 800 roentgen units, survival was deemed unlikely).

The Rongelap people were removed to Kwajalein two days after the Bravo explosion, and then allowed back three years later (1957), until they complained of sickness and radiation burns. The Utirik population was evacuated from their atoll three days after Bravo and returned home three months after the test. The people living on atolls farther east were not removed, though their health, and that of the Rongelap people, was monitored in subsequent years by agents for the U.S. Atomic Energy Commission.

Although officials of Operation Crossroads, as the 1954 series of tests was named, maintained a strict code of silence about the change in direction of fallout, twenty-three Japanese fishermen caught in the fallout zone alerted the worldwide community to the radiation burns they had experienced as a result. The effects on the forty-two thousand U.S. military personnel in the area have not been reported. Ironically the effects of radiation on plants and sea life were carefully monitored by the Applied Fisheries Laboratory at the University of Washington, but the human inhabitants of islands under the fallout were given low priority. Recently it has been suggested that they were indeed part of an experiment to find out the effects of radiation on the human body even though the experiences of the people of Hiroshima and Nagasaki, who suffered from the first nuclear explosion fallout in 1945, were available.

Health Effects

Radioactive fallout from nuclear testing in the northern Marshall Islands is now known to have adversely affected people and the environment in all the atolls, not just the northern five atolls, as originally claimed by the U.S. monitoring service. Morbidity rates for the total period since testing began continue to be revised, depending on the agency reporting them and the basis of their survey. At the end of 1996, 1,368 individuals had been identified as having medical conditions that were deemed to be related to the effects of fallout.[2] New medical conditions are being identified each year, more than forty years after the Bravo test, but no statistics are available to compare those under the Nuclear Claims Tribunal with those in the general hospital population. The compensation program run by the Nuclear Claims Tribunal acknowledges a connection between certain medical conditions and the nuclear testing program. These include acute radiation sickness, cancers of various parts of the body, and leukemia. The greatest number of medical conditions diagnosed have been thyroid nodules and cancers of the thyroid. Of the ill patients with new medical conditions receiving compensation, most awards (fifty-one) were for bronchial cancer.

Forty cases of ovarian cancer were also reported in 1996.[3] No further details are available on these women, but these cases are significant in terms of the overall effect of radiation from nuclear tests to the life of the Marshallese community. Not only was the reproductive life of these women severely affected, but their families suffered too. A child's death is mourned, but the loss of a mother is even more distressful. There is no information on what stage in their childbearing life these women had attained or on their earlier reproductive histories. Significant as well is the loss to the Marshallese matrilineages, so integral to the culture of these islands.

The women with ovarian cancer, together with another forty-four women suffering from breast cancer, have been acknowledged to have compensable conditions, but many more women, and their lost offspring, are not included for lack of hard evidence. Totally unknown is how many men's reproductive functions have also been reduced.

The Marshall Islands has a high rate of reproduction. On outer islands in 1981 women had seven to ten live children, and some had twelve to sixteen children.[4] Reduction in childbearing capacity is deplored. Although not officially acknowledged, radiation is commonly perceived as a cause of stillbirths and malformed fetuses, known as hydatidiform cysts, or "jelly babies," by Marshallese. One woman on Witje had seven miscarriages in nine pregnancies, and one of the live born babies, in utero at the time of the Bravo blast, is now a mentally handicapped middle-aged woman. Witje is now one of the atolls identified as having received radiation fallout in 1954. The link between fetal deaths and nuclear radiation in the Marshalls, according to epidemiologists, is tenuous.

Relocated Communities

The explosion of Bravo necessitated the removal of the people to make way for all the United States military and civilian activities associated with the nuclear testing program, known as Operation Crossroads. Jobs on Kwajalein atoll, which became the center of operations, contributed significantly to socioeconomic changes.

A distinction must be drawn between voluntary movement between atolls and forced relocations. Marshallese, as good navigators and experts in their canoe craft, have always moved between atolls visiting relatives whose hospitality is part of the Marshallese ethos. Forced relocation has had serious repercussions for the populations of Bikini, Enewetak, and Rongelap. Each population, still resident in their relocated places, has maintained a continuous struggle with the U.S. authorities expressing their desire to return to their home atolls. As James Matayoshi, mayor of Rongelap, notes, "Younger generations are growing up in ignorance of their atoll homes. . . . Their lives and use of resources were guided by an intricate body of traditional knowledge which is only held by the older generation.

The longer a return to Rongelap is delayed, the harder it will be for the younger generations to learn this knowledge and adjust to atoll life."[5]

In the time since the forced relocations took place, an entire generation of descendants of the original inhabitants of Bikini, Enewetak, and Rongelap has grown up not knowing the place of their ancestors. Half of the Bikinians still live on Kili, the Enewetak people are spread between their atoll and urban centers, and the Rongelap people live on Mejatto in Kwajalein atoll and Ejit in Majuro atoll. Other members of these atoll communities are spread over the other atolls of the Marshall Islands. They have lost the close ties with their home atoll that characterized the existence of previous generations.

Urbanization

With the creation of jobs associated with nuclear testing, particularly on Kwajalein, rapid urbanization has followed. Marshallese have poured in from all the other islands. Because they have no land rights on Kwajalein they are housed on Ebeye, an islet two miles long by a quarter of a mile wide, that is now "home" to ten thousand people. The U.S. military-built apartment-style dwellings are small and inappropriate for the Marshallese style of living, which focuses on the area around the dwelling house, and overcrowding is common. In contrast, on Kwajalein, U.S. personnel live with such amenities as a golf course, a supermarket/PX, wide roads, and palm trees around their houses.

The main attractions to migrate from relocation centers are employment, health facilities, and a secondary school. The one thousand or so jobs on Kwajalein are a good source of cash, so there are always plenty of applicants. Over the forty-year period of testing and continued military pressure, the number of jobs has fluctuated; however, the number of Marshallese seeking jobs increases.

Economic Fallout

Nuclear testing turned the Marshall Islands from a subsistence/cash economy to a million-dollar-a-year rent economy. Other significant pay-outs also have altered the Marshall Islands' economy. Dependency on cash and a consumer culture among the Marshall Islands' people are direct results of nuclear testing. Initially populations moved to new island spaces had no food or canoes for fishing, and the housing provided was unsatisfactory. The United States as administrator provided the funds and the labor. Slowly some crops and useful plants, such as breadfruit trees, have become established, but dependency on cash is the norm. What the economy of the Marshalls would be like today without all the pay-outs associated with nuclear testing is hard to imagine.

Monies received in the Marshall Islands can be placed in five categories and are distinct from the vast U.S. military bill for deployments on Kwajalein:

1. Rent for use of land on Kwajalein and other atolls is approximately $11 million per year, paid to the Marshall Islands' government.[6]

2. Income from nuclear program operations has been a significant feature both in giving the Marshallese access to cash, as well as in acting as a drawing card for people hoping to get such jobs on Kwajalein. Also, taxes on the salaries of Americans working on Kwajalein, wages paid to the Marshallese, and other services from the army, as well as the rent money, yield a total of about $25 million annually, or almost one third of government's annual operating budget.[7]

3. Kwajalein landholders have received annual rent payments since 1946 from the United States for use of their lands for military purposes, in addition to money paid to the government of the Republic of the Marshall Islands (RMI). Landowners, however, see a significant portion of the rental money for their atoll lands going into RMI government coffers and feel justified in asking for improved social services to accommodate the very densely crowded populace on the islet of Ebeye.

4. Compensation monies paid to Bikini, Rongelap, and Enewetak peoples total many millions of dollars. These payments include compensation for relocation, loss of use of their atolls due to nuclear testing, costs of establishment in the new location, and compensation for radiation contamination and loss of cultural heritage. Part of the compensation is paid to individuals; the balance is placed in trust funds that pay out quarterly to individual members of those communities. These sums do not include pay-outs for damage to health.

5. A trust fund set up by an act of the RMI government in 1986, managed by the Nuclear Claims Tribunal, was part of a political settlement designed to monitor claims associated with the United States nuclear testing program and its aftermath. The Compact provided a trust fund of $150 million that was invested to earn a total of $270 million, with $75 million for Bikini, $48 million for Enewetak, $37 million for Rongelap, and $22 million for Utirik. The Nuclear Claims Tribunal was assigned $45 million with $33 million designated for health care and monitoring of radiation levels. By the end of 1996, $55 million had been granted, but there were still many claims outstanding, including those for "class action property damage claims for Bikini, Enewetak and Rongelap atolls"[8] that have been given priority over individual property damage claims.

RESPONSE: STRUGGLES TO SURVIVE CULTURALLY

The people of the Marshall Islands have constantly struggled to draw attention to the fallout from U.S. nuclear testing on their islands. Many sectors of their lives have been drastically affected by irradiated soils, relocation, goitrous nodules and other health conditions, and the impact of a large military presence in these small islands. The Marshallese have maintained continued pressure on Washington, D.C., and in return have been granted desultory action for clean up and drip-fed sums of money as compensation. Can a group of people ever be recompensed for such total disruption to their life-style, and for the diseases and loss of life that so many Marshallese have endured? Money seems a paltry response. The people of the Marshall Islands, however, have learned to keep "asking for more." That has been their greatest means of survival. They have kept the issues alive, rather than allow themselves to be ignored.

The relocated communities have each fought their individual battles with Washington, D.C. The overarching desire is to return to their home atolls, and this has been asserted many times, in many different settings. At times the requests have been ignored, or answered with delaying tactics. In 1968 journalists from New York visiting the people of Kili informed them that they would be going back to Bikini. There was no celebration for those journalists to record as those people had become cynical, even then, about such messages from Washington. And thirty years later they were still being told Bikini is unsafe for their return. Yet, a scuba dive facility has been established, advertising for international travelers to visit.

Each of the three major communities affected by nuclear testing has formed its own lobby group, operating under the leadership of the mayor of each community, together with paid officials. The Rongelap, the Enewetak, and the Bikini people each have an office in Majuro district center where materials are collated for their claims, which are being pursued vigorously. Each community has its own set of lawyers. Each community has its own set of claims before the Nuclear Claims Tribunal. These agencies keep the interests of their individual communities alive. A major issue, the loss of cultural heritage, is still not resolved. It is most difficult to argue especially with regard to valuation of heritage and a way of life. There are few similar cases worldwide on which to base precedents.

Health issues still loom large, especially now that the entire Marshallese population is included in the claims. Those who have goitrous nodules have been screened at the hospital. In addition to United States agencies monitoring these radiation associated conditions, Japanese epidemiologists have brought new research findings to bear on the aftermath of fallout. These are supported by new findings released from Washington in confidential documents pertaining to the explosion of Bravo in 1954. Marshallese government officials are keen to use this new information for the benefit of their people. A study to follow up on those people who may have been exposed on atolls other than the northernmost ones is currently being planned between the RMI Department of Health and the Centers for Disease Control (CDC) in Atlanta, Georgia. Meanwhile Japanese health officials are also involved in monitoring health conditions.

The large sums of money paid to communities and individuals are bringing to the fore new ideological principles that contest traditional Marshallese principles of generosity and community sharing and caring. Clearly relationships between claimants and rights to be claimants rest on social principles, notably belonging to a matrilineage. The rights and responsibilities of kin to one another, whether coresident or living miles apart, are being preempted by the pressures for access to these large cash sums. As the population increases rapidly (4.2 percent per year) the shares in these pay-outs are becoming smaller.[9] At the same time, they become more precious.

Particular life-styles have been adopted by those communities that depend on compensation payments, income from trust funds, and rent for lands. Food consumption is based on imported foods, and money is spent on consumer goods, including alcohol and cigarettes. Health problems are being exacerbated by the new life-style, a matter that is yet again a concern for health services that are already underfunded but heavily in demand.

Dependency on a cash income with very few chances of employment or work has thus altered the life-style and ideology of these recipients. The principles of both those who govern and those lucky to have received their compensation money have been drastically altered by the economic fallout from nuclear testing. The only solace to their concerns is to maintain ties with their atoll communities and act collectively.

FOOD FOR THOUGHT

Bravo 1954 was the largest of a series of sixty-seven nuclear explosions in the atmosphere over the Marshall Islands. Fallout from that one test was particularly severe, dropping radioactive particles on people and their land and sea. The other sixty-six atmospheric nuclear tests between 1946 and 1958, and that in 1962 on Christmas Island, are also designated under the U.S. Radiation Exposure Compensation Act of 1990 as likely sources of additional contamination. After 1962 nuclear tests in the Marshalls were moved underground, thereby reducing the likelihood of atmospheric fallout.

The peoples of Bikini, Enewetak, and Rongelap were forced to leave atolls from which they derived their unique identity. They were separated from ancestral burial sites and their cultural heritage and ultimately forced to invent a new cultural base. Both physical and psychological suffering has resulted. Lives were lost and many people have suffered lifelong illnesses. Two generations have grown up not knowing their home atolls or the way of life before relocation. Future generations of Marshallese will carry the burden of the fallout from Bravo and will have difficulty in eradicating its impact on them physically, morally, and socially.

Compensation has been offered in various financial forms as the main solution to the cultural upheaval generated in 1954. The cash in hand and in trust has led to a strong capitalist ideology with its emphasis on consumerism. The Marshall Islands' government has found itself locked into the Compact of Free Association, which keeps that money flowing, as long as the United States chooses to test nuclear missiles.

Questions

1. How can the safety of nuclear residues be measured today?
2. How can the rights of small states with apparently no power be protected from external agents who have their own agenda, whether military or civil?
3. Is money an appropriate form of compensation for the dislocation and health damage caused by fallout from Bravo in 1954?
4. What, if anything, has the world community learned from the Bravo disaster?
5. What might the current generation of Marshallese tell their children about fallout from U.S. nuclear testing?

NOTES

1. Population statistics of the 1940s and 1950s are from Stewart Firth, *Nuclear Playground* (Sydney: Allen and Unwin, 1987), and Robert Kiste, *The Bikinians* (Menlo Park, CA: Cummings, 1974).
2. *Nuclear Claims Tribunal Annual Report*, Majuro, Marshall Islands, 1996, p. 4.
3. Ibid., p. 24.
4. Republic of Marshall Islands Census, 1981.
5. *Tok Blong Pasifik* (March 1997), pp. 11–12.
6. Giff Johnston, *Collision Course at Kwajalein* (Honolulu: Pacific Concerns Resource Center, 1984).
7. *Marshall Islands Guidebook* (Majuro, Marshall Islands, 1996), p. 53.
8. *Nuclear Claims Tribunal Annual Report*, p. 9.
9. Republic of Marshall Islands Census, 1988, p. 16.

RESOURCE GUIDE

Published Literature

Firth, Stewart. *Nuclear Playground*. Sydney: Allen and Unwin, 1987.
Hines, Neal. *Proving Ground*. Seattle: University of Washington Press, 1962.
Kiste, Robert. *The Bikinians*. Menlo Park, CA: Cummings, 1974.
Pollock, Nancy J. *These Roots Remain*. Honolulu: University of Hawaii Press, 1992.
Weisgall, Jonathan. *Operation Crossroads*. Annapolis, MD: U.S. Naval Institute Press, 1994.
Wulff, Stuart. *After the Bomb*. Special Edition of *Tok Blong Pasifik* 51, nos. 1–2 (March/June) Victoria: South Pacific Commission, 1997.

Videos

Half Life: A Parable for the Nuclear Age, 1985. Copyright Denis O'Rourke Associates Filmmakers, Pty Ltd., Australia. Australian Documentary, Channel 4. (PAL VHS) Length: 2 hours. Writer: Dennis O'Rourke. Film Editor: Tim Litchfield.

Strategic Trust, 1986. Copyright Aroha Productions, New Zealand. New Zealand Tuesday Documentary. (PAL VHS) Length: 57 minutes. Producer/Writer: David Rose.

WWW Sites

Bikini Atoll Homepage
http://www.bikiniatoll.com

Department of Environment, Safety and Health
http://www.eh.doe.gov./portal/

Chapter 6

The Marquesas Islanders
Jane Freeman Moulin

CULTURAL OVERVIEW

The Marquesas Islands lie in the Southeast Pacific, over nine hundred miles northeast of Tahiti and about six hundred miles south of the equator. The twelve islands—only six of which are inhabited—are part of French Polynesia, an overseas territory of France.

The early settlers in the Marquesas were the carriers of a Western Polynesian culture that they took with them from the area of Fiji/Tonga/Samoa. Through purposeful, two-way voyaging early Marquesans maintained frequent contact with people in what are now called the Society Islands and Cook Islands and contributed to the development of a culture that eventually became distinctive from that which they had brought with them. It was this new set of ideas, practices, and values that these Eastern Polynesians took with them when they later set out to the more remote, non-inhabited islands at the far points of the Polynesian triangle. And it is these unique cultural traits that unite the lands settled by these later migrations from the east—New Zealand, for example, home of the Maori, is located in the Western Pacific but is culturally Eastern Polynesian.

As one of the easternmost archipelagoes in the Pacific, the Marquesas Islands not surprisingly were the first to experience contact with European ships setting out from South America and Europe to explore the Pacific. In 1595 the first Europeans to arrive in the Marquesas were part of a Spanish expedition that drew near to the island of Fatuiva and then went ashore on Tahuata. Unfortunately, this initial contact was brutal, and a lack of cultural understanding and human empathy contributed to a particularly violent interaction. Almost 180 years passed before the next European ship

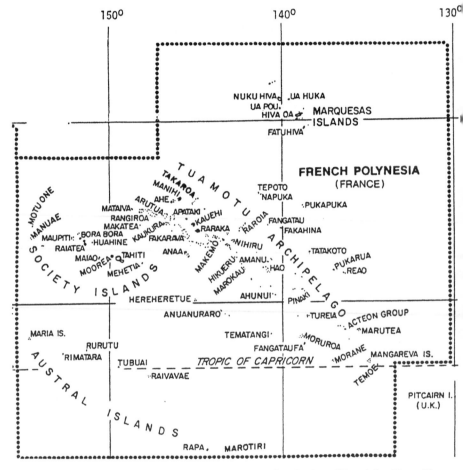

French Polynesia. Courtesy of the Hawai'i Geographic Society, Honolulu, Hawai'i.

appeared on the horizon, and the famous Pacific voyages of Captain Cook ushered in a new era of repeated contact with outsiders. Over the next century, the number of European ships entering the Pacific grew rapidly, and the Marquesas' position at the gateway to the Pacific made them convenient and popular ports of call—first for explorers, and then for whalers, sandalwood traders, and other commercial ships crisscrossing the Pacific in search of new products and new markets. The frequent and repeated contact with these ships caused widespread change in Marquesan society and cultural institutions. Political change occurred with the annexation of the islands by France in 1842. With this and the subsequent Christianization of the islands during the second half of the nineteenth century, the power of local chiefs, traditional rituals, and indigenous religion slowly disappeared.

In the late nineteenth century and throughout the twentieth century, the same extreme eastern location of the islands had a much different effect on the lives of Islanders. Sandalwood activity declined, whaling tapered off, and the center for regional commerce turned to Tahiti, the Marquesas Islands' distant neighbor in the Society Islands. With the French establishment of a colonial government on Tahiti, Tahiti's role as the central island of what was eventually called French Polynesia was secured. Ships bypassed the Marquesas in favor of the economic and political center, and the Marquesas Islands turned into a remote, "country" outpost—its dwindling population neglected and, in many respects, left to fend for itself. Even the advent of air traffic in the twentieth century did little to relieve the isolation and dependence of the Marquesans. With the only international airport located on Tahiti, contact with the exterior still today goes through Tahiti. Tahiti remains the filter through which all people, new ideas, money, and outside goods must pass.

The People

The oral traditions of the people as well as evidence from such fields as archaeology and linguistics support the idea that the original inhabitants of the Marquesas traveled by canoe from the Western Pacific. They remained in this eastern location for perhaps centuries before venturing to such islands as Hawai'i and Rapu Nui (Easter Island). Ongoing archaeological work in the archipelago continues to push the dates of first settlement further back in time, but most researchers agree that the islands were populated by the first century B.C., perhaps even as early as 500 B.C.

Today, a predominantly Polynesian population of seventy-four hundred inhabits the six main islands (Nukuhiva, 'Uahuka, 'Uapou, Hiva'oa, Tahuiata, Fatuiva). Improved medical care and living conditions have contributed to a steady population growth and an especially youthful population. In the 1990s more than 55 percent of the inhabitants were younger than the age of twenty years.[1]

The Setting

The people live in narrow, steep-walled valleys, most of which are separated from neighboring valleys by mountainous interiors and the lack of a coastal plain between the mountains and the sea. A system of ancient footpaths and, on some islands, unpaved roads provides overland links between communities. Unlike many Polynesian islands, the Marquesas Islands have no surrounding lagoons, and access by sea is along a dramatically spectacular coastline of steep cliffs that rise sharply from the ocean. On those islands without roads, people travel by canoe or speedboat when visiting friends or family in another valley; for land travel, islanders rely on horses and four-wheel-drive vehicles.

Young people begin their formal education in valley elementary schools. As teenagers, however, many must leave their homes and families to attend middle schools on other islands. Most boys are educated at the Catholic school in the island of Nukuhiva, and girls go to Catholic school on the island of Hiva'oa. Students who want to continue their schooling past the compulsory age of fourteen, however, must go to Tahiti. The move from a small, close-knit rural community in the Marquesas Islands to the hustle and bustle of the capital city of Pape'ete is a major, and sometimes difficult, change for Marquesan youth. Because there are no high schools, few jobs at home, and many young people competing for those jobs, however, many parents believe that this move is the only way for their children to gain the skills, education, and experience that may lead to good jobs and a better income.

Traditional Subsistence Strategies

Because the Marquesas Islands are located in an Eastern Pacific equatorial belt that is noted for irregular rainfall, intermittent drought, and lack of a coastal plain for cultivation, Marquesans do not practice extensive agriculture. Locally grown fruits and some root crops do supplement the canned and packaged goods found at the trade store in most valleys. Coastal shell life, deep-water fish, and wild pigs and goats provide protein in the diet, and men plan regular hunting and fishing excursions.

Breadfruit grows extremely well in this climate, and the paste made from the starchy fruit (*ma*) has traditionally been the staple of the Marquesan diet. Ancient Marquesans made large pits to store and ferment the paste, and this resource helped them to survive droughts, periods of population pressure, and those times when warring parties from neighboring valleys destroyed their food-producing trees. The preference for fermented breadfruit paste is still strong today, and *ma* remains a favorite food on the Marquesan table.

Social and Political Organization

Marquesan life in the past was organized around a system of tribes who occupied the different valleys. As in most Polynesian societies, Marquesan allegiance was to the tribe and its allied groups rather than to a larger sense of nationalism or widespread political unity. Intertribal conflicts were commonplace. Even though political alliances provided some measure of protection, these alliances did not result in widespread unification or even islandwide political control. Instead, control remained primarily with the valley *haka'iki* (chiefs).

Because the Marquesas are an overseas territory of France, a high commissioner represents the interests of the French state in the region, but most decisions concerning internal matters are made by an elected Territorial Assembly that meets hundreds of miles away in Tahiti. As in previous centuries, local politics revolves around the valley, but now an elected mayor replaces the hereditary chief. The French government appoints a resident official to the Marquesas. Although this person should ideally be in a position to aid the Marquesans by providing a direct link to the French government, a frequent turnover rate diminishes the effectiveness of the office and allows for little consistency in either policy or results.

Modern historical events and Western politics have grouped the Marquesas together with the Society, Austral, Tuamotu, and Gambier islands to create one political entity, but these five archipelagoes do not constitute a cultural unit. Marquesans, for example, are very different from their neighbors in both language and culture. The distinctive features of this difference, including in the performing arts, are more and more apparent as Marquesans step into the new millennium with an ever-growing sense of cultural pride.

Religion

The first Protestant missionary to the Marquesas, William Pascoe Crook of the London Missionary Society, arrived in 1797. The particular social organization of the Marquesas and the independent nature of the people, however, seem to have contributed to a very slow acceptance of the beliefs and practices of Christianity. Whereas Christianity was enthusiastically embraced in many parts of Polynesia, the missionaries to the Marquesas encountered overwhelming difficulties and strong resistance to religious change. Almost fifty years later, one remarked that there was little hope "the word of God had taken root in even one heart."[2]

A major setback in the Protestant effort to gain converts was the arrival of the French Catholic priests in 1848. The two groups set up opposing camps and accused each other of all sorts of improprieties and falsehoods. By the end of the nineteenth century, however, Catholicism was firmly established on all islands. By the 1990s about 95 percent of the residents were Catholic, although the strong Protestant-Catholic division and currently a certain element of distrust from those former years remain.[3]

Several of the early priests left important documents that tell us about Marquesan culture during the second half of the nineteenth century and express dismay and shock at the extreme violence in Marquesan life brought on by the widespread political, social, and religious changes of the times. During this same period, the French also enacted laws that forbid many traditional practices—such as tattooing, chanting, drumming, wearing perfumed oils and flowers, and holding elaborate funeral feasts. It is hardly surprising that much of indigenous culture either disappeared or went into hiding as a result of both church and French disapproval.

The church is perhaps the most important organization in the community, but there is an interesting tension that exists between Christian beliefs and indigenous culture. In valleys where tikis (religious figures), ancient feast places, and archaeological sites are omnipresent features of the landscape, residents today are constantly reminded of the past. They believe in Christianity but also tend to believe that the past and objects related to it have power. Today, because of religious conversion, this is usually interpreted to be negative power and contributes to a situation in which Marquesans do not treat the past lightly. There is a respect for the past and people are reluctant to do things that might be considered "messing around" with it—through participating in certain traditional practices, associating with historic objects, or consciously changing old things that have been passed on (especially important chant texts and certain dances).

THREATS TO SURVIVAL

Current Trends

In the last quarter of the twentieth century, issues of cultural identity became increasingly important in many parts of Polynesia. It was a notable change for Islanders, because it meant purposefully stepping back and observing and thinking and talking about culture rather than just living it. It meant, in many cases, that people were looking at their lives, seeing the multiple and rapid changes taking place, and seriously questioning the impact of these new ideas and practices on their lifeways. Uncomfortable with many elements attributed to progress, many Islanders began to examine the importance of tradition in a modern world and question the extent to which they would participate in, and ultimately be defined by, outsiders' notions of who they are—for example, deciding whether they wanted to be the seductive hula dancers on the tourist poster conforming to European ideas of a flashy and exciting show or the performers of traditional songs and dances that embrace island culture and values. In addition, as increased travel and contact throughout the region contributed to the widespread exchange and borrowing of artistic ideas throughout the region, many Polynesians began to react to what they believed was a blurring of the distinctiveness between their individual cultures. In other words, emerging issues on one hand dealt with Polynesia's relationship to the outside world and, on the other, with interactions among island communities.

The motivation for a renewed emphasis on traditional culture—and on a clear definition of what is "theirs"—varied from island group to island group. The renewed emphasis on traditional culture was prompted and shaped by such realities as Islander attempts to alter established political relationships (independence for the Cook Islands and growth of the sovereignty movement in Hawai'i), a sense of helplessness in the face of actions taken by an external power (nuclear testing in French Polynesia), artificial groupings of people based on historic colonial ties (the division of Samoa and American Samoa, but the uniting of Marquesans and Tahitians), a resurgence of pride in Polynesian culture among Islanders who have become minorities in their own lands (Hawai'i and Aotearoa), and the increasing impact of foreign, global culture on small island societies throughout the region.

The history of colonialism in the Pacific and the very real fear of being subsumed under a foreign culture underlie all these reasons for validating tradition and underscore the desire of contemporary Polynesians to highlight and nurture what is distinctively theirs. The word *hegemony* is a particularly useful one when talking about situations in which one group of people has authority and control over another or one group imposes its thoughts and ideas upon another. There are many different kinds of hegemony, or many different ways in which one group of people can exert control over another, for example, political, economic, or cultural hegemony. This chapter looks at interactions between two Polynesian cultures and at how the Marquesas Islanders use cultural icons—including traditional music and dance—to help accomplish their political goals. In the process, they both define their unique culture for others and affirm for themselves the important role of tradition in modern life.

Tahitian Hegemony

Tahiti is the government center and the most populous island in the territory. In addition, it has an international airport and established shipping links and interacts directly with the outside world. This means that Tahiti holds both the reins of political power and enormous economic strength. It also means that Tahiti, Tahitian interests, and Tahitian culture tend to dominate the concerns of the country—and it is this hegemonic stronghold that Marquesans increasingly resent and resist. Tahitian domination is evident in many areas; those that are particularly threatening to the Marquesans center around economic development, political goals, and cultural identity. To understand the resentments Marquesans have, it is necessary to contrast life in Tahiti with life in the Marquesas.

Pape'ete is a modern, sophisticated, Europeanized town. Although buildings are not higher than about five stories, there is a developed downtown area with numerous stores, businesses, restaurants, and all the modern conveniences as well as parking hassles, commuter traffic jams, and other congestion problems. In families both parents work and many children participate in organized after-school activities such as sports or classes in foreign language, dance, music, or computers. Most young Tahitians speak French at home and school and learn Tahitian almost as a foreign language, unless they are in homes in which Tahitian language is valued or have Tahitian grandparents with whom to converse. Stores stock the latest fashions from France or local copies with an added Polynesian flare, restaurants support the French love of gourmet food and wine, nightclubs offer the hottest music from America and Europe, car and motorcycle dealers advertise the year's new models, and television stations broadcast French satellite emissions of current European and world events into living rooms throughout the territory. Sustained for years by large sums of money from France, Pape'ete is definitely plugged in, turned on, and going somewhere.

In contrast, life in the Marquesas is like a step backward in time. Whether transporting copra (dried coconut meat) on horseback, sitting in the shade to make the fragrant *mono'i* oil or leis of sandalwood shavings, hunting wild pig and goats, finding shrimp in the freshwater streams, or catching the small crabs that scamper along the rocky shore, there is a calm to the tempo of daily life. Teenagers gather by the roadside in the evening to sing songs, play their boom boxes, and just pass time together. They are bilingual—generally using Marquesan with their friends and families, but speaking French at school. Life is rich in strong interpersonal relationships. With extended families and as few as five hundred people on the whole island, people cooperate to accomplish individual and community projects.

But there are very real problems as well. Most islands have just a few miles of paved road. Small hospitals exist on two of the six islands and are unable to handle emergencies. Television and telephone arrived only in the late 1980s, and some villages still do not have twenty-four-hour electricity. Interisland flights are offered once or twice a week, and two inhabited islands are accessible only by sea. Many valleys have no boat dock, making it difficult to import some items, and the cost of clothes and food is prohibitive, because of transport costs. Businesses are few in number, so there are few jobs. Marquesans travel back and forth to the capital, but the high price of getting to the remote archipelago coupled with the lack of any developed infrastructure to support tourism means that visitors to the islands are infrequent. Those tourists who do arrive on the one tourist ship per month stay as little as four or five hours in a particular valley before taking off again, so there is little outside money entering the economy.

And—worst of all from a Marquesan perspective—there has been very little effort in the territorial government to address these issues that touch so deeply Marquesans' quality of life.

Politics

Severe depopulation of the archipelago has affected Marquesan society in a multitude of areas, not the least of which is contemporary politics. From a low of only 2,094 people in 1926, the population has grown steadily. Nevertheless, Marquesans today represent only 4 percent of the total French Polynesian population. Even with an elected delegate to the Territorial Assembly, the Marquesan voice in the government is extremely limited, and Tahitians tend to view the Marquesans as a very small minority group living on the periphery of a Tahiti-centric country. Tahiti, with 70 percent of the territory's population, is obviously the dominant power.

From a Marquesan perspective, Tahiti receives substantial amounts of money from France, takes the lion's share, and then sends the leftovers out to the remaining 129 islands of the territory. Marquesans distrust Tahitian motives and intent, largely because they see how Tahitians have exploited the pearl farms of the Tuamotu Islands at the expense of the indigenous residents. Given their small population base, however, Marquesans remain dependent upon the actions and largesse of the numerically larger and politically stronger Tahitians, noting all the while that the cessation of nuclear testing and the subsequent cutback in the amount of money coming from France will make competition for the remaining funds even tougher in the future.

One political faction in Tahiti is pushing for French Polynesian independence from France, and this is a special worry to Marquesans. Marquesans recognize that life under French rule is not ideal, but they also believe that being governed by Tahiti—especially a bankrupt Tahiti—would spell certain disaster for the archipelago. They feel a very real need for political action.

Economic Crises

Many of the Marquesas Islands' current problems focus on economic issues—a lack of jobs, high cost of living, limited economic opportunity, absence of local industry or commercial development, no infrastructure to support development, and no direct international connections. Marquesans are constantly reminded of the contrast between the comfort of Tahitian life and their struggle for the basic necessities.

This fact is driven home on a daily basis. With so few businesses in the Marquesas, the main employer is the French Polynesian government (medical clinics, schools, various government bureaus, post offices). Yet, in order to qualify and compete successfully for the limited number of available government positions, applicants must take civil service exams that are administered only in French or Tahitian. Marquesans, therefore, are required to take their examinations in what is a second or third language and are at a definite disadvantage. A similar situation affects Marquesan students at the Teachers' College, where exams for teachers include a compulsory section in Tahitian. Requests to offer the exams in Marquesan fall on deaf ears in the capital, and Marquesans are reminded of it every time they are forced to encounter a Tahitian who has filled one of the few precious jobs in the Marquesas.

With such a limited economic base in the islands, Marquesans are forced to rely on many government services, many of which are ultimately controlled by Tahiti. For example, one government-funded boat previously traveled between the islands on a regular basis; another serviced the airport on Nukuhiva. This latter was a crucial duty, since the airport is located on the opposite side of the island from the main village. Because there is no paved road, it is considerably faster, cheaper, and more comfortable for arriving passengers to take a boat. When the French funds dried up, however, the ship was recalled to Tahiti, and Marquesans are now forced to take a three-and-a-half-hour ride over unpaved wasteland in order to reach the airport. Similarly, the scheduled boat service between the islands came to a halt, leaving interisland travelers from the two islands without airports reliant on the once-weekly trip of the mayor's thirty-five-passenger tuna boat. For people who dream of selling their crafts on Tahiti or welcoming the occasional tourist to their island or seeing their families, the removal of government-funded boats was like the cutting of a life line.

Cultural Crises

Marquesans believe they have been treated as second-class citizens of French Polynesia for decades. When they move to Tahiti in search of jobs, they encounter subtle and overt forms of social discrimination. In earlier years, Tahitians often referred to them as "savages." Today, they are more likely viewed as unsophisticated "country folk."

Tahitian cultural domination is evident throughout the territory, especially in the widespread presence and acceptance of Tahitian music and dance in all of the archipelagoes. For example, Tahitian dance was imported to the Marquesas as early as the 1880s; by the 1920s, it had virtually replaced Marquesan performances on most public occasions. Scholars writing in the 1920s and 1930s predicted the death of the language and the demise of anything resembling traditional Marquesan culture.

It is easy to see why Tahitian models became so popular. Given the French laws, the disapproval of the church, and the disparagement of the Tahitians, Marquesans dropped many of their traditional practices. They

Marquesan youth playing *pahu* drum. Courtesy
of Danee Hazama.

did what was allowed and appreciated, adopting in the process a completely different culture from the politically dominant Tahitians.

There were, thus, two processes that took place: cultural dispossession,
or the attempt to strip away the indigenous culture of the Marquesans, and
cultural replacement, the process of substituting Tahitian ideas and values.
It was easy for Tahitian culture to take hold because it was reinforced by
its social and economic predominance throughout the territory, radio (and
eventually television) broadcasts from Tahiti, and a church structure that
was very closely allied with Tahiti. Fortunately, Marquesans did not completely throw away their own ancient arts, however. They guarded them
as if they were fine china or heirloom silver, bringing them out only for
the most special occasions and the most worthy guests.

Historically, Marquesans were fine carvers who, with complex geometri-
cal designs, turned utilitarian objects such as bowls, poi (pudding made from
processed root crop) pounders, and ornaments into highly admired works of
art. In the 1960s, a special school was opened in the Marquesas with govern-

ment funds. The purpose was to teach young boys how to carve so that they could sell their work to the tourist market in Tahiti. Many fine artists came out of this school, and Marquesan *tiki* (religious figures) and *umete* (bowls) became cherished objects for both locals and visitors. Works by carvers of the Kimitete family were especially treasured, and government officials in the capital often chose these carvings as gifts to visiting dignitaries.

In the 1980s, the ancient art of tattooing became increasingly popular once again across the Pacific. Tahitians, who had given up this body decoration long ago and even denigrated Marquesans for their love of tattoos, were interested in publicly displaying their interest in Pacific culture. With little knowledge of their own traditional patterns, they once again turned to the Marquesas to supply artistic models.

Now the Marquesans were confronted with another cultural threat. In addition to dispossession and replacement, they now faced the likelihood that the arts they had preserved would be appropriated by Tahitians. Indeed, stores in the capital were full of Marquesan objects that were already passed off as "Tahitian." Tahitian choreographers were looking to traditional Marquesan dance for ideas but not acknowledging the source of them, and scores of young Tahitians were now claiming the right to wear traditional Marquesan tattoo patterns. Even more alarming to Marquesans, many Tahitians viewed this submersion of Marquesan identity into a larger French Polynesian culture as completely normal.

RESPONSE: STRUGGLES TO SURVIVE CULTURALLY

Separate Status, Separate Identity

Marquesans were not prepared to allow themselves to be further dominated by Tahitians or culturally merged with Tahiti or blended into an artificial pan–French-Polynesian identity, particularly one controlled by Tahiti. In the mid-1980s, they knew the time had come to act. With little hope of radically changing their economic situation as long as the power remained in Tahiti, they decided to focus their efforts on the political arena.

The 1980s and 1990s were a time when the voices supporting independence for French Polynesians became increasingly louder and more vocal. Yet Marquesans repeatedly voted *against* independence for French Polynesia, a vote that is sometimes difficult for outsiders to understand.

In many ways, their position is perhaps more anti-Tahitian than pro-European. Marquesans know that they do not have a sufficient economic base to be able to survive on their own at this point. They also realize that if French Polynesia were to gain independence as a country, Marquesans would remain under Tahitian control—but, in this case, without any funds from France. Seeing that they receive little from Tahiti as it is, Marquesans justifiably question what could they possibly hope for if Tahiti could no longer rely upon French money. Given the choice of rule by an independent Tahiti or a wealthy European country, Marquesans overwhelmingly choose the latter.

In 1989, the Marquesans asked France to recognize their island as a new Overseas Territory, one separate from that of Tahiti. The request was not granted. In some ways it is difficult for the French administrators back in Paris to view the Marquesans as a distinct people. With such a small population, some might think it hardly worth the trouble to divide these people from their neighbors. After all—they are all Polynesian!

Marquesans continue to claim their cultural heritage and to state their complaints and concerns loudly in the capital. They also continue to ask for separate political status. A flowering of Marquesan culture began to emerge in the late 1980s with the help of a new cultural organization known as Motu Haka, the efforts of local schoolteachers, the blessing of Bishop Monseigneur Hervé-Marie Le Cléache, and the dedication of a concerned group of Islanders. They held large festivals to show off important archaeological sites and to demonstrate the singular beauty of Marquesan music, dance, and visual arts. And, in an effort to fight Tahitian cultural hegemony at home, they began to hold summer camps to teach their youth the legends, songs, and dances of their homeland.

Language is one of the most obvious ways for a people to mark their separateness and one of the most essential ways for them to maintain crucial ties to the meaning and importance of their patrimony. Although Marquesan children have always heard and spoken the Marquesan language at home, the language is essentially an oral one, and their schooling is in French. Furthermore, with students spending more time in school and often removed from their families, the rich storytelling tradition and the ancient knowledge of the islands were not passed on.

The language issue reached into the church as well, for there was no Marquesan translation of the Bible. Written religious expression for these devoutly Christian people relied on French or Tahitian. For many years, religious songs were sung in Tahitian.

In the 1980s, Tahitians pushed to have compulsory Tahitian language study included as part of the school curriculum. Obviously, this was not what Marquesans wanted. They took advantage of this opening, though, to fight for the inclusion of their own language in Marquesan schools and were eventually successful in that effort. Symbolically this was an immensely important step. The reality, however, is that Marquesan language instruction is limited to only about three hours per week, and there are genuine challenges. For example, because of its oral nature, there are almost no written materials for teaching the Marquesan language. The few books that do contain ancient stories in Marquesan were written by foreigners for their purposes, not for language instruction. Often the content is not appropriate for language study or is not interesting for children. Many times the language used is different from contemporary speech, and there are words that young people no longer use or understand. Finally, because Marquesan was always passed on orally, there are no standard rules for writing it down. What happens when people simply cannot agree on the proper way to transfer the sound to paper? At present, there are three different systems used for writing Marquesan. What happens to students when teachers prefer—and teach—different systems?

Slowly but surely, progress is being made. People are increasingly interested in the language, and writings in Marquesan are gradually beginning to appear. In 1993, the former bishop of the Marquesas—Monseigneur Hervé Le Cléache—finally finished the translation of the Marquesan Bible, a task that required years of devotion and effort. Songs in Marquesan are a normal part of worship services in the Catholic church, a far cry from years ago, when Monseigneur Le Cléache first arrived in the Marquesas and admonished the Marquesans, "Each bird has its own unique song. Why do you welcome me with Tahitian songs?"[4]

FOOD FOR THOUGHT

Twenty-five years ago in French Polynesia, no one talked or thought very much about the Marquesas Islands or the people who lived there. With the exception of beautiful wood carvings and an occasional decorated bark cloth, the islands had little to offer city dwellers. Marquesans who traveled to the capital were noticeably different from the Tahitians and, as with many minority groups who clung to older ways of doing things, were looked down upon and generally thought of as unsophisticated and inferior.

Then, in the 1980s, a new Pacific began to emerge as Islanders placed renewed importance on indigenous traditions and Pacific ways of doing things. Tradition and traditional arts became increasingly valued as they looked to their ancient legends and practices to instill a sense of cultural pride. Tahitians looked at their own culture and realized how much they had lost. They also saw that many of the things they had previously denigrated—including the large tattoos, traditional costumes, and vigorous dancing style of the Marquesas—suddenly had meaning and value.

Questions

1. The desire for hegemony, to retain power and control, is not limited to European colonial governments. Can you think of other instances in which the people of one ethnic group are in a position to control others? What kind of control do they exert? Why are they able to maintain this control?

2. In what ways do you have a unique cultural heritage that is different from that of some of your friends? How was knowledge of this culture passed on to you—from your grandparents, your parents, your community, your church? What

parts of this identity do you think are important for you to learn more about? What do you think is the best way to do that?

3. If you lived in a place where there were few jobs and where most of the good jobs were for people who spoke another language, how would you respond? What would you be willing to sacrifice in order to have a better job—being near your parents, your siblings, your lifelong friends, your homeland, other people who think and act as you do, people who speak your language, people with whom you feel you belong?

4. When there are limited resources, who should determine where the money or materials should go? Are there different levels of economic reliance that developed in French Polynesia? Is this reliance negative or positive? Can or should these reliance patterns be changed? How?

5. What can people who are a minority in number do to ensure that their complaints, needs, and concerns are heard by those in power? Are there situations in which the issues of the minority group should take precedence over those of the majority?

NOTES

1. *Résultats du Recensement Général de la Population de la Polynesie Française* (Papeete: Institut Territorial de la Statistique, 1998), p. 64.

2. G. Stallworthy, letter to the missionaries of the American Board, July 3, 1846 (Armstrong letters, American Board of Churches for Foreign Missions, Hawaiian Mission Children's Society Library, Honolulu).

3. Monseigneur Guy Chevalier, personal communication, July 1989.

4. Monseigneur Hervé Le Cléache, personal communication, August 1995.

RESOURCE GUIDE

Published Literature

Dening, Greg. *Islands and Beaches, Discourse on a Silent Land: Marquesas 1774–1880.* Honolulu: University of Hawaii Press, 1980.

Handy, E. S. Craighill. *The Native Culture in the Marquesas*, Reprint. New York: Kraus Reprint, 1971.

Handy, Willowdean C. *Tattooing in the Marquesas.* Honolulu: Bishop Museum, 1922.

Melville, Herman. *Typee: A Peep at Polynesian Life.* New York: Viking, 1996.

Moulin, Jane Freeman. "Marquesas Islands." In *The Garland Encyclopedia of World Music*, vol. 9, *Australia and the Pacific Islands*, Adrienne L. Kaeppler and J. W. Love (eds.), pp. 889–96. New York: Garland, 1998.

Tahiti Tourist Promotion Board. *Marquesas Islands Guide.* 1992.

Audio Recordings

Te Ka'ioi. Cassette recording C013. Eleven examples of traditional Marquesan music, including *hakamanu, maha'u* ("pig dance"), *putu, ru'u, tapeka, mave, mauta'a*, and *hakapahaka*. Océane Production, 17 rue Jeanne d'Arc, Pape'ete, Tahiti, French Polynesia. Telephone: 42–69–00.

Rataro, *Marquises Terre Sauvage*. Compact disc OCN CD 38; *Kaoha, les Marquieses*. Compact disc OCN CD 17. Contemporary music by Rataro, a Marquesan singer who is one of Tahiti's recording stars. Océane Production, 17 rue Jeanne d'Arc, Pape'ete, Tahiti, French Polynesia. Telephone: 42–69–00.

1980—Année du Patrimoine: Iles Marquises-Tahiti. Cassette recording MC 3.038. Side 1 contains examples of both traditional Marquesan music and song genres borrowed from Tahiti. Manuiti Productions Musicales Polynésiennes, B.P. 755, Pape'ete, Tahiti, French Polynesia. Telephone: 42–82–39. Fax: 43–27–24.

Videos

Contact the following for a current list of videotapes on the Marquesas (available in NTSC, PAL, and SECAM):

Institut de la Communication Audiovisuelle (ICA)
B.P. 519
Pape'ete, Tahiti
French Polynesia
Telephone: 43–85–00

WWW Sites

Isles of Hiva
http://leahi.kcc.hawaii.edu (then search hiva)
http://leahi.kcc.hawaii.edu/org/pvs/hiva.html
An overview of the Marquesas Islands with separate pages concerning geography, life today, language settlement, prehistory and archaeology, life of the land, religion, social structures, warfare, canoes, voyaging traditions, Western contacts and colonization, and bibliography.

Marquesas Studies Institute
http://www.alptuna.com/public/dadd/studies.htm
The Marquesas Studies Institute is dedicated to mutual cooperation and understanding between the people of the Marquesas Islands and the rest of the world. Teachers are encouraged to visit the Teacher Support web page and may post questions about the Marquesas to a specialist in the discipline concerned.

Organizations

Marquesas Studies Institute
P.O. Box 1206

Kuristown, Hawaii 96760
E-mail: daddison@hawaii.edu

Mayor's Office
Maire de Taiohae
B.P. 28
Taiohae, Nukuhiva,
Iles Marquises
French Polynesia
Telephone: 92–03–01

Office Territorial d'Action Culturelle (OTAC)
B.P. 1709
Pape'ete, Tahiti
French Polynesia
Telephone: 54–45–44

Service Territorial du Tourisme
B.P. 4527
Pape'ete, Tahiti
French Polynesia
Telephone: 50–57–00

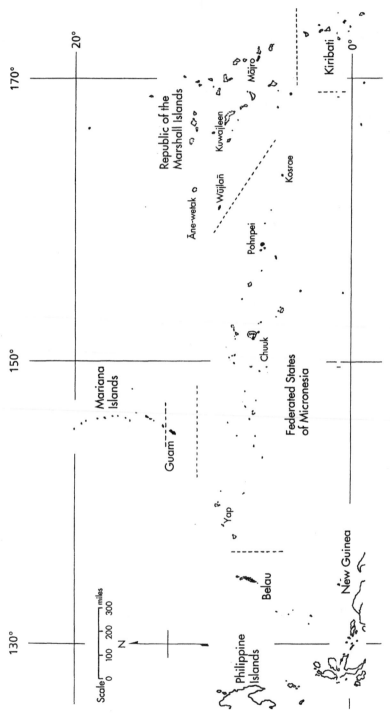

Atolls and islands of the Central Western Pacific. From L. M. Carucci, *Nuclear Nativity* (De Kalb: Northern Illinois University Press, 1997). Copyright © 1997 by Northern Illinois University Press. Used by permission of the publisher.

Chapter 7

The Micronesians

Glenn Petersen

CULTURAL OVERVIEW

The People

The islands of Micronesia are still almost entirely inhabited by indigenous Micronesian peoples, with the key exceptions of Kwajalein (site of a U.S. missile range), Saipan (where immigrant laborers work in garment factories), and until more recently Palau (which now imports foreign workers for its service and production sectors; also known as Belau). Although these Micronesian societies experienced devastating depopulation when Europeans first arrived on their shores, today their populations are robust and the islands that serve as administrative centers tend to be in danger of overpopulation.

The Setting

The name *Micronesia* has a range of geographical, cultural, historical, and political meanings, depending on the context in which it is used. Geographically it includes Tungaru (Gilbert Islands) and Nauru. Today *Micronesia* is often used as a shorthand for the Federated States of Micronesia, a much more constricted term. In this chapter it refers to the island chains known as the Carolines, Marianas, and Marshalls, all of which were, until recently, part of what was the United States Trust Territory of the Pacific Islands.

To examine the impact Micronesia's location has on the well-being of its people, it is useful to begin by focusing first upon three distinct elements of Micronesians' relations with their lands and surrounding waters. Their islands and waters provide most of their subsistence, the symbolic underpinnings of their social groups and thus significant elements of their identities, and their sovereignty as peoples in a world where international law is based upon an assumption that nation states form the natural units of legitimate government.

Traditional Subsistence Strategies

The degree to which Micronesians remain subsistence farmers and fishers capable of supplying themselves with most of their daily needs varies enormously from island to island and from family to family. What farming there is in the Marianas tends to be of either the kitchen garden sort or very small-scale commercial operations: There are few—if any—true subsistence farmers left. In the two population centers of the Marshalls, Majuro (the capital) and Ebeye (adjoining the Kwajalein missile range), there is little more than kitchen gardening. In the towns on some of the larger islands (Kolonia in Pohnpei, Moen in Chuuk, Colonia in Yap), relatively large populations of immigrants from outlying atolls generally lack access to enough land to farm and instead depend heavily, even entirely, on wage labor. On the more isolated atolls in the Marshalls and the Carolines, and in rural parts of the larger islands, on the other hand, most of the population remains engaged in traditional subsistence farming practices, augmented by the wage-labor employment of a few extended-family members. Virtually everyone in Micronesia eats imported rice, but most families also produce substantial stocks of the local staples: breadfruit, bananas, pandanus, dry and wet taro, and/or yams. Even on the largest islands there are no settlements without access to marine resources, though access and resources are not necessarily distributed equally. Although families seem increasingly to be consuming fish sold locally by the foreign commercial operations (China, Taiwan, Japan) that haul in vast quantities of deep-sea species, most remain capable of, if not actively engaged in, reef fishing for subsistence purposes.

Social and Political Organization

Most Micronesians are like rural peoples in the rest of the non- or semiindustrialized world because they do not depend exclusively on their own production. Exchange networks of various kinds link families, lineages, communities, and islands. On the islands particularly subject to typhoon damage, as the central Carolines atolls are, life is possible only because of these links. Everywhere these linkages are embedded in layer upon layer of social, political, and ritual meaning. Theirs is a political economy in the true sense of the term. Society is bound together by the constant

Chief Soulik Anastasio Dosalwa of Upper Awak on Pohnpei, Federated States of Micronesia, 1975, weaving baskets to be used in food redistribution at a community feast. This kind of communal interdependence is being replaced by reliance on outside aid. Courtesy of Glenn Petersen.

movement of subsistence items; this in turn ensures everyone survival in times of shortage.

These networks are interwoven with a series of political and ritual obligations. The elements of clanship are shared throughout the area and are organized around political and ritual hierarchies. Micronesian chieftainship depends upon important assigned principles for its framework and moral force, and in its daily operations it relies heavily upon competitive production and generosity. Those who would be chiefs must consistently produce more and give away more than their neighbors. On the smaller atolls fishing often occupies this same central focus of meaningful activity, and although the competitive feasting may be less rigorously organized, the underlying ritual principles remain much the same. On the largest islands elaborate systems of formal rank have developed.

An individual Micronesian's social status derives from a variety of factors. Most obvious is one's genealogy, but preeminent among the activities that promote individual effort and success are ritual knowledge and economic prowess. It is not exaggeration to say the ability to produce local produce and/or fish and a grasp of how to distribute them appropriately among others lie at the heart of one's membership in a community and thus provide a foundation for both individual and group identity. To be *udahn ohl en Pohnpei* ("a real Pohnpeian man"), for instance, requires a lifetime of agricultural and feasting activity. Thus the act of cultivating the land not only provides subsistence but goes a long way toward establishing the meaning of a person's life.

Religion and World View

There are strong physical and spiritual ties between the people and the land they inhabit—these are by no means distinct categories.

Although there has certainly been continual interaction among the peoples of the region's many islands, no archaeological or linguistic evidence suggests that any of these populations has ever been displaced by invaders from other islands. Even the so-called Yap Empire of the central and western Carolines appears to have been the product of mutually beneficial and largely voluntary voyages of outer islanders to Yap, not a consequence of any sort of Yapese invasion.

Micronesian mythohistory and cosmology organize the archipelagoes' physical features and legendary history into a web of interconnections that almost seamlessly bind the islands and the cosmos. According to these accounts much of the physical character of the islands themselves is the product of construction projects of sorts, undertaken by legendary ancestors. Because they believe their ancestors made—or at least substantially enlarged and improved—these islands, and because their populations have not been displaced during the course of the two to three thousand years they have been inhabited, modern Micronesians truly do have virtually timeless ties to their homelands. It seems entirely likely that modern Kosraens, for example, are the direct lineal descendants of the people who first settled the island. And because nearly every square inch of most of these islands has been transformed by the cultural and subsistence activities of their ancestors, almost every physical feature on them tells them a story about them and their heritage. Micronesia's landscape is authentically hallowed ground.

Finally, Micronesian leaders who have studied abroad, primarily at the University of Hawaii (but in Guam and the mainland United States as well), consistently report that their understanding of American colonial history has been deeply influenced by U.S. relations with the indigenous peoples who originally inhabited the lands the expanding United States has occupied. To the extent that Native Americans, native Hawaiians, and Guam's Chamorros have lost control of their lands, they have become minority peoples in their own homelands, lost the physical bases of their sovereignty, and thus been disenfranchised. During the course of their negotiations with the United States, most Micronesian leaders never lost sight of the absolute imperative of regaining and securing full legal title to their lands. They had never lost moral title to it, they were certain, but the long period of U.S. unwillingness to recognize Micronesian sovereignty served only to convince the Micronesians that unless they could establish legal title to their lands, they were likely to find themselves in the same sorts of predicaments that have reduced other former non-Euro-American subjects of the United States to their current marginal status.

THREATS TO SURVIVAL

At the end of World War II eleven League of Nations Mandates were reestablished as United Nations (UN) Trust Territories. One of these was assigned a unique status: The Micronesian islands became a "strategic" trust territory administered by the United States, with minimal—at times virtually no—UN oversight. Micronesia's tortured legal status as a strategic territory resulted from a compromise struck between the U.S. Navy and the Department of State. As long as the United States did not annex the Micronesian islands outright, the military would be guaranteed absolute sway over them. This arrangement was hammered out in 1947, with the cold war at its most intense and the United States acutely concerned with retaining strategic control over the approaches to East Asia. Today most of the Micronesian islands are included within three independent republics—Palau, the Federated States of Micronesia, and the Marshall Islands—and the most immediately threatening aspects of the cold war have become history. It would be easy to assume, therefore, that Micronesia's strategic location has become irrelevant. This is not the case. Among the many problems the Micronesians confront, the strategic character of their location may be the most problematic. It is not only that another war could destroy them entirely but that there is so little they can do to protect themselves.

Other potential threats to contemporary Micronesian populations include overpopulation and rising sea levels resulting from global warming, but these are hardly peculiar to the region. Its strategic position is.

Upon its demise, which took place in a halting fashion between the mid-1970s and the early 1990s, the former area was reconstituted as four separate polities: the Commonwealth of the Northern Marianas Islands (CNMI), the Republic of Belau (Palau), the Federated States of Micronesia (FSM), and the Republic of the Marshall Islands. The former is an American commonwealth; the latter three are technically known as *freely associated states*, a relationship with the United States that is in fact as ambiguous as that of commonwealth. These freely associated states seem simultaneously to be independent, dependent, and American protectorates. The absence of certainty in this matter of political status plays a central role in the themes of this chapter, the interrelationships between strategic location and political status.

The American Presence in Micronesia

The American presence in Micronesia is sometimes described as accidental, implying that the United States occupied the islands entirely as a consequence of its battles with Japan. Nothing could be further from historical reality. The United States has sought the China market since the earliest days of the republic and has consistently pursued the goal of establishing secure access to it in the Western Pacific, via the Philippines, Guam, and Micronesia.

Little has changed in the intervening years, despite termination of American trusteeship over Micronesia. Major changes in the technology of warfare, including submarine-launched ballistic missiles, have not had much impact on the U.S. commitment to retaining control over the region. The American position there has long been known as *strategic denial*, a concept harkening back to the Spanish position in Guam, first established in the eighteenth century. The island approaches to East Asia have been dubbed a *rimland* by political geographers, who describe American leaders as struggling desperately to maintain control of the area. As long as the United States retains Guam, and now the Northern Marianas Commonwealth, the Carolines straddle its most secure forward bases in the Western Pacific. Cold war confrontations in the East Asian rimland were at least as profoundly shaped by geopolitical factors as they were by ideological tensions, and the end of the bipolar competition between communism and capitalism portends little change in the ongoing rivalries in this rimland. Arguments about the irrelevance of Micronesia to superpower rivalries do little to clarify the situation there. Indeed, the tangle of disputes now manifesting themselves in the area suggest that with the retreat of cold war polarization, conflicts calling for the deployment of conventional forces may well become *more* common.

The possibility of readily exploitable petroleum deposits at certain sites increases boundary disputes between China and a host of Southeast Asian states over the South China Sea's Spratly and Paracel archipelagoes, and among Japan and the two Chinas over the Senkaku/Diaoyu islands between the Rikuyus and Taiwan. Japan and Russia remain at odds over disposition of the southernmost islands of the Kurile chain and agitation for an American pullout from Okinawa shows no signs of subsiding. The reversion of Hong Kong to China may in time result in disturbances that draw outside attention, and Indonesia's changing relations with East Timor have brought the area under closer scrutiny. The so-called rimland remains fissured with cracks that the United States intends to keep under close surveillance.

The Micronesians' Dilemma

The end of the United States' trusteeship has done little to diminish the U.S. role in Micronesia. The United States interprets any real exercise of autonomy by the Micronesians as a challenge to its security interests in the islands. The U.S. government's insistence upon its rights to intercede in any activities it might choose to define as security matters was spelled out at hearings Congress held before it ratified the Compacts of Free Association. It is in Micronesian disagreements with this interpretation of the compacts that the question of Micronesian sovereignty becomes most salient. And the Americans' insistence upon their alternative interpretations is the reason that Micronesian apprehensions are so great.

The Micronesians' dilemma is this: That which confronts them with one of the greatest threats to their continued survival on their islands—that is, their strategic location—has also proved to be the source of their most substantial forms of revenue, American transfer payments as recompense for the United States' right of strategic denial in the region. Many Micronesian leaders view the potential for military conflict in the Pacific Basin as considerably more than just a vague possibility. There are a number of concrete historical reasons for this outlook, which seems to derive not so much from any sort of indigenous world view as from practical experience.

The majority of the problems confronting the Micronesian nation states are by no means peculiar to them. Many of these difficulties are experienced by small states in general and most of them plague all but a few small island states. Their locations make shipping prohibitively expensive; all but the largest lack efficiently exploitable natural resources; the islands are, however, usually endowed with fertile enough resources and communitarian enough economies to have bred cultural resistance to sweatshop labor and other forms of industrial drudgery. Opportunities for economic development in all these locales are severely limited. There are, however, several aspects of the Micronesian situation that differ distinctly from the common lot of small island polities.

Micronesians face an additional array of problems not ordinarily encountered in the adjacent areas of Polynesia and Melanesia for several key reasons. First, Micronesians had to struggle much longer and with much greater tenacity than those small-island colonies to achieve self-government. Second, Micronesians have become vastly more dependent upon financial subsidies from the former colonial power as the consequence of a long trajectory of budget increases that accompanied U.S. endeavors to sweeten the pot and thereby forestall Micronesian demands for autonomy and independence (the Trust Territory budget increased tenfold between 1961 and 1975). Most significantly, however, few if any Pacific island territories occupy such strategically crucial locations. Both U.S. opposition to Micronesian autonomy and the Micronesians' successes in raising the financial stakes as high as they have are consequences of the islands' strategic location, and the nature of the final trade-off is well understood by all concerned parties. But the Micronesians now have to experience the consequences of their relationship with the United States. The strategic character of their location means their islands can reasonably be perceived as posing threats to adjacent regions, and they must therefore cling all that much tighter to their relations with the United States.

There can be little question about the value U.S. military planners have placed on the Micronesian islands, in terms of both what it cost in "blood and treasure" (to use the common martial jargon) to acquire them and their importance to U.S. strategic planning for East Asian and Western Pacific operations. Micronesia's leaders are as fully aware of these factors as anyone else. Indeed, having experienced the destruction—sometimes near-total in its scope—wrought by battles fought on land and seas that not only have provided them and their families with subsistence but also serve as the symbolic foci of their lineages and the entire social order, Micronesians must be acknowledged as the best judges of the costs they have incurred. And, moreover, they must calculate the benefits to be reaped from any ongoing political relations with the United States against the possibilities that such calamities might again be visited upon them.

Any doubts Micronesian leaders might possibly have entertained about the degree of importance U.S. military planners ascribed to their homeland were dispelled during the course of their political status negotiations with the United States in the mid-1960s through the early 1990s. The United States initially insisted upon retaining powers of eminent domain over all the so-called public lands of the Trust Territory, areas that had been under the direct control of the Japanese and that accounted for approximately 70 percent of the land in the territory. When negotiators for the Congress of Micronesia made it clear that they would not agree to eminent domain, the U.S. military undertook a series of studies in the region and in short order spelled out rather precisely its requirements, including major bases in Palau and the northern Marianas. Indeed, one of the major precipitating factors leading to the break-up of the Trust Territory into the four separate political entities was the differential U.S. interest evidenced in bases in the various archipelagoes and the amounts of payments it might potentially be willing to make in return for its use of these sites. Furthermore, the breakup underscored regional and ethnic separatism.

Micronesian evaluations of their location's strategic implications require no hypotheses about possible permutations of geopolitical forces. Their outlook is rooted in personal experience and direct observation. These tell them a story best summarized with an aphorism borrowed from a distant part of globe, but one that has shared much the same sort of colonial history, Africa: When elephants fight, it is the grass that suffers.

RESPONSE: STRUGGLES TO SURVIVE CULTURALLY

Some may wish to discount the lingering consequences of World War II, but recent studies demonstrate that for many in Micronesia the war's aftermath remains current, continuing to shape Micronesian outlooks on contemporary political process. Micronesians suffered doubly during the war. U.S. island-hopping strategy left most of them cut off from all outside supplies for several years, imposing dreadful privations upon them, in addition to invasions and bombardments.

Today, older Micronesians tell of how during attacks they tried to make themselves invisible behind thin coconut tree trunks, under shallow breadfruit roots, or in swampy taro patches. Those who experienced especially heavy bombardments were sometimes forced to escape to the forests; some lived under trees or rocks or huddled in caves during bombings. The combination of these two sorts of atrocity was at its worst where major battles were fought. On Saipan, which had a large Japanese civilian population, one-third of the civilians who died were Micronesians. Most horrifying, perhaps, was that "Micronesians everywhere suspected that the Japanese were planning to exterminate them."[1] In the 1970s preoccupation with this threat of extermination remained a major topic of conversation and concern in Pohnpeian communities.

These lessons persist: "Wartime experiences certainly play an important role in the decisions Micronesians now face."[2] Describing the dances a troupe representing Yap performed at the dedication of the Federated States of Micronesia (FSM) capital in 1989, which were conscious commentaries on World War II and changes it wrought on their island and the rest of Micronesia, one Yapese remarked that "they intend that these memories act not only as a warning to future generations in their own land,"[3] but as a reminder to foreigners as well.

These intensified anxieties and reservations have sometimes been expressed boldly. A Palauan woman, Gabriela Ngirmang, told the U.S. Senate that her people "assume that if you seek options on Palauan land, you at some point will use them." She later elaborated on her opposition. A compact with the United States would draw in the military and "big changes would happen. Then Palau would serve U.S. interests rather than our own." The military would occupy the best parts of the islands. "Palauans would be pushed and pushed" until they became "a minority in [their] own land." In sum, she asked, "Would we take money and then have a missile wrapped around our necks?"[4]

Or as the former FSM president Tosiwo Nakayama explained in response to a question about his insistence on as much Micronesian independence from the United States as possible: It was motivated by Americans' attitudes toward Micronesians. "That and the fear of the loss of the land."[5]

These Micronesian analyses of their predicament have been ignored or discounted, but indigenous philosophers there are no less thoughtful and perspicacious than the superpowers' geopolitical thinkers. We would do well to remember that President Nixon's secretary of the Interior, Walter Hickel, responsible for the administration of the Trust Territory, was once rebuffed by the National Security adviser, Henry Kissinger, who said of the Micronesians, "There are only 90,000 of them. Who gives a damn?"[6]

The Micronesian Perspective on Political Status

Micronesians would like to be out of harm's way. To the extent that they can reduce the degree of American domination in their islands, they can reduce the number, variety, and intensity of the threats confronting them. Because of their location, they realize, they will always be vulnerable. What they seek to do, therefore, is simultaneously reduce these threats and maximize the benefits they accrue as a consequence of being subject to them. But the greater the support they receive from the United States, the greater their reliance upon America and the greater the danger they find themselves in.

Quite understandably, Micronesians have no desire to see anything like World War II again befall them. All of their subsistence and moral rationales for pursuing the autonomy of national independence are paralleled by a wish to see any impetus for another war removed: to be rid of any alien presence that might draw attacks similar to the American invasion spawned by the Japanese occupation of their islands. It is rare to encounter a Micronesian who took at face value American claims that a U.S. presence was necessary for the defense of Micronesia. Just whom would they be defending us from? people asked. The only threat they pose to anyone, many Micronesians explain, is as a direct consequence of the American presence in their islands. To the extent that Micronesians can ease the United States out of their islands, then, they believe they can reduce the likelihood of precipitating another invasion.

At the same time, however, they recognize that they cannot escape this U.S. presence. Guam, which the FSM straddles, remains entirely an American territory. It is armed to the teeth and there is virtually no likelihood of an American withdrawal. On Guam itself local concerns are for a more clearly defined relationship with and more local autonomy from the United States (including control over immigration from Micronesia). The missile testing site on Kwajalein continues in its strategic role. The Marshallese people and their government derive most of their income from the lease of Kwajalein and from reparations for the consequences of nuclear testing on Bikini and Enewetak. FSM leaders have at times described their location as akin to the Straits of Gibraltar—that is, they occupy a strategic location significant because most of it is situated between these two key positions, Guam and Kwajalein. During the plebiscite on political status in 1983, one of them expressed this sense of vulnerability in describing the FSM: "We're the hole in the donut."[7]

Whether the Micronesians like it or not, then, they are situated between two strategically important positions as well as lying along a historically important strategic route and will continue to be endangered because of this location. Because strategic considerations place them in what seems to be a long-term—if not a permanent—state of vulnerability, they believe themselves, quite reasonably, entitled to recompense. In the course of their negotiations with the United States they simultaneously pursued two goals, seemingly contradictory, but that make considerable sense when considered in this light. Micronesians insisted both upon total autonomy and sovereignty *and* upon a relatively high rate (by Pacific island nation state standards) of financial support from the United States. With what seemed at the time brilliant foresight, these transfer payments were arranged in a stepped-down series of five-year increments on the assumption that the Micronesian economies would thereby grow progressively less dependent upon American funding by the end of the fifteen-year Compacts of Free Association.

Unfortunately, these economies, in common with the economies of nearly all the other small Pacific island nation states, have experienced little or no growth in their primary and secondary sectors: They are totally dependent upon what are known as *MIRAB monies* (migration, remittance, aid, and bureaucracy). When the FSM's compact with the United States expires in the year 2001, the country will have only fishing royalties from its extensive maritime exclusive economic zone as a source of any but utterly minimal amounts of financial support. In the Marshalls the compact with the United States is for thirty years; thus monies from reparations for damages sustained on Bikini and Enewetak during nuclear testing and rent for the missile base on Kwajalein will continue to be paid; and Palau's compact is for fifty years.

At the same time, however, the transfer payments have been undergirded by financial strictures that stipulate certain performance standards for the Micronesian national economies. If these governments abrogate their fiduciary responsibilities to the United States by modifying, for instance, tax structures or nationalizing businesses, the United States can withhold payments. Moreover, the uncertainty inherent in the continuity of these payments, as well as doubts about renewal of the compacts after they expire, ensure that the Micronesian governments do little to antagonize the United

States, either at the United Nations or elsewhere in international venues. The Micronesians are in some ways even more bound to the United States than they were before the end of trusteeship. Now, however, the United States has bilateral arrangements with the governments, allowing it to cut them off without international oversight. It can be argued that in having chosen to retain these close ties to the United States, rather than having had them imposed arbitrarily upon them, the Micronesians make themselves, if not more vulnerable, then at least more culpable in the eyes of their neighbors. As allies—rather than unwilling subjects—they do not occupy precisely the same moral ground.

FOOD FOR THOUGHT

It may seem contradictory for Micronesians to claim simultaneously that they are fully sovereign and independent, and that they have no choice in the character of their relations with the United States. This is, nevertheless, precisely the nature of their ties to the United States. Micronesians pursue sovereignty as a means to remain true to their own traditional values, to free themselves from some of the risks their colonial status has exposed them to, and to enhance their ability to negotiate their future situation.

Questions

1. Many Micronesians experience threats to their rights over their lands as endangering their identity as a people. What factors lead them to do so?
2. Is the Micronesian situation unique, or even particularly unusual, in that their primary source of cash income (in this case, their strategic location) is also the source of the greatest threat to their well-being?
3. Micronesians have traditionally depended upon the peoples of other islands for refuge during or after natural disasters. How might this affect their attitudes toward their economic dependence on the United States?
4. Each colonial government that has controlled Micronesia has portrayed itself as serving Micronesian interests. But the Micronesians see these colonial regimes differently. How has their experience of past wars shaped their expectations about future possibilities of a war being fought in or near the islands?
5. Sovereignty is not, in real-life politics, an absolute status. Nevertheless, most Micronesians place a high value upon it. Why?

NOTES

1. Suzanne Falgout, Lin Poyer, and Lawrence Carucci, " 'The Greatest Hardship': Micronesian Memories of World War II," *Isla* 3: 211–16, 1995.
2. Ibid., p. 217.
3. Lin Poyer, "Yapese Experiences of the Pacific War." *Isla* 3: 251, 1995.

4. Lynn Wilson, *Speaking to Power* (New York: Routledge, 1995), pp. 36, 170–72.

5. P. F. Kluge, *The Edge of Paradise* (New York: Random House, 1991), p. 108.

6. Walter Hickel, *Who Owns America?* (Englewood Cliffs, NJ: Prentice Hall, 1971), p. 208.

7. Kluge, *Edge of Paradise*, pp. 25–26.

RESOURCE GUIDE

Published Literature

Enloe, Cynthia. *Bananas, Beaches, and Bases*. Berkeley: University of California Press, 1989 (a general consideration of the impact of American military bases abroad).

Hayes, Peter, Lyuba Zarsky, and Walden Bello. *American Lake: Nuclear Peril in the Pacific*. New York: Penguin, 1986 (on strategic issues throughout the Pacific).

Kiste, Robert. *The Bikinains*. Menlo Park, CA: Cummings, 1974.

Kiste, Robert. "Termination of the U.S. Trusteeship in Micronesia." *Journal of Pacific History* 21: 127–38, 1986.

Lutz, Catherine, ed. "Micronesia as Strategic Colony." *Cultural Survival Occasional Paper 12*. Cambridge: Cultural Survival, 1984.

Petersen, Glenn. "Dancing Defiance: The Politics of Pohnpheian Dance Performances." *Pacific Studies* 15(4): 13–28, 1992.

Wilson, Lynn. *Speaking to Power: Gender and Politics in the Western Pacific*. New York: Routledge, 1995.

WWW Sites

Central Intelligence Agency—*The World Factbook 1999*
http://www.cia.gov/cia/publications/factbook/fm.html

Federated States of Micronesia Homepage
http://www.fsmgov.org

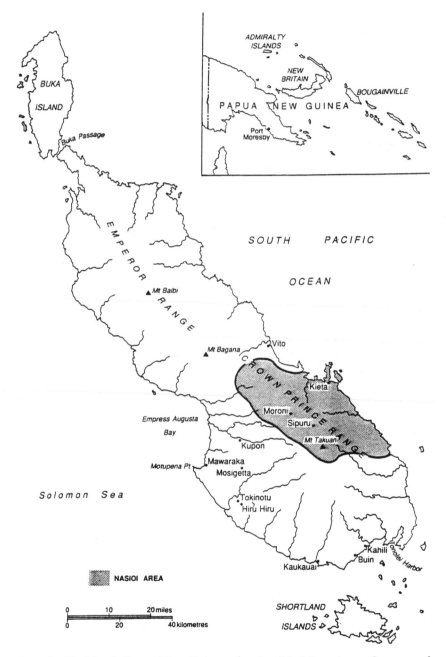

Bougainville Island, Papua New Guinea, showing Nasioi territory. Courtesy of Eugene Ogan.

Chapter 8

The Nasioi of Papua New Guinea

Eugene Ogan

CULTURAL OVERVIEW

The People

Nasioi is a language spoken by people living on the island of Bougainville, which in 1997 formed part of the North Solomons Province of the independent nation of Papua New Guinea. Nasioi speakers, who form the largest linguistic group, live in the south central portion of the island; sixteen other languages are spoken on the island. Like all of the island's indigenous population, Nasioi are characterized by very dark skin, distinguishing them from other citizens of Papua New Guinea. Archaeologists believe that the ancestors of these islanders migrated from Southeast Asia to Bougainville more than thirty thousand years ago.

The Setting

Nasioi villages extend from the coast through the valleys up to altitudes of more than 2,500 feet above sea level, occupying several different environmental niches. The climate is warm and humid, and temperatures can vary more widely in a 24-hour period than in terms of average monthly differences. Temperatures also decrease with altitude so vegetation changes from coastal to mountain villages. The annual rainfall of approximately 120 inches is distributed more or less evenly throughout the year.

Traditional Subsistence Strategies

In spite of all the changes caused by outside influences, most Nasioi continued to provide much of their subsistence by traditional gardening as late as the 1960s. They practiced shifting cultivation within particular localities, clearing new gardens and harvesting one or two crops before moving on. Men did the heavy work of clearing the forest and building fences; women performed the routine daily tasks that provided households with food. Originally only simple tools like stone axes and digging sticks were used. The starchy root taro was a staple crop until a plant blight swept through the island during World War II; after that, sweet potatoes became more important. Coconuts, sago palm, and betel nut were raised at lower altitudes. Villagers traded items like pottery or bows and arrows that were produced in one area but not in another.

Social Organization

Whether they lived along the coast, in the valleys, or on mountain slopes, Nasioi dwelt in small, scattered settlements, often consisting of no more than one or two households, where a married couple and their immature children resided. Occasionally an aged person or other relative might join the household, which was the basic unit for producing daily subsistence needs. Every Nasioi was also a member of a larger kinship group, a clan; clan membership was inherited from one's mother. Ideally, a man or woman had to select a spouse from another clan, so an individual's father would belong to a group different from his or her own. Certain kin were favored as marriage partners, and this practice tended to produce a continuing relationship between two clans exchanging spouses over generations. However, members of any single clan lived in settlements spread over all Nasioi territory, and the entire clan membership never got together to perform social or political tasks.

Rights to garden land were primarily inherited through the female line, so that a man would expect to inherit from his mother's brother, rather than his father. Because of the importance of women in the kinship and inheritance system, and in the provision of most daily subsistence, relations between the sexes tended to be complementary. Unlike in other parts of Papua New Guinea, Nasioi women had status and rights comparable to those of men.

This absence of strict social ranking was general in traditional Nasioi society. There were no chiefs like those found in some other parts of the Pacific. Rather, villagers recognized what are often called by anthropologists "big men." These were individuals who among Nasioi established their influence by hard work, generosity (especially in giving feasts), and knowledge of local affairs. They did not have widespread authority to command others; if a "big man" became too overbearing, other villagers might simply move away from him because land for gardens was relatively plentiful. A guiding principle of social life was that interactions between individuals and groups should be in balance. The marriage pattern in which two clans exchanged brides and grooms over time is an example of this goal and balanced exchange. Since no individual or group could wield much authority over others, one of the sanctions that enforced harmony in the village was the fear that an offended person might work sorcery on someone guilty of antisocial behavior.

Religion

The exception to this notion of balance and relative equality in life occurred in the area of traditional religion. Nasioi believed in the superiority of ancestral spirits who could aid them in everyday activities. Though they recognized the need for energy and skill in producing the necessities of life, they did not think real success was possible without the aid of supernatural help from these spirits. Special qualities of individuals, such as ability to heal or perform sorcery, were also believed to derive from such help. Villagers entreated spirits for their assistance by making gifts of valuable food such as pork, which they set out in small household shrines.

THREATS TO SURVIVAL

Threats to the Nasioi way of life began more than a century ago when outsiders began to divide up the Southwest Pacific into European colonies. These threats have taken different forms at different times, as the activities of outsiders have changed through history. The physical survival of Nasioi was especially endangered in World War II, but the thirty-five years that followed created forces that could destroy not only Nasioi population and culture, but their natural environment as well.

In 1884 Germany claimed the northeastern part of the large island of New Guinea (present day Papua New Guinea) and some islands to the east; Bougainville was added two years later. By creating this artificial boundary, Germany separated Bougainvilleans from the rest of the Solomon Island chain and from those people with whom they had the closest cultural ties. The new colony, called German New Guinea, was supposed to produce wealth for the colonizers by exploiting the indigenous population's land and labor. One factor that made Nasioi particularly subject to colonialism was the existence of a good natural harbor at Kieta, so the first European settlers on Bougainville entered there. These settlers were Roman Catholic missionaries, who began spreading the Gospel to Nasioi in 1902. In 1905 Germans set up an administrative headquarters in Kieta, and other Europeans began to establish coconut plantations on Nasioi land in 1905.

Nasioi escaped the severe population declines from introduced diseases suffered by other Pacific Islanders such as Hawaiians. The same scattered settlement pattern that prevented the development of epidemics and their decentralized social organization made armed resistance to colonization impossible. On the other hand, these conditions also made colonial administration more difficult. The administrative staff was always small in relation to the area they had to cover, and mountain villagers were less subject to interference with their lives.

Plantation Colonialism

Although Australia became the colonial power ruling Nasioi and the rest of what had been German New Guinea after World War I, the threat to traditional life remained the same for more than thirty years. This took the form of a particular kind of political economy, based on plantations producing copra, the dried meat of the coconut. Bougainville's rich volcanic soil, together with Kieta's harbor, made the Nasioi area particularly attractive for creating plantation agriculture. It was fairly easy for prospective planters to "buy" Nasioi land cheaply, because villagers did not have any concept of a sale that permanently alienated such a basic resource. The villagers could not foresee a future shortage of land, which had always been abundant for their needs.

Indeed, planters were able to acquire more land than they could easily develop because conditions such as endemic malaria made it unlikely that there would ever be a large European settlement on Bougainville. A persistent problem for planters was obtaining an adequate labor supply. The understaffed colonial administration could not force Nasioi to work, and there were few incentives for villagers to enter a money economy so long as they could fill their basic needs through traditional subsistence activities. Only the desire for imported goods could persuade Nasioi to engage in regular employment.

The planters' problem was solved by adopting copra as the basic plantation product. Copra production does not need a highly trained or well-organized labor force in order to be profitable. The tasks required are simple and can be performed in a relatively casual manner. From a Nasioi point of view, the presence of plantations on their land was as much a source of confusion as of any kind of "economic development," since they learned little about modern technology from their plantation jobs. Plantation work did not educate, but more often raised questions. Who were these strangers with such unfamiliar wealth as metal tools, kerosene lanterns, and tinned food, and what was the source of their power?

Unlike planters, missionaries saw their goal as bringing the blessing of salvation to Nasioi, but inevitably they too represented a threat to traditional culture. For the first twenty years of colonialism, missionary efforts were in the hands of Roman Catholics. Later, Methodists and Seventh-Day Adventists worked among Nasioi, but most of the population was nominally converted to Catholicism. Nasioi tended to interpret Christian doctrine in terms of their original world view: God, Jesus, and the Virgin Mary were seen as superancestral spirits, whom villagers could ask for practical benefits, as they had in the past. This mixture of supernaturalism and a search for material wealth was later to be called "cargo cult" by outsiders. Missionaries, such as planters and administrative officers, enjoyed a material life-style that remained tantalizingly out of Nasioi reach. Missionaries were not always free of the race prejudice that was more commonly expressed by the other kinds of colonizer. All colonizers had European ideas of male dominance as well, and the status of local women suffered accordingly. Nothing could have been less like life before European settlement than the sharp inequality between colonizer and colonized that Nasioi now experienced in many forms.

War and Its Aftermath

Plantation colonialism disturbed Nasioi life without yielding the improvements, especially in their material standard of living, that villagers sought. This situation lasted for almost forty years, until World War II introduced new invaders, the Japanese, to Bougainville. As soon as Japanese forces bombed other parts of New Guinea, the small colonizer community around Kieta began to flee the island. This abrupt departure had a demoralizing effect on Nasioi, who had been led to believe that these Europeans were much more knowledgeable and powerful than they. They were now faced with a completely new threat for which nothing had prepared them.

Once again Kieta's harbor made the Nasioi area a natural point for invasion and settlement. Villages and individuals tried different strategies for dealing with these invaders. Some cooperated with the Japanese as fully as they could, and others secretly assisted the few Europeans who had remained behind. The latter included for a time missionaries as well as "coast watchers" who observed Japanese shipping and troop movements and sent radio reports to Allied forces.

Because Bougainville was a major Japanese base, the island was subject to heavy bombing by American planes. This bombing not only harmed villagers directly but also drove them from their gardens to seek shelter wherever they could find it. As people said in the 1960s, "We lived in the bush like wild pigs."[1] Children and pregnant women suffered most, and the postwar population distribution was skewed as a result. In late 1943 American forces landed on the west coast of Bougainville just north of Empress Augusta Bay. Once an Allied base had been established, Nasioi joined other Bougainvilleans visiting the camps, attracted by the stories of food and supplies they heard could be obtained from the generous troops. Later Allied "mopping-up" operations took place mostly outside Nasioi territory, and Australian administration was restored in 1946. What had originally been German New Guinea, then a League of Nations Mandated Territory, became a United Nations Trust Territory under Australian administration. This continued to include Bougainville, though Nasioi had never seen themselves as truly connected with the rest of that political unit, recognizing instead their affinity to the Solomon Islanders immediately to the south.

Nasioi had already become disillusioned with decades of a colonial experience that seemed to disrupt their lives without improving them. Their abandonment by their former colonial "masters" followed by wartime suffering added to their deep dissatisfaction. As one village man said in the 1960s:

When my grandfather was alive and my father just a little boy, the Germans came. They gave us steel axes and "laplaps" [cloth to wrap around the body]. Then the Australians came and drove away the Germans. Then the Japanese came and drove away the Australians. Then the Americans drove away the Japanese so the Australians could come back. Now my grandfather is dead, my father is an old man, and I am a grown man. And what do we have? Nothing more than steel axes and "laplaps."[2]

A New Threat to People and Environment

In 1964 a chain of events that created an entirely new kind of threat to Nasioi life began. Australian geologists began searching for minerals on Nasioi land, where an occasional prospector had panned for gold before World War II. These new prospectors were able to do so without asking villagers' permission because Australian mining law, imposed in the 1920s on what had been the Mandated Territory of New Guinea, allotted all subsurface mineral rights to the government. This was not in accordance with Nasioi ideas about land rights, but they were essentially powerless to resist.

Prospecting was carried out by subsidiaries of Rio Tinto Zinc, an English multinational mining firm. Geologists found a multibillion-dollar deposit of low-grade copper, containing significant quantities of gold and silver as well. The deposit was profitable to exploit because of new technologies developed after the war. The minerals legally belonged to the government, so the agreement to develop the mine was negotiated between Australian civil servants (acting as trustees for the Territory of New Guinea) and lawyers employed by Rio Tinto Zinc. No Nasioi was ever consulted or otherwise involved in these negotiations.

The agreement had to be ratified by the first democratically elected House of Assembly in New Guinea. When debate began, it appeared that only those landowners directly affected by construction of the mine and associated facilities would receive any payment. This would be compensation for loss of land and other property, assessed at a minimal level. The lone Bougainville member of the House of Assembly (not a Nasioi) was able to obtain a royalty for the landowners, amounting to 5 percent—not of the value of minerals produced but of the government's royalty of 1.25 percent. In other words, Nasioi were to receive a little more than 6 cents per 100 dollars of the value of minerals taken from their land! This agreement was unanimously approved in the House of Assembly in August 1967.[3]

From 1968 to 1972 a tremendous technological effort went into the construction of the mine, brand new port facilities north of Kieta, new towns, and a road system to connect all this new construction. This construction period was unlike anything seen before on the island. The mine and the road to the port had to be carved out of rough terrain, much of it covered by huge stands of primary tropical forest, in an area where 120 or more inches of rain fall every year. At a time when the total population of Bougainville was less than eighty thousand—Nasioi making up perhaps fourteen thousand of that total—some ten thousand construction workers from all over the world, including the main island of New Guinea, flooded into the Kieta area and inland to the mine site at Panguna. This invasion transformed a peaceful part of the island to a place where public drunkenness, violence, and attempts to obtain sexual favors from Nasioi women were all too common.

Construction also involved massive changes to the environment. Land leased by the mining company, now organized as Bougainville Copper Limited (BCL), amounted to more than thirty-two thousand acres. Small Nasioi villages had to be relocated to make room for the mine. Additional land was taken over by the administration for new towns and other facilities. Loss of Nasioi land was felt even more keenly in the face of a rapidly growing population. After wartime losses, improved medical care and other factors had boosted natural population growth to an estimated 4 percent per year, one of the highest rates in the world. Nasioi themselves had also reduced the amount of available garden land by beginning to plant cash crops of coconut and cacao. By the 1970s, even unsophisticated village folk at some distance from the mine began to appreciate the increased pressure of so many young people in their territory. At the mine site itself, women said, "We weep for what is being done to our land."[4]

The mine started production in 1972, and within a few years the environmental damage was visible to all. Open-cut mines like that created by BCL wreak extraordinary destruction on the landscape. The huge hole from which ore is taken simply grows larger and larger, with no hope of restoring the area to productive use when the ore deposit is exhausted. Mining operations have produced hundreds of millions of tons of waste material.

Panguna mine site. Reproduced with consent from the *Bougainville Copper Limited Annual Report*, 1987.

Initially this was simply piled up around a river at the mine site, but eventually it had to be dumped into a larger drainage system flowing westward to the sea. All the natural life in this entire river system was thereby destroyed, so west coast villagers from other language groups also received a taste of the disruptive effects of mining.

At the end of its first full year of production, Bougainville Copper Limited showed the highest profit in the history of Australian-owned mining. Part of this great profitability was the result of the very advantageous agreement negotiated by the multinational parent firm's lawyers. What would become the nation state of Papua New Guinea was now moving rapidly toward independence, and new political leaders in the House of Assembly began to call for renegotiating the original agreement. The new agreement was more favorable to Papua New Guinea but added nothing to income received directly by Nasioi, who bore the brunt of all the environmental and social damage produced by the mine.

However, BCL had early learned that they had to deal directly with Nasioi individuals and groups as well as with central administration if they wanted their operation to be profitable. Profitability was also increased by localizing the mine's work force as much as possible, though Nasioi were less willing to accept BCL employment than were other Papua New Guineans. BCL provided financing and assistance to Nasioi who wanted to set up small businesses such as trucking, and Nasioi together with other islanders might take advantage of education and training schemes financed by the company. Many forms of compensation for damage to Nasioi land, in addition to royalty payments based on value of minerals produced, had been paid during the years since production began.

Ironically, these new sources of income increased the dissatisfaction many Nasioi felt, because the financial rewards were distributed according to Western legal practice, in sharp contrast to the traditional values of a social life based on balanced exchanges that spread benefits equally. New social divisions developed among the Nasioi themselves, particularly between the generations, which had been affected in different ways by the mine, as well as by other social changes, such as cash cropping and new educational opportunities.

RESPONSE: STRUGGLES TO SURVIVE CULTURALLY

Because threats to the Nasioi way of life during the past century differed, their responses have also changed through time. Nasioi have never agreed on any single best strategy. Faced with outside powers greater than they could muster, they nevertheless have always tried to adjust, to adapt, to survive. From a Western point of view, some of these attempts might seem strange or futile, but they show that Nasioi were never simply passive or unthinking victims. Rather, they continually sought to solve the problems that colonialism produced.

Adapting to Plantation Colonialism

Earliest invasion by colonizers found Nasioi ill prepared to resist. Their technology was barely removed from a Stone Age level. Bows, arrows, and wooden spears were no match for German firearms. Their scattered settlement pattern with its decentralized "big man" political organization could not mobilize any sort of combat force of a size capable of overcoming this disadvantage. In addition, Nasioi and speakers of other languages living along the coast around Kieta were eager to obtain the new trade goods that the colonizers could provide. After some initial efforts at resistance, coastal villages began accommodating themselves to the colonial presence. Nasioi in the mountains farther from Kieta tried to avoid contact with colonizers as much as possible, using traditional exchange practices with lowland villagers as a means to obtain new goods.

These strategies continued for decades. When Australians took over the Bougainville administration at the end of World War I, avoidance was at first even more successful. Nasioi in coastal and valley villages misled Australian patrol officers whenever possible, saying that the mountains were uninhabited and not worth visiting. In the 1930s, there was only a handful of colonizers living on Nasioi land. Missionaries, administrators, and planters each had different goals in interacting with villagers, who were sometimes able to play one group against the other.

Colonizers typically use means other than force to maintain their control, including efforts to convince the colonized that their best interests are served by cooperation. For some time, such efforts were successful with Nasioi, who worked on plantations, followed administrators' orders, and attended mission services, in the hope that they would achieve the material prosperity the colonizers represented. Such hopes were doomed to disappointment by the very nature of colonialism, which operates to benefit outsider interests. The flight of the colonizer community in the face of Japanese invasion was a crucial lesson to the Nasioi that they must change strategies to achieve their own goals.

Postwar Strategies

Nasioi began to express their disenchantment with colonialism in a variety of ways soon after Australian administration was reestablished, as planters and missionaries also returned to the Kieta area. Nasioi were no longer willing to work on plantations in return for the kind of treatment they had received in the past. Plantations that had existed on Nasioi land for decades had to import labor from other parts of New Guinea. Mutual resentment between planter and villager increased.

Administration policy in what was now the United Nations Trust Territory of New Guinea changed considerably in the postwar era. Great emphasis was placed on "development," especially economic development. This included more government expenditure on education, which had in the past been left in the hands of missions. At the same time the United Nations' (UN) pressure to move the territory toward independence increased. To Nasioi it seemed that the administration was more intrusive than ever, just when villagers were less willing to believe that such interference was to their benefit.

Most Nasioi simply refused to participate in administration-sponsored projects. These included elected councils, with the power to tax and carry out local development projects, and cash crop producers' cooperative societies. Nasioi also resented, though they could not resist without open rebellion, new public health efforts such as spraying villages with insecticides to get rid of malaria-carrying mosquitoes.

In the early 1960s, Nasioi had not yet organized themselves to carry out effective political or economic action. Rather, many villagers were seeking more supernatural solutions to their problems. Small groups would try to combine economic efforts such as cash cropping with religious practices that joined traditional with missionary ideas and rituals. These groups were attacked by the administration as "cargo cults," and leaders were sometimes jailed. Though irrational from an outsider's viewpoint, this response—which Nasioi called in pidgin *longlong lotu* or "crazy church"— did focus resentment, and it helped link villages in a way that traditional political organization had not.

A more recognizably political response occurred in 1962, when a UN fact-finding team visited Kieta. At a public meeting, some Nasioi braved colonizer anger by asking the UN to remove Australia as administering authority and to substitute the United States. This proposal reflected memories of American troops' wartime generosity with food and supplies. It also showed that many Nasioi still believed outside help was necessary to achieve their goals. Typically, Nasioi were not united on the issue; others were equally outspoken in favor of continuing Australian control.

New Political Responses

Rapid social change in the 1960s, especially but not exclusively associated with mining development, began to move Nasioi to more political forms of action. Although initially resisting the idea of the first House of Assembly election in 1964, because they associated it with local government councils, most Nasioi eventually voted for the winner, from a different language group. Villagers often emphasized their choice's experience as a former Catholic seminarian, implying he had supernatural knowledge that could help them.

Nasioi learned more about modern politics from this leader, but also from younger islanders who took advantage of new educational opportunities. In addition to mission schools, some Nasioi now went to the government high school recently established on Buka Island. Young Bougain-ville men were well represented when the University of Papua New Guinea opened at the end of the decade, though the proportion of Nasioi students was relatively small. In the 1968 House of Assembly election, a majority of Nasioi overwhelmingly voted for the Bougainville incumbent, though they did not necessarily understand or approve of his role in the original mining agreement.

This political leader was a key figure in the formation of an organization called Napidakoe Navitu, centered in Kieta. This was the most modern political organization in which Nasioi participated as a majority. In the 1972 election, Navitu's candidates were successful, although new electoral boundaries meant that Nasioi could not vote for their 1964 and 1968 choice. Most Nasioi backed these candidates even though they were from other language groups.

Few of Bougainville's political spokesmen who emerged in the 1970s were Nasioi; perhaps this reflects the inhibiting effect of the long dominant colonial presence in and around Kieta. But Nasioi participated in new institutions and activities, whether these were educational, political, or economic. When Papua New Guinea became independent in 1975, Nasioi were the strongest supporters of a movement demanding Bougainville's secession from the new nation. This movement was appeased by creating a form of provincial government. Bougainville became part of a new North Solomons Province, with its own executive and legislative institutions, though subject to the central authority of Papua New Guinea's prime minister and House of Assembly in Port Moresby. North Solomons Province also received mining royalties originally given to the central government; however, this did not provide any additional revenue directly to Nasioi landowners.

The "Bougainville Crisis"

By 1988, a combination of factors created what came to be called by outsiders the "Bougainville Crisis." Nasioi resentment of the mine's social and environmental effects continued to grow. Review of the mining agreement, scheduled for 1981, did not take place, partly because of general landowner resistance to any further projects. Differences between the central and provincial governments over divisions of mining revenue continued. BCL no longer gave the same attention to community relations that had characterized the 1970s. But the first acts of violence demonstrated new social divisions within the Nasioi community.

The Panguna Landowners Association (PLA) was created in 1981 by Nasioi as an organization to represent landowners in negotiating with others, especially BCL. The PLA succeeded in obtaining a new compensation agreement with the company, establishing a trust fund with some of the money otherwise paid to individuals. Despite initial successes, disagreements arose within the PLA, particularly between younger and older members, over issues such as distribution of funds.

A new group of younger, educated Nasioi appeared to contest the leadership and policies of the PLA. That one of these was a young woman suggests that the importance of women in traditional life never completely disappeared. Representatives of this "new PLA" presented their grievances to consultants employed by BCL in November 1988 but rejected the consultants' responses. From this point, increasing violence spread from Nasioi territory throughout Bougainville and would last almost a decade.

First targets were mining installations and equipment, blown up by explosives stolen from BCL. Mining operations were interrupted but resumed when additional police were sent in to improve security. Their attempts to arrest the alleged ringleader, a Nasioi associated with the "new PLA" and a former BCL employee, were unsuccessful. This same Nasioi, Francis Ona, was believed to have kidnapped and perhaps murdered his uncle, an older PLA leader. These acts are further evidence that differences among Nasioi landowners were a primary cause of what later became a much wider conflict.

Violence escalated when police and Papua New Guinea soldiers were sent in to restore order and reopen the mine. The human rights organization Amnesty International later reported that police and military were guilty of many human rights violations, including torturing prisoners. These offenses created wider support for what was now called the Bougainville Revolutionary Army (BRA), led by Ona. Nasioi formed the core of BRA, though men from other language groups joined, as resentment of PNG soldiers' mistreatment of civilians spread throughout Bougainville. Other young men began to take up weapons in random acts of violence, sometimes claiming BRA connections.

Continued attacks on BCL installations caused the mine to close in May 1989, creating a crisis for the Papua New Guinea government. In its last full year of operation, the mine had provided 8 percent of the nation's gross domestic product and 12 percent of all government revenue.[5] Unable to accept such severe financial costs, the central government kept shifting policies, sometimes trying military solutions, at others attempting a negotiated settlement. Nothing succeeded in preventing the spread of violence, which eventually destroyed many modern facilities, including the Kieta airstrip.

In the meantime, divisions appeared within the population. Buka residents favoring peace invited central government troops back into their island. The BRA called for complete secession from Papua New Guinea; some Nasioi who disagreed were killed by their own compatriots. The central government blockaded the island. When Bougainvilleans seeking shelter or supplies crossed the southern water border into the Solomon Islands, government troops pursued them, creating an international incident. The "Bougainville Crisis" had grown far beyond that island, involving many forces, but Nasioi remained the core of resistance to colonialism and its legacy.

After nine years, journalists estimated the conflict had caused from ten thousand to twenty thousand deaths, directly or as a result of lack of medicine and other necessities.[6] Though earlier peacemaking efforts had failed, conditions began to change in 1997. People on all sides were fed up with the destruction and misery. Women, from Nasioi and other language groups, were prominent in calling for peace. Elections created a new government in Papua New Guinea, and both New Zealand and Australia became more directly involved in truce negotiations. On April 30, 1998, a truce was signed by Bougainvilleans, including representatives of the BRA and other Nasioi, and Papua New Guinea's prime minister. Significantly, Francis Ona boycotted the ceremony and continued to call for secession, but he can only speak for a minority of Nasioi. There are no immediate plans to reopen the copper mine.

FOOD FOR THOUGHT

The struggle of Nasioi to achieve their goals continues. The Nasioi case is distinctive in the Southwest Pacific because these people have been subjected to many different kinds of colonial impact, from plantations to a world war to high-technology mining. However, similar events have taken place and continue to occur in other parts of the world. It remains to be seen whether Nasioi provide lessons that can inform other endangered peoples about how to respond to threats to their way of life.

Questions

1. Colonialism is often defined as political control by an outside power. Nasioi are now citizens of an independent Papua New Guinea. Is it accurate to describe their present condition in terms of colonialism?

2. Open-cut mining is much more destructive of the physical environment than is plantation agriculture. Have the social effects on the Nasioi also been more destructive?

3. What factors seem to have been most important in causing Nasioi to shift their responses to colonialism over time?

4. At least some of the Nasioi, some of the time, were willing to cooperate with

different colonial agencies. If this is true, can one speak of "exploitation" of Nasioi by others?

5. Societies change over time, but there are also continuities in the midst of change. What aspects of Nasioi social life show the greatest continuity during the past one hundred years?

NOTES

1. Eugene Ogan, *Business and Cargo: Socio-Economic Change among the Nasioi of Bougainville* (Canberra: Australian National University Press, 1972), p. 76.

2. Eugene Ogan, *The Bougainville Conflict: Perspectives from Nasioi* (Canberra, Australia: Research School of Pacifica and Asian Studies, Australian National University, 1996), p. 4.

3. Douglas L. Oliver, *Black Islanders: A Personal Perspective of Bougainville 1937–1991* (Honolulu: University of Hawaii Press, 1992), pp. 134–35.

4. Ogan, *Bougainville Conflict*, p. 6.

5. Oliver, *Black Islanders*, p. 121.

6. Michael Field, "The Lincoln Agreement," *Pacific Islands Monthly* 68 (3): 17, 1998.

RESOURCE GUIDE

Published Literature

May, R. J., and Matthew Spriggs, eds. *The Bougainville Crisis.* Bathurst, Australia: Crawford House, 1990.

Ogan, Eugene. *Business and Cargo: Socio-Economic Change among the Nasioi of Bougainville.* Canberra: Australian National University Press, 1972.

Oliver, Douglas L. *Black Islanders: A Personal Perspective of Bougainville 1937–1991.* Honolulu: University of Hawaii Press, 1992.

Spriggs, Matthew, and Donald Denoon, eds. *The Bougainville Crisis: 1991 Update.* Bathurst, Australia: Crawford House, 1992.

Wesley-Smith, Terence, ed. "A Legacy of Development: Three Years of Crisis in Bougainville." Special Issue on Bougainville of *The Contemporary Pacific* 14 (2): 1992.

Films and Videos

My Valley Is Changing, 1970, Distributed by Film Australia Pty. Ltd.
Tukana: Husat I Asua?, 1984, Distributed by Ronin Films

WWW Site

Papua New Guinea Homepage
http://www.png.com

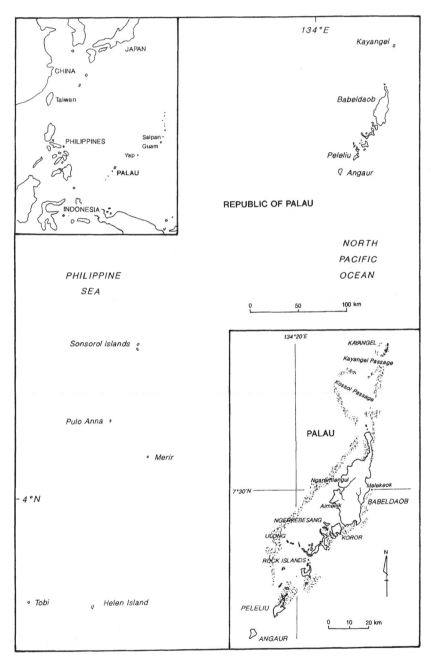

Republic of Palau. Copyright © Joan Lawrence, Department of Anthropology, University of Auckland, New Zealand.

Chapter 9

The Palauans

Karen L. Nero

"Chad er a Belau" and "Palauan" are not just different ways of saying
"Palauan" but may also be seen as representing a transformation of
mindset, lifestyle, and values.

Howard Charles, Palauan musician and
social scientist, 1998[1]

CULTURAL OVERVIEW

The People

The people of the world's newest nation—the Republic of Palau—are endangered even though they enjoy a high standard of living, booming economy, and cultural and political autonomy. According to the United
Nations' Human Development Index (HDI), which attempts to assess real
standards of living based on human (education and health) as well as economic indicators, Palau ranks second among fifteen Pacific Island nations,
and fifty-fifth of 174 nations around the globe, higher than many of the
world's industrialized nations. In what ways, then, and why, are Palauans
struggling to sustain cultural survival?

The issues that confront Palauans today—high levels of foreign workers;
long-term out-migration; transformations of economic, employment, and
political structures; shifts from rural to urban life-styles; economic and cultural influences from abroad—are those that affect many of the world's
nations. They differ significantly from the issue of political autonomy that
first brought Palauans to international attention as an endangered people

when they passed the world's first nuclear-free constitution in 1980, on a collision course with their United Nations' administering authority, the United States. At that time Palau was part of the U.S. Trust Territory of the Pacific Islands (USTTPI), which also included the Marshall Islands; the Northern Mariana Islands, except Guam; and the remaining Caroline Islands, which now form the Federated States of Micronesia. For nearly two decades Palauans fought a series of bitter confrontations both among themselves and with various parts of the U.S. government and military, which wanted to retain the option of military access to Palau. After the end of the cold war, Palauan and American leaders negotiated a series of compromises that resulted in the end of the world's last trusteeship as Palauans voted to enter into a Compact of Free Association with the United States. The Republic of Palau became independent and joined the United Nations in late 1994.

Palau's over-riding national goal is to meet the basic needs of her people from domestic resources in a manner that preserves the Palauan culture and environment for future generations. The Palauan people then stand at the center of development; their well-being is the purpose for which development is pursued; they are the instruments through which development should occur. In the context of this policy document, "population" means the balance between people, their activities, and their resources.[2]

THE SETTING

Palau is a small island archipelago north of the equator about five hundred statute miles east of the Philippines and north of New Guinea. Archaeologists believe the islands were settled about thirty-five hundred years ago by peoples from Island Southeast Asia and Philippine region. The entire island group is less than two hundred square miles (2.5 times the size of Washington, D.C.) and includes volcanic and coral platform islands and a number of coral atolls. Ten of Palau's sixteen states are on the main island of Babeldaob, but over two-thirds of the resident population of 17,225 people live on the adjacent five-square-mile island of Koror, currently the nation's capital. Extending several hundred miles farther to the southwest are the coral islands of Sonsorol, Hatohobei (Tobi), Pula Anna, Merir, and Helen, whose inhabitants form a cultural minority within Palau. Like other Palauans, most of the residents of these two states reside on Koror and speak Palauan and English, Palau's two official languages. The government estimates that there are 7,000 overseas Palauans, mostly in long established communities on the neighboring islands of Guam, Saipan, and Yap, and on Hawaii and especially the West Coast of the United States.

The wealth of the island nation is its people, along with its land and especially its lagoon and sea resources. Enclosed within the main barrier reef is an extensive lagoon of 560 square miles, and Palau's 200-mile Exclusive Economic Zone (over 235,000 square miles) has rich marine resources, particularly pelagic species such as tuna. More than fifteen hundred species of fish, seven hundred species of coral and anemones, the rare *Tridachna* giant clam, dugong, and saltwater crocodile all contribute to Palau's reputation as one of the world's best scuba-diving spots. The three hundred mushroom-shaped limestone islands, collectively known as the "Rock Islands," are a world-renowned tourist destination. Palau has a warm, tropical climate with high rainfall (except during El Niño droughts) but rarely experiences major typhoons. It is a fragile environment, requiring careful management.

Traditional Subsistence Strategies

The sea has always been an important resource, and archaeologists have found evidence that lagoon fisheries resources were overexploited until Palauans developed conservation practices, many of which continue to this day. Men are responsible for line and spear fishing in the lagoon and deep-sea trolling—providing the all-important protein foods that balance starch foods such as the taro root grown by women. Although in the past all adult men and women, assisted by youth, were responsible for fishing and farming, there were recognized experts. Master fishers had in-depth knowledge of the characteristics of the many species of fish harvested, their spawning cycles, and where and when they might be found. Senior women had expert knowledge and developed intensive deep-soil cultivation methods for the purple taro, *Colocasia esculenta*. The women of the villages maintained large taro patches, cultivated and fertilized over generations and sustained by irrigation, which provided rich yields. Giant swamp taro was grown on the borders of the patches; bananas and myriad fruit trees surrounded both houses and gardens. Breadfruit trees provided another seasonal starch food.

Rather than being a subsistence system in which each family produced its own needs, production in Palau was spurred by a system of exchanges organized around the brother-sister pair and their respective spouses. If a woman and her brother provided sufficient food and labor for her in-laws, then they could look to these affinal relatives (relatives by marriage) for economic support and the provision of Palauan valuables (land, shell and bead monies) to support their matriline (female descent group) and the children of the union. Similarly intervillage alliances among Palau's villages and as far as the neighboring island of Yap, 250 miles to the northeast, circulated both valuables and foodstuffs. Competition for money, prestige, and power spurred production of foodstuffs and local, intervillage, and interisland wealth exchanges.

Social and Political Organization

Palauans recognize a series of political eras in their history. The most recent consolidation of power was complete by the early to mid-eighteenth century. Palauan villages comprise small nucleated settlements, which in the past were situated predominantly in the islands' interiors for defensive purposes, with canoe and young men's houses found on the shores and village perimeters. A number of extended families, residing in lineage (descent line) houses on associated stone platforms, are located around a central meeting house and platform. Palauan social organization is characterized by the principle of what is called *balanced oppositions*. In general, each village is divided in half and the two sides are governed by central chiefly councils and associated age-graded clubs working in friendly competition. The principle of balanced opposition permeates all structures, from the gendered food production already discussed, to the sides of the village, to the chiefly governing structures. Inheritance of title and lands is through the maternal line. The female heads of each matriline select the male and female titleholders, who represent the clan in the complementary male and female chiefly councils that govern each village.

On the model of the four cornerposts of the chiefly meeting house, the *bai*, each village has four primary "cornerpost" governing clans among the councils that generally comprise ten titleholders. Similarly, there are four ranking villages, each conceived of as "children" of the founding goddess of the current era, *Milad*. The eldest brother is Ngeremlengui; followed by Melekeok; the only sister, Aimeliik; and the youngest brother, Koror. Reflecting the propensity for dual organization, the Palauan islands are themselves ordered into "side heavens" (the two sides) of shifting village federations led by the two paramount chiefs, Reklai of Melekeok and Ibedul of Koror. Although Palau in 1980 established a constitutional government with elected president and members of legislature, and an appointed judiciary, the paramount and village chiefs governing structures and intervillage relationships still hold some importance.

The island polity is strongly hierarchical, and individuals, lineages, organizations, and villages are ranked. However, social mobility is possible through hard work. Residence is flexible, with wives joining their husband's household, and males often moving when taking high-ranking titles in their matrilineage. It is rare for one's rank to be uniformly high in all social settings. Both personal autonomy and lineage autonomy are highly valued.

Religion and World View

Each of the villages recognizes a primary god and/or goddess, although certain villages share gods, furthering intervillage alliances. Ancestral and village spirits are recognized. In the past the chiefly titles were in turn counterbalanced by priests and representatives/embodiments of the gods; each meeting house had an associated god's shrine. Today the majority of Palauans are Christians, relatively evenly distributed among Catholics, a number of Protestant sects including prominently the Seventh Day Adventists, and *Modekngei*, which comprises both Christian and indigenous elements, the syncretic Palauan religion.

The most important life-cycle celebration of this island nation is the woman's First Birth Ceremony. After a period of special care, seclusion, and hot herbal baths, the young woman is presented to the public on her family's stone platform, while the clans joined by marriage exchange foods and valuables. Large festive exchanges of valuables, pigs, turtle, taro, other special foods, and betel nut also accompany events such as the taking of a title, the construction of a meeting house, the purchase of a house, or village to village exchanges. In the past the dances, food exchanges, and such festivities of these village-level occasions could continue for weeks. Today these feasts and celebrations are organized around national occasions such as Constitution Day as well.

THREATS TO SURVIVAL

Palauans have maintained a dynamic, vibrant culture, creatively and selectively incorporating wealth, ideas, and people from abroad for centuries, even millennia. Although the degree of outsider control of Palau during the past two centuries has had devastating effects, at present Palauans have achieved a degree of political autonomy. Can the short-term economic capital Palau now commands be used to achieve longer-term economic autonomy for the benefit of Palauans?

Demographic Trends

Historically the greatest threat to the Palauan people was depopulation after exposure to European diseases in the late eighteenth century. From perhaps fifty thousand people Palauans were reduced to just over thirty-seven hundred by 1901. Throughout successive Spanish, German, and Japanese colonial administrations the population slowly began recovering, although Palauan cultural institutions such as the indigenous religions and the chiefly institutions were severely eroded by Christianity and the powers of the foreign political administrators. Between World Wars I and II Palau was the capital of the Japanese South Seas Empire. In the prewar era Palauans to a certain extent benefited from the roads, electricity, stores, newspapers, and other amenities of the Japanese. But they were considered third-class citizens, after the Japanese and the Okinawan laborers. During

Ngasech (first birth ceremony), Angaur, Palau, early 1980s. The young mother has just descended from the platform from which she has been presented to the community, and the senior women of her husband's and her lineages are washing her with herbs and dancing to her. Copyright © Karen L. Nero.

the Japanese military buildup prior to the war Palauans were used as little more than slave laborers; then Palau became the site of one of the Pacific's bloodiest battles, on Peleliu. Both Japanese and Palauans starved as the United States maintained a strict embargo on supplies to Koror and Babeldaob and carried out daily bombing raids.

After an initial recovery period and provision of medical services immediately after the war, the islands entered a long period of economic stagnation under the early U.S. administration. Beginning in the 1950s a number of Palauan families moved to Guam to find employment, and U.S. families there sponsored a few young students.

It was not until the early 1960s that Palauans routinely had access to education higher than the primary level. Educational services further expanded with aid from the United States under the Kennedy and Johnson administrations. The general extension of U.S. educational programs introduced many new values and concepts. Beginning in 1966 U.S. Peace Corps volunteers were dispersed throughout the villages helping upgrade the educational, health, and general government systems.

Thus higher education joined the other benefits of life in the urban center of Koror—new employment opportunities within the expanding U.S. administration now committed to training Micronesian workers, and access to the only hospital, not to mention the excitement of theaters and clubs where Palauan music and contemporary dancing could be enjoyed. The bright lights of Koror drew ever-increasing numbers, with the balance of population shifting from rural to urban villages in the mid-1960s. The composition of the rural villages became skewed toward the elders and the young children, as school age children and young workers gravitated to Koror, even though the new immigrants' affection generally remained strongest for their home villages.

The concentration of 71 percent of Palau's resident population on the Koror islands has severely taxed these islands and surrounding lagoon area. Despite increasing conservation measures, there are pressures on marine and fisheries resources through commercial and subsistence exploitation. Increased recreational use has resulted in noise and gas pollution from the fleet of speedboats and added to depletion of reef fish, shellfish, and corals. There are inadequate facilities for the disposal of solid waste, and threats to the marine ecosystem from sand and coral dredging and from runoff into mangrove swamps and the lagoons. The construction of the new national capital in Melekeok should help population redistribution but will require the extension of roads, facilities, and sewage, solid waste, and water treatment facilities now centralized in Koror.

Beginning in 1986 but especially after Palauan independence in 1994, the number of foreign workers rapidly increased. By 1995, foreigners, mostly workers and their families, accounted for 24 percent of the population. Palau's overall growth rate of 2.8 percent per year is due to this immigration.[3] A number of major development projects have been undertaken, including planning and constructing the new capital, building a paved road connecting all of the states of Babeldaob, and replacing the Koror-Babeldaob bridge. There is also a tourism boom; another hotel has just been completed and more are planned. Even if Palau could persuade all overseas Palauans to return, skilled and unskilled construction workers would still be required. Most of the migrant workers are drawn from Asian countries. In the private sector Palauan entrepreneurs turn to foreign workers for construction as well as sales and service jobs and hire foreign farmers and deep-sea fishers.

Shift to Wage Labor

Wage labor also introduced an expanded set of values. As the U.S. administration in the 1970s sought to include Micronesian workers at all levels, Palauans were disproportionately successful in obtaining positions with the United Nations Trust Territory administration on Saipan in Guam. Overseas Palauans began to create new elites based on U.S. models of monetary wealth counted in U.S. dollars, and the level of job one was able to obtain.

Although most villages still maintain some of their established deep-soil taro patches, few women today work full time in the back-breaking labor, and much of the taro, as well as other starches and vegetables, is grown in dry-land patches by Filipino and Chinese men. Gardening skills are no longer as central to a Palauan woman's identity and reputation. Palauan men and women continue to farm and fish, but mainly as avocations in addition to wage employment. In the past, one's primary identity was through one's father's and mother's villages and lineages. One's position in life was based on hard work within the family and lineage, one's skill as a fisher or farmer, and one's fulfillment of the various responsibilities of family life.

Loss of Language

As both Palauan men and women are active in wage labor, and many of the young people are overseas, few extended family members are available to care for children and elders. Increasingly Palauan families are turning to foreign domestic helpers, generally from the Philippines. Parents and educators fear the potential cultural and language losses of children who spend much of their day in the care of foreigners. The Palauan language is changing at a dramatic rate with the incorporation of loan words and concepts from Spanish, German, Japanese, and English. Bi- and multilingualism is common and highly valued. Although there have always been dialect differences among the states, there are widening differences in the language of the elders and the youth, the rural communities and the urban centers. Certain linguistic practices that are core to Palauan understandings—ways of enumerating human beings as opposed to different classes of objects— are being eroded and lost.

Racism

Especially to the extent that the expanding economic benefits of the expanding economy are not evenly distributed among Palauans (growing inequities exist, despite a general prosperity), issues of racism are now a public concern. Although Palauans historically employed household servants and foreign workers prior to the arrival of Europeans, most were Palauans, often distant relatives, and servant status was not necessarily a life-long classification. Under colonial government, members of the islands (now states) of Sonsorol and Hatochobei became cultural minorities within Palau. Palauans also grew familiar with other cultural minorities. The Filipino community has been gradually established in Palau since the 1970s, and the languages and cultures of Palau and the Philippines are similar. The valence of Japanese/Palauan and American/Palauan relationships has now been transformed by political independence, and many Palauans are fluent in Japanese and English and have become accustomed to American and Japanese world views. In contrast, many of the recent workers imported as household servants and unskilled or semiskilled workers speak languages unknown to Palauans (and the reverse) and come from considerably different cultures and world views. Whereas in the past Palauan culture was flexible in incorporating foreigners and training them to act in culturally appropriate fashion if they were to remain, the sheer number of foreign residents and the short-term nature of many of their contracts make this unlikely today even if it were desirable.

Tourism

By far the fastest-growing sector of the economy today is tourism. Long a favored destination for scuba divers and wealthy international tourists, Palau now offers increased numbers of low-cost package tours. Visitor arrivals have been increasing at a fast rate from a base of 5,640 in 1980 to 73,719 in 1997.[4] It is estimated that tourism might account for about 11 percent of gross domestic product.[5] There are currently around eight hundred rooms available, mainly on Koror, including the international standard Palau Pacific Resort and the new Palasia Outrigger. Another twenty-six projects were on the drawing boards in December 1996, six of which are on the scale of five hundred to nine hundred rooms, including a number of golf courses to serve a predominantly Japanese clientele. Palauans are understandably concerned at the levels of foreign investment required, as well as the high numbers of foreign workers required for the construction of the facilities and as service providers at the rate of three to four per room once the hotel is opened. They worry that this massive tourism investment could result in a second Saipan (a major resort destination for Japanese tourists), where the indigenous Chamorros and Carolineans became a minority within a decade. Current legislation attempts both quality control and protection of Palauan interests, but there are no absolute limits set on what tourism levels the islands might be able to sustain. Regulatory boards are not empowered to limit and choose among proposals. It is also difficult to control under-the-table deals with Palauans that subvert the strong controls on foreign ownership.

RESPONSE: STRUGGLES TO SURVIVE CULTURALLY

Just as the current threats to Palauan cultural survival have developed over the past century, so have the responses.

Economic Safeguards

During a period when most economies were struggling to maintain a stable or small 3 to 4 percent growth rate in gross domestic product (GDP), in 1995 and 1996 the Hawaiian Bank estimated that Palau experienced growth rates in excess of 24 percent per year.[6] This rate is too large for either the economy or the people to absorb and threatens Palauan cultural practices in multiple ways.

To a certain extent, Palau is well poised to control the situation. The nation is independent, yet enjoys a relationship with the United States that has provided both physical and economic security for the new nation. Part of the compact funding established a trust fund to provide operating capital during the subsequent period when these funds are no longer provided by the United States. However, it is all a precarious balancing act.

Conservation Efforts

Marine conservation of lagoon resources was highly developed in Palau prior to colonial administrative disruptions. Historically economically important fish, turtles, and dugong were managed by indigenous political (e.g., chief) controls, such as seasonal bans on fishing. Palau's long-established 70-Island Reserve in the Rock Islands, which restricts all visits and resource utilization, was the region's first marine wildlife reserve. Today the traditional controls have had to be integrated within new national administrative bodies. The erosion of traditional knowledge, however, is even more critical, as children spend more time in schools than in the lagoons and on land learning well-established practices from their parents. International organizations such as the Worldwide Fund for Nature, Nature Conservancy, and Sierra Club have provided technical support to Palauan conservationists since the 1970s. The Palauan Noah Idechong won the prestigious international conservation Goldman award in 1995 and used the substantial grant to found the Palau Conservation Society, which is working to integrate more traditional conservation practices with present-day requirements.

Food Production

Palau's traditional and current strength has been its ability to support a growing, healthy population from its rich sea and land resources, absorbing new production techniques and crops. In the 1980s the development of fishing and farming cooperatives and central marketing systems supported diversification of family farming. Today foreign workers provide much of the labor as 60 percent of Palauan men and women have entered into the wage labor force.[7] Those who farm, fish, and prepare food for cash as well as family needs are able to enjoy a high standard of living. However, the expanding local food market requires constant vigilance and protection. In the early 1990s the high export levels of reef fish to Guam threatened Palauan access to fresh fish, until controlling legislation was enacted. Also, open markets allow less expensive imported white rice and tinned fish, which are less nutritious than local taro and fish, into the system.

Family Planning

Successful family planning programs, introduced in 1974, in combination with outmigration have resulted in an overall 2.8 percent fertility rate. The influx of foreigners, however, keeps the numbers high. The median age in 1990 was 25.7 years—high for the region, but still lower than that of established market economies.[8] The fast-growing segment of the population is foreign workers, who by law cannot become citizens. Palau is currently experimenting with legislation to control the number of foreign workers as well as their dependents residing in Palau. Study groups, including the Palau National Committee on Population and Children, which presented its report and policy recommendations in March 1997, have been established because of local concern about the population issues.

Education Reform

After years of foreign dominated educational systems, the Ministry of Education is actively supporting the development of Palauan educational materials. A revised Palauan-English dictionary and teaching grammar have been completed, and a Palauan-Palauan dictionary is nearly complete. The entire curriculum is being revised with local community participation to center teaching within Palauan models, while retaining access to advanced mathematical and language skills.

Palauans are industrious and well educated. The government administration and ministries, the judiciary, and the legislature are led and staffed by capable Palauans. There is a strong Palauan private sector. The relevant ministries and government agencies are actively monitoring the economy and providing a forum to increase public awareness and participation. Palau has a significant resource in its overseas population, many of whom are also well educated and well employed.

FOOD FOR THOUGHT

Today Palau is a multicultural independent nation closely linked economically and politically with the United States. The economic transfer provided under the compact is on a declining schedule, which could promote economic independence if Palau is able to use the coming decade to balance population and natural resource utilization and create a truly sustainable life-style. Large foreign investments in tourism and other businesses both support and may undercut such balancing attempts. Will Palau be able to take short-term advantage of foreign investment and labor while maintaining the controls necessary to ensure that it is the Palauan people who are at the heart of such development? The record from neighboring islands is not encouraging.

What does it mean to "be a Palauan?" What does cultural survival mean to those residing at home and abroad? In the past *chad er a belau* were farmers and fishers who developed and protected Palau's rich natural resources during intensive competitions for prestige, power, and wealth, but such prestige and power were achieved in a large part through fulfillment of one's familial and community responsibilities for the welfare of others. Competition for prestige, power, and wealth is still an important incentive, but today's forms of wealth are easier to hide away, and it is easier to point to government responsibilities for social welfare. In today's widening world, Palauans include cultural minorities within the nation, and Palau is host to thousands of foreign workers, just as thousands of Palauans reside, study, and work overseas. Palauans have chosen to be part of the international movement of people, wealth, and ideas.

Questions

1. What is cultural identity? All cultures are constantly changing and are defined by present practices and increasingly by international influences. How do Palauans keep their cultural traditions?

2. In most societies there are many different cultural groups living together, with one or two that may hold significant political and economic power. Yet all contribute to the community. Especially across differences of language, class, and social practices, how can the Palauans avoid racism and class distinctions, learning to treat others as individuals and to value their particular contributions?

3. How important is language to cultural identity? How important is it to be fluent in more than one language, and what is the situation in Palau today?

4. Palauans enjoy one of the world's most spectacular natural environments. How can it be protected not only as a world heritage site but as a means to meet primarily local needs?

NOTES

1. Personal communication, 1998.
2. The Palau National Committee on Population and Children (CoPopChi), *Population and Development: Toward a Palau National Policy for Sustainable Human Development* (Koror: Palau National Committee on Population and Children, March 1997).
3. CoPopChi, *Population and Development*, 1997.
4. Palau 2020: National Master Development Plan (NMDP). Revised Draft Final Report, 1996.
5. Palau 2020, 1996.
6. Republic of Palau Economic Report. Honolulu: Bank of Hawaii Economics Department, 1997.
7. Palau 2020, 1996.
8. Palau 2020, 1996.

RESOURCE GUIDE

Published Literature

Barnett, Homer G. *Being a Palauan*. New York: Holt, Rinehart & Winston, 1960.
Johannes, Robert Earle. *Words of the Lagoon: Fishing and Marine Lore in the Palau District of Micronesia*. Berkeley: University of California Press, 1981.
Nero, Karen L. "The Breadfruit Tree Story: Mythological Transformations in Palauan Politics." *Pacific Studies* 15(4): 235–60, 1992.
Smith, DeVerne Reed. *Palauan Social Structure*. New Brunswick, NJ: Rutgers University Press, 1986.
Wilson, Lynn B. *Speaking to Power: Gender and Politics in the Western Pacific*. New York: Routledge, 1995.

Films and Videos

Islands on the Edge of Time. Options 2000, distributed by PIC, 1995.
Palau: Conserve Our Precious Environment, distributed and produced by Bureau of Resources and Development, Koror, 1990.

WWW Sites

Culture and History of Palau
http://www.visit-palau.com

Moving Cultures: Remaking Asia-Pacific Studies
http://www.hawaii.edu/movingcultures/

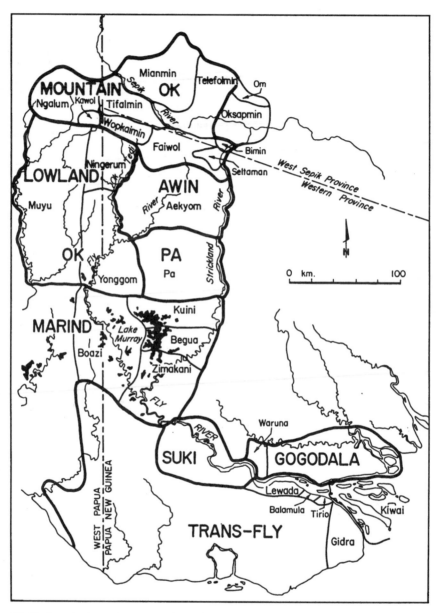

Ok Tedi and Fly River socioecological region. Courtesy of David Hyndman.

Chapter 10

The Peoples of Ok Tedi and Fly River, Papua New Guinea

David Hyndman

CULTURAL OVERVIEW

The People

Within the core Ok Tedi region in Papua New Guinea (PNG) there are Mountain Ok peoples consisting of some 700 Wopkaimin, Lowland Ok peoples consisting of some 3,000 Ningerum and 2,200 Yonggom, and some 6,000 Awin peoples primarily Aekyom. Within the greater impact region, the Marind peoples of the Middle Fly region include some 2,000 Boazi and 1,500 Zimakani, and the region south of the Strickland confluence includes some 1,000 Suki, 3,300 Waruna, and 7,000 Gogodala. The Trans Fly people of the Lower Fly consist of 200 Lewada, 170 Balamula, 280 Tirio, and 23,000 Kiwai.

The Wopkaimin of the upper Ok Tedi River and the Yonggom of the lower Ok Tedi River emerged as the main indigenous stakeholders in the Ok Tedi crisis, precipitated by environmental damage caused by a mining operation. The Wopkaimin are a Mountain Ok people and the Yonggom are a Lowland Ok people. Current political borders between Indonesia and PNG bisect their homelands, in the center of the island of New Guinea.

The Setting

Commoditization of Natural Resources in Papua New Guinea

The Australian colonial administration laid the groundwork for the production of commodities for export and promoted the use of natural resources to finance economic development. Since independence in 1975,

PNG has opened a mining resource frontier for the world market and imported to supply the home market. Foreign companies, who bring in capital and technology, are allowed to exploit the gold and copper resources. PNG then extends concessions, extracts a portion of the revenues from production and export, and redirects the available resources for national development.

Since the start of the Ok Tedi mining project, PNG has followed a typical mining trajectory whereby the state takes the subsoil minerals while being vague about protecting indigenous peoples against resulting ecological devastation. Clause 29.13 of the 1976 Ok Tedi agreement refers to "the limited present use of the area" and to the "effect the project must 'necessarily' have on the environment."[1] From the beginning of the project the state and the developer prioritized company profits and increased state revenue well ahead of environment and systems of subsistence production of local landowners.

Kennecott was the first transnational to test drill in 1969 on Mt. Fubilan, the mining site on Wopkaimin land now commonly referred to as the "Pot of Gold." To the exploration geologists, it was a 7,216-foot peak situated on the extremely rugged and unstable Star and Hindenburg Mountains, which received over 429 inches of rainfall every year, making it the wettest place recorded anywhere in the world. Exploration between 1969 and 1971 costing about A$13 million (at the time approximately U.S. $18 million) determined that an extremely ambitious engineering project could convert Mt. Fubilan's 137 million tons of 0.88 percent copper ore containing 0.66 gram per ton of gold into a profitable mining project. To the Wopkaimin landowners, Fubilan is their sacred mountain sitting on top of the land of the dead.

After prolonged deadlocks at the negotiating table, Kennecott's prospecting authority was withdrawn in 1975, and in March 1976 PNG signed the Ok Tedi Agreement with Dampier Mining Company. The transnational Broken Hill Pty Ltd (BHP), the "Big Australian," became the lead developer in 1979, but soaring gold prices finally prompted creation of the transnational Ok Tedi Mining Limited (OTML) consortium in 1981 to develop the project. The German-based industrial conglomerate Kupferexplorationsgesellschaft (KE) and the United States–based Amoco (Standard Oil of Indiana) were eventually attracted by PNG to the consortium. BHP and Amoco both took a 30 percent share, but BHP has always operated the consortium. The German KE took a 20 percent share, as did the PNG state. Although excluded from the consortium, the Wopkaimin as landowners received modest compensation in rent and royalties. Much greater social impact on the Wopkaimin occurred from the expanding mining frontier of the world capitalist system than their encapsulation in the newly independent PNG state.

Wopkaimin house being built on the Tabubil plateau, 1975. It is thatched from sago groves. Courtesy of David Hyndman.

Traditional Subsistence Strategies and Social Organization

Before the mining project some seven hundred Wopkaimin of the upper Ok Tedi River maintained a system of subsistence production in scattered hamlets in the surrounding mountains. Membership in a local kinship group provided the basis of claiming land and resource rights, and social class was absent. Men monopolized public life and formal religious activity in the secret Afek cult. Men rose through Afek cult initiation and competed for status and leadership (*kamokim*) within the kin group. Women participated in decision making on matters other than the secret male cult. There were separate masculine and feminine spheres of production in the kinship relations of subsistence production. Men dominated the hunting of game; women specialized in growing *Colocasia* taro, the staple food, and raising domestic pigs.

Before mining, twenty-three hundred Yonggom practiced subsistence production on the lower Ok Tedi River. Staple food gardens of bananas and sago palm groves were located extensively along the riverbanks. Systems of political authority were restricted to the level of the immediate kin group. Yonggom men exercised leadership through control of sacred knowledge, persuasion, and achievement, not through competitive economic exchange.

The PNG government decided for the indigenous peoples of the Ok Tedi

139

River that their natural resources were to become national resources. It was stipulated in the 1976 agreement that a permanent tailings dam be constructed on the Ok Ma to prevent mining wastes, sediments, and chemicals from entering the Ok Tedi River systems. However, once the Ok Tedi project started in 1981 it was specifically exempted by the newly independent PNG government from the state's own Environmental Protection Act of 1978. Even the "excellent environmental protection" alternative in the Ok Tedi Environmental Study predicted that some 200 million tons of sediments would enter the Ok Tedi River system from waste dumps and that aquatic life from the Ok Tedi would be contaminated with dissolved copper 62 miles downstream to the territory of the Ningerum.

From the beginning of construction in 1981 the Ok Tedi project was built on the "fast-track" approach in which the engineer and construction company are the same. The Ok Tedi mine was required to report their accumulated and analyzed environmental impact data to the state at six-month intervals. The heavy metals and sediment levels introduced into the river system during the severe El Niño drought period from July to December 1982 were unreported for a year. The company routinely kept the state out of technical review. For example, early in 1983 construction on the Ok Menga hydroelectric facility was terminated as a result of the movement of a massive block of land. During the same year, with major schedule delays, cost overrides, and construction on the Ok Ma tailings dam uncompleted, the Ok Tedi mine presented the PNG government with an Accelerated Gold Production Scheme. Initially the request was rejected by then–Prime Minister Somare, who issued a stern reprimand stating that "it is important that developers understand the strong view that government has on environmental protection. They must also understand that the government expects developers to adhere to agreements."[2]

The mining plan to extract gold and copper from Mt. Fubilan involves a three-stage process that started in 1984 with gold removed from the top of the mountain for the first five years using a carbon-in-pulp cyanide leach treatment. Gold production ceased in 1989 with the leveling of the summit, and it is now obtained only as a by-product of copper smelting using standard sulfide flotation techniques. Gold and copper reserves are expected to continue until 2005, by which time the mountain will be transformed into a 3,937-foot-deep mining pit.

THREATS TO SURVIVAL

"Impossible to Build a Safe Dam": Creation of an Environmental Crisis

Mining requirements for capital, labor, and food for workers for the Ok Tedi project, as well as the physical output of its operation, have integrated environment and peoples throughout the Ok Tedi and Fly rivers into a single socioecological region. Weak environmental protection plans coupled with a long series of ecological disasters starting in 1984 have endangered natural resources sustaining over thirty thousand indigenous peoples of the socioecological region. By 1989 continued sediment and chemical discharge from the Ok Tedi mining project threatened subsistence production throughout the area.

In January 1984 a 50-million-tonne, 3,280-foot-long landslide on the Ok Ma essentially destroyed all prospects of a permanent tailings dam. Irwin Newman, the first general manager of OTML, stated, "It will be impossible to build a safe dam in the area."[3] The PNG government approved the AGPS, even though the aborted Ok Ma and Ok Menga dams left the project without hydroelectric power or environmental protection.

In the first half year after the start of the AGPS operation, the Ok Tedi mine assessed that it would have "moderate to severe biological impact on the lower Ok Tedi and a minor impact on the Fly River."[4] The scheme was accepted knowing it involved releasing undesirably larger quantities of sediment, tailings, and chemical wastes into the Ok Tedi River. According to the PNG government's own independent report these levels were "10,000 percent, 2 orders of magnitude, over reasonable criteria; 7500 percent over predictions for the original tailings dam; and 650 percent over the maximum total from all sources predicted in the original environmental study."[5] By assuming a role as resource owner and shareholder (20 percent) in the Ok Tedi project, the PNG government was compromised in their duty to protect the health, well-being, and resources of the Wopkaimin and other indigenous peoples of the Ok Tedi and Fly River socioecological region.

In June 1984, a few months after the Ok Ma landslide disaster, a barge transporting chemicals for the mine overturned in the Fly River estuary, losing 2,700 sixty-liter drums of cyanide, the single largest loss of the world's most dangerous poison, as well as several stainless steel containers of hydrogen peroxide. After recovery of only 117 cyanide drums, the Ok Tedi mine terminated the recovery operation, leaving thousands of cyanide drums in the river. In July the PNG government temporarily shut down the Ok Tedi project because of a second cyanide spill at the headwaters of the river system. Some 1,310 cubic yards of highly concentrated cyanide waste was released into the Ok Tedi River. The Ok Tedi mine was silent about their cyanide spill for two weeks, until dead fish, prawns, turtles, and crocodiles started floating downstream of the mine as far south as Ningerum. In their required six-monthly environmental report covering this period, the Ok Tedi mine acknowledged failure of their detoxification system but remained silent about their cyanide drums lying on the bottom of the Fly River estuary, and it was concluded that the environmental impact during this time was not of great magnitude and the fish in the Lower Ok Tedi were overall unaffected. In one critical incident after another the Ok Tedi mine placed environmental protection as a low priority.

Because of low world prices in copper, the Ok Tedi mine did not want to proceed to stage two of the project once they had stripped the more valuable gold resource from the top of Mt. Fubilan. In January 1985 the PNG government refused to renew the mining operation, not because of pollution but for contractual failure to develop a long-term copper mine. Full operations resumed in April 1985. Two Amoco secondhand copper rolling and grinding mills from the United States were relocated to Tabubil, and a 106-mile-long copper slurry pipeline was constructed from Mt. Fubilan to Kiunga. Under the sixth supplemental agreement, the second stage of mining commenced in September 1986 to process 30,000 tons of gold and 70,000 tons of copper per day. The Ok Tedi predicted the lower Ok Tedi River fishery would be reduced from good to between poor and extremely poor.

Astonishingly, the Ok Tedi project went ahead without a permanent tailing dam, hydroelectric scheme, or ocean port, thus making a complete mockery of the 1982 Ok Tedi Environmental Statement. During the course of the 1980s an impressive infrastructure of roads, town, pipeline, river port, and power station was slowly created for the needs of the mine and its employees. Limited use was granted to landowners of the socioecological region and the provincial government. The PNG government as consortium partner advanced U.S. $50 million for road construction and met, or cofinanced, other infrastructure running costs. Tabubil remains a totally artificial mining town, and it and other infrastructure will no longer be required or maintained once mining is completed. Moreover, the crucial dam and retention basin for tailings for environmental protection have never been constructed.

Copper concentrated in the mountain mining town of Tabubil is trucked and piped over 93 miles down a newly constructed all-weather road to Kiunga and then transported by barge to the mouth of the Fly River, where it is transferred to ocean vessels for delivery to copper refineries in Germany, Japan, and Korea. KE became responsible for marketing the concentrate in 1988.

"The Place without Work": Wopkaimin Changing Relations of Production and Social Protest

Ok Tedi mining operations centered in Tabubil created a mining frontier that ushered in a clash between kinship and capitalist relations of production that has threatened Wopkaimin social and cultural reproduction. By the time the mine started extracting gold in 1984 most Wopkaimin relocated to two roadside shanty towns near Tabubil, which had expanded from a former sago grove and hunting shelter into an instant township with over five thousand residents, nearly all males.

By the time of the second-stage copper mining operation, the Ok Tedi mine became known to the Wopkaimin as "the place without work." Job training in the mining enclave consigned the Wopkaimin as apprentices to a succession of authoritative, mostly white expatriate outsiders. Enthusiasm for meager wage-earning opportunities in new capitalist relations of production rapidly diminished with the realization that vast disparities in wealth and status separated them from the white controllers of the mining enclave. There continued to be a separation between masculine and feminine spheres of production in the roadside villages. Women controlled subsistence gardening for home use. Their gardens were planted at lower altitudes of around 1,968 feet (600 m) with new root-crop staples. As menial work disappeared, men had less and less of wage earnings, but exercised control over beer and compensation money.

Wopkaimin culture had a limited capacity for exercising social control in the new roadside villages. There was little new social unity fostered through commitments and obligations to the mine or the government, because the majority of the Wopkaimin were never severed from controlling their own means of production. Two competing social protest movements arose among the Wopkaimin: an indigenous Christian movement known as *rebaibalists* (revivalists) and a decentralization movement associated with a revitalization of the Afek cult. The *rebaibalists* supported rapid socioeconomic change in the roadside villages, whereas proponents of decentralization advocated return to the traditional hamlet structure segregated into men's and women's houses. Under decentralization, the Wopkaimin moved from their roadside villages to their Kam Basin hamlets, thereby enhancing the significance of the Afek cult as the supreme marker of their distinctive identity. Few Wopkaimin liked the *rebaibal* movement because it jeopardized the status they exerted as the indigenous owners of the mine. Social protest by the Wopkaimin against rapid socioeconomic change was realized through continuation of the Afek cult. Through decentralization and continued commitment to the Afek cult, the Wopkaimin were able to carry past traditions forward to retain a sense of place and cultural identity.

"Environment of Economy"

The move to stage-two copper mining production ensured that pollution was no longer confined to the Wopkaimin, Ningerum, and Aekyom peoples of the upper Ok Tedi River area of the socioecological region. Neither the PNG government nor the Ok Tedi mine accepted responsibility for compensating peoples downstream of the project, because they did not want to establish a precedent for any payments to affected peoples throughout the greater socioecological region.

Outrage escalated among peoples in the lower Ok Tedi and Fly River socioecological region as the environmental crisis increased. In 1989 the PNG government was forced to reassess the environmental impact of the Ok Tedi project independently. By the end of July the national government's choice between total discharge into the Ok Tedi or closure of the mine was expressed as an "environment or economy" decision for the peoples of the Ok Tedi and Fly River socioecological region. According to the state-sponsored environmental consultants, pollution would produce a staggering 60 percent fish kill for the life of the mine downstream from continued production with total discharge. This affected international pollution control commitments and jeopardized Australian domestic prawn, lobster, and barramundi fisheries in the Torres Strait.

The Ok Tedi mine's environmental and management program minimized the dangers their mining operation posed to the Fly River socioecological region. The PNG government is simply informed by the Ok Tedi mine that environmental damage from their mining is temporary and unpreventable and APL compliance standards are ever increased. PNG was concerned that in closing the mine they would lose four thousand jobs, reduce the rate of the state's economic growth, and hamper their international image. Finally on September 29, 1989, Jim Yer Waim, the former minister for environment and conservation, announced, "We decided in favor of the people."[6] A Lower Ok Tedi–Fly River Development Trust Fund of kina $2.5 million (approximately U.S. $2.5 million) was created out of a levy paid to the state for each ton of ore processed and waste mined. The PNG government envisioned offsetting the loss of fish with fish ponds, chicken farms, and piggeries to provide alternative sources of protein.

The 1989 Ok Tedi environmental report and tailings dam debate saw sustained political pressure from Western Province politicians. Parry Zeipi, then member of Parliament for South Fly and minister for environment and conservation, warned the government that "if it is not careful in its dealings on the Ok Tedi environmental situation, another potential Bougainville scenario is brewing."[7] The decision "in favor of the people" was also one of political expediency motivated by the violent closure of the Panguna mine on Bougainville, the only other mining project then in PNG.

The state's desperation to retain revenue flow from the Ok Tedi project jeopardized the livelihood, welfare, and health of the thirty thousand people in the Fly River socioecological region. Particulate pollution and heavy metals in the Ok Tedi–Fly River system are not derived from tailings alone; a substantial amount comes from the mining waste dumps. The dumps will continue to pollute long after mining operations have ceased. By 1989 the PNG government had only taken in Kina $19 million (approximately U.S. $19 million) in revenue, a return inadequate even to meet daily food needs of the peoples of the region whose subsistence-based production systems had already collapsed as a consequence of mining.

Ecological Disaster for the Yonggom

The Ok Tedi mine's annual release of 30 million tons of tailings and 40 million tons of waste rock into the river system has created an ecological crisis, especially in the lower Ok Tedi–Fly River. The ecological crisis was and continues to be centered on the peoples of the lower Ok Tedi River, which is the homeland of the Yonggom people. Mine sediments deposited on Yonggom land along the lower Ok Tedi River formed 16- to 33-foot-wide stretches of knee-deep mud, and when the river overflowed the banks the waste sediment destroyed fertile garden land. Fish have disappeared from the lower Ok Tedi, and heavy rains upstream cause mine sediment to wash into the streams feeding the lower Ok Tedi, threatening prawns, lobsters, and bivalves. It is impossible to drink from the river, and the Yonggom cannot swim, bathe, or wash clothes in it. The Yonggom homeland was ecologically sacrificed for continuation of the Ok Tedi project. Bumok Dumanop, a Yonggom woman from Dome village, told the anthropologist Stuart Kirsch on August 7, 1996:

I'm unhappy with what the company has done. They have spoiled our way of life. Before we lived easily: food from the gardens was plentiful, as was the wild game. The river was fine: you could see the fish, the turtles and all the other animals living there. But now it is all gone and it's hard. We're suffering.[8]

RESPONSE: STRUGGLES TO SURVIVE CULTURALLY

The Ok Tedi project typified the manner whereby the resource owner (the state) and the resource developer (the transnational) fail to extend compensation to communities living downstream of mining projects in PNG. As the landowners surrounding the mine, the Wopkaimin enjoyed monetary compensation not received by those living downstream of the project. Explanations usually stress the social consequences of mining impact and relate conflict primarily to poor distribution of economic benefits. This partially accounts for Wopkaimin social protest, which was essentially a reflection of rapid socioeconomic change. The Wopkaimin revitalized their Afek cult to promote their cultural identity and asserted their status as the key landowners of the mining project. By the beginning of 1990, however, the new protest movement of landowners was in conflict with the mining company. The popular ecological resistance movement, which emerged in the lower Ok Tedi–Fly River socioecological region, was primarily a response to the Ok Tedi environmental crisis.

Landowners, Ecological Activists, Anthropologists, and Lawyers: Global Alliance of Radical Environmentalism

Concerns grew for over a decade about the destruction of their environment by the mine, and Yonggom petitioning of the mine increased in magnitude, keeping pace with the level of damage from the mine. Through the emergence of astute new political leaders, the Yonggom refined their popular ecological resistance movement by communicating their concerns beyond the mine to national and international audiences and by adopting more effective strategies of political engagement.

The Yonggom petition of early 1989 was the first document to link ecocide directly to a compensation claim for Kina $13.5 million (approximately U.S. $13.5 million). In a Ningerum Council meeting of March 1989 involving Yonggom villages it was noted that the councilors would threaten to block the Kiunga-Tabubil road, Kiunga airport, and Kiunga wharf if the government and Ok Tedi Mining did not find a suitable solution for the pollution of the Alice–Fly River system. The demonstration that occurred on December 12, 1990, galvanized the popular ecological resistance movement and is documented in OTML Community and Business Relation files as follows: "[A]t about 10 o'clock this morning around 600 to 800 people mostly led by youths and women staged a rather noisy but peaceful and orderly demonstration march to present their petition or sets of demands to OTML and the Government. . . . The demonstration leaders Alex Maun, Rex Dagi, and Joe Tata with the help of Peace and Good Order Committee under the watchful eyes of police kept the crowd under control. . . . The presentation lasted for less than half an hour and the crowd marched off towards the Government Offices to present their copy of the petition."[9]

The localized forms of popular ecological resistance that followed consisted of petitions, roadblocks, and demonstrations. In January 1991 over two thousand landowners responded to the decision to continue mining production with total discharge by blocking all access roads and closing the mine. The Workers Union and the Ok Tedi National Staff Association of OTML supported landowner protest for better compensation to offset environmental destruction; in Port Moresby, the capital, at the University of Papua New Guinea, a large student demonstration against the ecocidal decision to continue mining was held in support of peoples of the socioecological region, especially the Yonggom. From 1992 to 1994 compensation packages were allotted; however, demonstrations always followed to protest irregularities of assessment and retention of compensation money by provincial bureaucrats.

The Yonggom popular ecological resistance movement gave rise to a new generation of political leaders with a much-enlarged political base embracing the entire population of some twenty-two hundred. Alex Maun and Rex Dagi combined being traditional initiation cohorts with government-sponsored, small business–based, and mine work experience to emerge as the new, incorruptible leaders (*nup korok*) of the popular ecological resistance movement. A massive class action suit against BHP, the leading partner of the Ok Tedi Mining consortium, ensued.

Harry Sakulas and Lawrence Tjameri of the Wau Ecology Institute published their "Ecological Damage Caused by the Discharges from the Ok Tedi Copper and Gold Mine, Case Document for the International Water Tribunal" in 1991.[10] Dagi and Maun, supported by the institute report, presented their concerns regarding ecocide from mining before the second International Water Tribunal, which was held in the Netherlands, February 1992. An independent international jury heard the case of water mismanagement and aquatic pollution and found the Ok Tedi project guilty of disrupting the socioecological region's fragile ecosystem; the PNG national government was criticized for encouraging it.

Also in 1992 Dagi attended the Earth Summit in Rio de Janeiro. Later that year he presented landowner concerns before the Amoco meeting held in Washington, D.C., to consider any future investment in the Ok Tedi mining consortium. As a result of the deliberations, Amoco withdrew from the consortium. Meanwhile scientists from the Max Planck Institute in Germany, Otto Kreye and Lutz Castell, produced the *Starnberg Report*, which appeared in Papua New Guinea in a special issue of *Catalyst* in 1991. Maun attended the release of the *Starnberg Report* in Germany and expressed Yonggom concerns, which were substantiated by the report. The report together with Maun's testimony proved crucial in the subsequent investment decision of KE to withdraw from the consortium. The Australian Conservation Foundation (ACF) in 1993 conducted their first international environmental impact assessment in Papua New Guinea in response to the Yonggom popular ecological resistance movement and the published studies substantiating ecocide down the river.

Still in 1995 the Australian-owned BHP refused to alter their perspective and claimed before the Mining and Petroleum Investment in Papua New Guinea conference held in Sydney that there was a "lack of any clear evidence of permanent environmental damage"[11] from the Ok Tedi project. BHP was of the opinion that compliance with particulate load standards agreed to with the PNG government would exonerate them from landowner attack and possible litigation.

The Alien Tort: Collective Action against BHP

Exposure to national and international nongovernmental organizations (NGOs) enhanced the Yonggom's political acumen and eventually put them in contact with the Australian legal firm Slater and Gorton in 1992. Unlike Papua New Guinea–based legal firms, Slater and Gorton possessed the resources and proven track record to prosecute class-action claims against transnationals. A Slater and Gorton lawyer assessed the case for one year and held a series of village-based clan meetings along the entire river system over the next year. This process eventually led Slater and Gorton to take out a class-action claim representing six hundred clans and thirty thousand people in the Fly River socioecological region against BHP.

The protracted two-year battle that ensued constituted an *alien tort*, because it took place in the Supreme Court of the state of Victoria, in Melbourne, Australia, rather than in PNG as Victoria is the location of the corporate headquarters of BHP. BHP lost the media battle in Australia and increasingly appeared to be uncaring environmental vandals. Their attempt to refute the jurisdiction of the Supreme Court of Victoria was rejected and ultimately BHP was found in contempt for drafting legislation for use in PNG to criminalize Papua New Guineans who sued the company. The Supreme Court of Papua New Guinea was hearing landowner appeals against such legislation criminalizing their legal claims when an out-of-court settlement reached in June 1996 committed BHP to implementation of a feasible tailings containment system, payment of K40 million (approximately U.S. $26 million) by way of compensation to the worst affected areas of the Ok Tedi, and payment of K110 million (approximately U.S. $72 million) to all affected persons.

Thousands of landowners, OTML, BHP, and PNG government personnel spent several months attempting to reach consensus. An out-of-court settlement was reached in early 1997 for trust funds to be controlled by landowners, 10 percent of the government's equity in the Ok Tedi mine to be transferred to the people of the Western Province, dredging of the Ok Tedi River, and another feasibility study for impounding tailings. At best, the settlement alleviates some of the environmental damage; the package falls well short of meeting the real costs of the downstream environmental impact of the mine.

The alien tort case against the transnational BHP made it accountable in its home country for the environmental impact it caused in PNG. The environmental compliance standards adhered to in PNG permitted BHP to generate levels of pollution in their mining operation that would never have been possible in Australia. The alien tort against BHP propelled the popular ecological resistance movement of the Yonggom and the Fly River peoples into the global arena and established a significant precedent for cases in which indigenous peoples claim environmental degradation in the courts.

BHP contended that as loss of amenity related to personal injury, any claim, therefore, was contingent on resultant economic loss. Furthermore, BHP deemed that because the thirty thousand landowner claimants resident in the ecological disaster zone were subsistence dwellers, they consequently suffered no economic loss. Slater and Gorton successfully argued for applicability of attachment to place through nonprofit resource and spiritual and religious use and asserted that a thing is economic even if it does not pass through the monetary system. Value would have to be placed on the subsistence system as a result of environmental destruction. The claim of "public nuisance" was also upheld. This was significant because it recognized that land and aquatic tenure systems operating among the claimants were communal rather than private. Therefore, it was accepted that environmental damage to a general communal area was as compelling as private nuisance dependent upon ownership. Thus, the court recognized the communally-based kinship mode of production of the Yonggom and their fellow claimants.

The Yonggom held out and received an extra K40 million (approximately U.S. $26 million) and compromised for an out-of-court settlement expecting the Ok Tedi project to honor its commitment to tailing containment. In May 1997 Alex Maun concluded his workshop presentation on the Ok Tedi settlement held in Canberra, Australia, as follows:

Our main concern is with our means of survival. What we have been given is compensation. Compensation money cannot be a substitute for a means of survival. Survival means we survive for our life and the next generation continues the means of survival until the end of the world. Compensation is a short-term benefit, so our concern is that we want to receive the maximum benefit.[12]

Drought from El Niño closed the mine for several months in 1997; by 1998 dredging of the lower Ok Tedi River had commenced, but the feasibility for tailings containment was still being considered.

FOOD FOR THOUGHT

The Ok Tedi case significantly raised the international profile of environmental debate and galvanized a Yonggom-led global alliance of Papua New Guinea landowners, ecological activists, anthropologists, and lawyers. The PNG Compensation (Prohibition of Foreign Legal Proceedings) Act of 1995 bans the successful alien tort claim as precedent for other rural communities. Although this step may be seen as a backward strategy by the PNG government in order to achieve its goals of national development, it leaves the door open for future violent resolutions of resource conflict as occurred with the Bougainville and Freeport mines. As an out-of-court settlement, the Ok Tedi alien tort was only moderate in its achievements. Amungme landowners across the border in West Papua followed with another alien tort against the American transnational Freeport-McMoRan at their corporate headquarters in Louisiana. Although the judge dismissed the environmental claims of the Amungme, he agreed to reconsider the case on the grounds of possible Freeport complicity in human rights violations. When compared to the armed social protest movement that closed the mine on Bougainville, the alien tort case opportunities against the Ok Tedi and Freeport mines illustrate that there are alternatives to violence.

The popular ecological resistance movement has demonstrated a form of political power gained without resorting to violence to achieve political ends. The popular ecological resistance movement transcended the Fly River regionally and demonstrated the value of global institutions and strategies for resolving environmental conflict. The tenacity of the Yonggom leaders in pursuing their environmental claims clearly globalized their struggle. The legacy of the popular ecological resistance movement led by the Yonggom is that transnational mining companies such as BHP can be held accountable for their actions on a global level.

Protest against the Ok Tedi mine has been misinterpreted as a regional socioeconomic contest over access to services and economic opportunity, rather than as a global environmental crisis. Conflict between indigenous peoples, resource developers, and states and popular ecological resistance are truly global phenomena. The clear lesson from the Ok Tedi crisis is that what goes around comes around. The Ok Tedi mine has come full circle and has the potential to become the first transnational mining operation in PNG to stop dumping tailings and waste rock into local rivers and to account properly for the environmental costs of resource extraction.

Questions

1. What would be the most appropriate level of analysis for conflicts such as the Ok Tedi crisis? Take into consideration that similar conflicts involving indigenous communities, natural resource developers, and states have become increasingly common around the world.

2. How did the globalization of markets, labor, capital, and commodities affect the Ok Tedi and Fly River ecosystem?

3. How did the powerful stakeholders in the Ok Tedi crisis—states and their legal systems, transnational corporations, the media, and international conservation organizations—mediate the impact of global forces on local communities?

4. How has the category of "indigenous" become a political designation for the Yonggom as they were forced to become players on the global scene? Consider how this posed a double bind for indigenous peoples such as the Yonggom as their autonomy, based on their ability to control their own environment and resources, became dependent on their effectiveness as global political activists.

5. How did the Yonggom-based popular ecological resistance movement and alien tort case function as valuable political resources in the peaceful pursuit of reform?

NOTES

1. The Independent State of Papua New Guinea, *Mining (Ok Tedi Agreement) Act of 1976* (Port Moresby: Government Printing Office, 1976).
2. *Pacific Islands Monthly* 1984: 29.
3. Ibid., 31.
4. Ok Tedi Mining Limited, *Report to the Department of Minerals and Energy, Addendum No. 1, October*, Papua New Guinea, 1984.
5. Australian Mineral Development Laboratories, *Interim Tailings Disposal Scheme (Ok Tedi Mining Limited), Impacts and Legislation*, (Boroko: Papua New Guinea Department of Minerals and Energy, 1984), p. 42.
6. *Post Courier*, September 29, 1989.
7. Ibid., July 27, 1989.
8. S. Kirsch, "Is Ok Tedi a Precedent? Implications of the Lawsuit," in *The Ok Tedi Settlement: Issues, Outcomes and Implications*, G. Banks and C. Ballard, (eds.), p. 123 (Canberra: Australian National University, 1997).
9. J. Burton, "Terra Nugax and the Discovery Paradigm: How Ok Tedi Was Shaped by the Way It Was Found and How the Rise of Political Process in the North Fly Took the Company by Surprise," in *The Ok Tedi Settlement: Issues, Outcomes and Implications*, G. Banks and C. Ballard, (eds.), pp. 45–46 (Canberra: Australian National University, 1997).
10. H. Sakulas and L. Tjamei, "Ecological Damage Caused by the Discharges from the Ok Tedi Copper and Gold Mine," Case document for the International Water Tribunal (Wau: Wau Ecology Institute, Papua New Guinea, 1991).
11. Stuart Kirsch, personal communication, July 1997.
12. Alex Maun, "The Impact of the Ok Tedi Mine on the Yonggom People," in *The Ok Tedi Settlement: Issues, Outcomes and Implications*, G. Banks and C. Ballard (eds.), pp. 116–17 (Canberra: Australian National University, 1997).

RESOURCE GUIDE

Published Literature

Craig, Barry, and David Hyndman, eds. *Children of Afek: Tradition and Change among the Mountain-Ok of Central New Guinea*. Oceania Monograph No. 40. Sydney: Sydney University Press, 1990.

Hyndman, David. *Ancestral Rain Forests and the Mountain of Gold: Indigenous Peoples and Mining in New Guinea*. Boulder, CO: Westview Press, 1994.

Hyndman, David. "Digging the Mines in Melanesia." *Cultural Survival* 15(2): 32–39, 1991.

Kirsch, Stuart. "Acting Globally: Ecopolitics in Papua New Guinea." *Journal of the International Institute* 3(3): 1, 14–15 (also available in *Active Voices: The Online Journal of Cultural Survival*, part 2 of "Eco-Politics in Papua New Guinea," issue no. 1, September 1997, http://www.cs.org).

Kirsch, Stuart. "The Yonggom of Papua New Guinea and the Ok Tedi Mine." In

State of the Peoples: A Global Rights Report on Societies in Danger, Cultural Survival Staff (ed.). Boston: Beacon Press, 1993.

WWW Site

Papua New Guinea Homepage
http://www.png.com

Chapter 11

The Samoans in New Zealand

Cluny Macpherson

CULTURAL OVERVIEW

The People and Setting

The Samoans, a Polynesian people whose ancestors moved from south China into the Pacific Ocean, settled the Samoan archipelago around thirty-five hundred years ago. Samoan identity rests on a distinctive history, culture, and language that evolved in the Samoas, a group of ten volcanic islands, in the Central Pacific. Most people lived in permanent coastal settlements until European colonization. A number of descendants of these island people immigrated to New Zealand. Today they number more than ten thousand and reside primarily in urban centers.

Traders and missionaries started work in Samoa in the early 1800s. From 1900, first Germans and then New Zealanders, who administered Western Samoa under a League of Nations mandate and later under a United Nations trusteeship, encouraged Samoans to become increasingly involved in cash cropping and whetted their appetite for material prosperity. During World War II, U.S. forces were stationed in Western and American Samoa, and postwar economic development further stimulated the Samoans' interest in travel and material prosperity.

After World War II, the New Zealand economy was restructured and diversified. Labor was sought for the new industries that were established in urban centers in New Zealand throughout the 1950s, 1960s, and 1970s. Because of long-standing relationships between New Zealand and Pacific Islands states, New Zealand looked to the islands as a source of well-

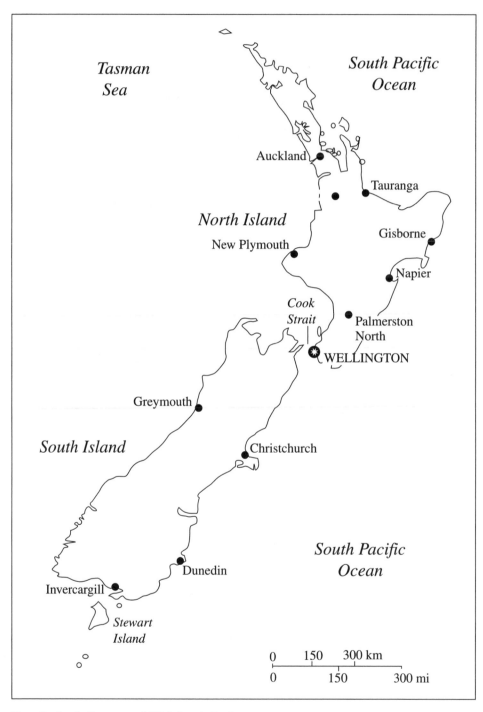

Tasman
Sea

South Pacific
Ocean

Auckland

Tauranga

North Island

New Plymouth

Gisborne

Napier

Cook
Strait

Palmerston
North

WELLINGTON

Greymouth

South Island

Christchurch

South Pacific
Ocean

Dunedin

Invercargill

Stewart
Island

| 0 | 150 | 300 km |
| 0 | 150 | 300 mi |

New Zealand. Courtesy of Nighthawk Design.

educated, docile labor. Western Samoans moved to New Zealand in growing numbers to take up newly created semiskilled and unskilled jobs.

Traditional Subsistence Strategies

Economic activity in the islands was primarily for subsistence, but small surpluses were produced and used in exchanges intended to establish and maintain stable political relationships between social groupings. Root crops, such as taro *(Colocasia)* and yams *(Dioscorea)*, and tree crops, such as breadfruit *(Artocarpus)*, bananas *(Musia* spp.), coconuts *(Cocos nucifera)*, mangos *(Mangifera)*, and papaya (*Carica payaya*), were cultivated in plantations on land behind the villages. Women gathered mollusks, crustaceans, echinoderms, and acalephae in shallow water inside the reef. Men hunted fish, octopi, and turtles in waters between the shore and the reef and, occasionally, beyond the reef. Diets were supplemented by birds and flying foxes trapped in the mountain forests.

Social and Political Organization

The basic units of precontact Samoan society in the islands were extended families, or *aiga*, who lived in more or less autonomous villages, or *nu'u*. Occasionally, groups of villages combined as a district, when their common interests were threatened by other entities. Extended families were headed by chiefs, or *matai*, who were chosen by the family, and villages were controlled by councils of chiefs, or *fono matai*, which were led by a high chief, or *ali'i*, and comprised the heads of each of the families in the village.

Migrant community formation started in the 1950s, and by 1956 nearly four thousand Samoans were concentrated, spatially and occupationally, in two cities, Auckland and Wellington. This occurred because the earliest migrants found work and accommodation and then sponsored the migration of other members of their families and villages. In many cases they found work within the same company and accommodation in the same, or nearby, suburbs. This process of chain migration led over time to concentrations of Samoans in particular suburbs and in certain work places within industries that were growing quickly.

Many of the migrants who were sponsored were chosen by their families because they were seen to be committed to Samoan social values and norms. Among these values was the commitment to service to the family, or *tautua*, and generosity to those relatives in need and to the village and church. Families valued these attributes in migrants because they believed that such people would continue to support their families, village, and church in Samoa and would be role models for others.

The growth of critical masses of migrants who were committed to Sa-

Samoans have become very much a part of the New Zealand urban landscape and emerging culture. Courtesy of Cluny Macpherson.

moan values contributed to the maintenance of the language and values because new arrivals had opportunities to meet and socialize, to use the Samoan language, and to organize a range of activities along Samoan lines. Various family, village, religious, and other voluntary associations sprung up within these Samoan enclaves. The Samoan language and principles of social organization were used to organize many activities in these contexts, and, for a while at least, the culture seemed to have survived its transposition from small-scale, rural agricultural village to large-scale, urban industrial city largely intact and to have been transplanted into conditions in which it was likely to be reproduced.

A major social survey of the Samoan population, carried out in the early 1970s, showed most of those interviewed were determined to maintain their culture and social organization. Time would show, however, that the culture's survival in the new setting would be threatened from both within and without.

Religion

Samoans had a polytheistic religion when Christian missionaries from the London Missionary Society started work in Samoa in 1830. Samoans, under the leadership of their chiefs, embraced Christianity quickly. Later in the nineteenth century missions of the Methodist, Roman Catholic, and Latter-Day Saints churches were established. Missionaries, settlers, and later colonial powers encouraged Samoans to increase production of crops such as coconut meat (copra) and coconut oil, which were traded for cash and manufactured goods. The new religion and the transition from a subsistence economy to mixed subsistence and cash cropping produced significant changes in Samoan society.

THREATS TO SURVIVAL

Exposure to Alternatives

In the cities of New Zealand many young migrants had the opportunity to compare their life-style of work and service to their family and church with that of non-Samoan workmates and friends. Many were surprised, for instance, by the level of control that their workmates had over both their income and their nonwork life. Other Samoans, accustomed to the principle of gerontocratic authority (leadership by elders), were exposed for the first time to the principle of meritocratic authority (leadership by the talented). Still others, accustomed to life in which religion played a central part, were shocked by the highly secular society that they found. Although many accepted that their relatively heavy commitment of time and resources to family, village, and church and acceptance of gerontocratic and religious authority were features of their culture, more began to think critically about them.

This questioning of the control that elders, churches, families, and villages exerted over their migrant members, and implicitly, the culture that legitimated this, could only occur once alternative world views and associated life-styles were readily apparent. In that respect migration and exposure to other cultures produced some internal challenges to the formerly unquestioned acceptance of the "correctness" of Samoan culture. The radio, television, and print media regularly provided windows on new world views and alternative ways of life that would have been inconceivable in Samoa and held out new possibilities in a number of areas of life.

Intermarriage

The exposure to new ways of life was exacerbated by intermarriage. Samoans were not bound, by cultural or religious beliefs, to marry other Samoans, although some believed that in-marriages were more likely to be successful for purely practical reasons. Samoan migrants began to marry out in relatively large numbers: One out of every three official marriages in the 1970s was to a non-Samoan.

This practice ensured that Samoans' unquestioning adherence to the precepts of their culture was under constant challenge from non-Samoan spouses and families, many of whom were committed to a more individualistic life-style centered on the nuclear family. Non-Samoan spouses challenged the extent and form of service, or *tautua*, that Samoans were called to provide for their villages, families, and churches both in New Zealand and back in Samoa. Samoan spouses had, for the first time in many cases, to justify values and practices that they had taken for granted.

Most non-Samoan spouses spoke little or no Samoan and English usually became the language of the home. In these cases there was, for both the Samoan spouses and their children, a consequent reduction of exposure to Samoan language and social activities. For children this was especially serious because they were, in many cases, denied opportunities to learn the language and to see the culture in action.

Language Loss

Language is central to cultural survival because it is the embodiment of certain concepts that make up a world view that legitimates a set of institutions and practices. Although many preschool children learned Samoan at home as their first language, once they reached schools in which the language of instruction was English and started to establish social networks that extended beyond the Samoan enclave, opportunities to use the language, and indeed the perception of its utility, began to change.

This condition was made worse by some parents who determined that their children would be more successful in their new society if they concentrated on learning the language and culture of their hosts. Even though migrant parents continued to take part in Samoan activities, many discouraged their children from doing so and encouraged them instead to become familiar with the dominant culture. A growing number of New Zealand–born Samoans who were, as a consequence, less fluent in the language stayed away from activities in which Samoan was used and, ironically, cut themselves off from opportunities to hear the language used and to see the "culture in action."

Dispersal

The loss of language accelerated as Samoans began to leave the cities and move to smaller regional centers in which they found employment; better, less-expensive housing; and less suspicion than they had encountered in the city. They found better material conditions, but they often found very few other Samoans in the area. Consequently there were few opportunities to speak Samoan, and their New Zealand–born children had few opportunities to associate with Samoans and to be a part of the Samoan culture.

Certain external forces were also threatening the viability of Samoan culture in urban New Zealand.

Prejudice

Samoan migrants encountered a certain amount of prejudice and discrimination early on. Some of the hostility arose out of perceived social characteristics of the Samoans. Later on, as the economy contracted, Samoans found themselves in competition with working-class New Zealanders for jobs that were once plentiful, and for housing and social services.

The informational foundations of these social stereotypes were laid and reproduced by the news media. Many created and reproduced negative social stereotypes of Samoans and, indeed, other Pacific Island migrants. The dominant European population, many of whom had little daily face-to-face contact with Samoans, formed their stereotypes of them on the basis of media images and, later, of the claims of populist politicians who sought to convert this fear into electoral advantage.

Negative stereotypes shaped educators' expectations of Samoans' educational potential and neighbors' and police expectations of conduct. This, in turn, led some Samoans to avoid the vigorous assertion of Samoan identity and downplay elements of Samoan culture. It also influenced the formation of New Zealand–born Samoans' identity.

Formal Education

New Zealand–born Samoans were exposed to a monocultural, monolingual education system that sought to produce an "integrated" New Zealand society. The integration was in practice to be achieved by de facto assimilation of ethnic minorities as had been the policy with the Maori, the indigenous people of the island. The national school curriculum was drafted largely by education administrators of European heritage and interpreted and taught largely by teachers of European heritage and reflected central values such as individualism, meritocracy, and the "Protestant ethic." There was little in the curriculum that spoke to, or positively valued, ethnic minority world views or life-styles. There was not a deliberate government policy to suppress minority culture and identity; rather it was assimilation by default.

The process, however, had a profound effect on the viability of Samoan culture. Those who were educated in New Zealand schools became increasingly familiar with the world view and life-style of the dominant society, which seemed to be a prerequisite for upward social mobility, and increasingly ambivalent about and critical toward their parents' culture, which seemed to be the subject of negative social stereotypes. Their increasing familiarity with New Zealand culture had a cost. With time, as a consequence of this formal education, many New Zealand–born Samoans found that they had less and less in common with island-born Samoans and lacked the opportunity and motive to reclaim their parents' culture.

Many Samoans found themselves in a somewhat ambiguous social position. To those of European extraction, they were clearly not Europeans and to their parents they were no longer Samoans. In practice, they had more in common with other New Zealand–born Pacific Islanders who had similar upbringings and faced similar dilemmas about their identities.

This ambivalence was resolved in part by creating an intermediate identity as New Zealand–born Pacific Islanders within which people distinguish among New Zealand–born Samoans, New Zealand–born Cook Islanders, New Zealand–born Tongans, and so on. This recognizes commonalities and acknowledges differences. Although this "solution" reflects reality, it means that many New Zealand–born Samoans are generally less familiar with the language and culture than previous generations.

RESPONSE: STRUGGLES TO SURVIVE CULTURALLY

The future of Samoan culture looked rather more promising from 1980 onward. This was less a consequence of deliberate, organized national Samoan political action than of a series of related developments that, on one hand, influenced the structure of Samoan migrant society and, on the other, shaped the ways in which Samoans were perceived by the dominant ethnic group in new Zealand society.

The Growth and Role of the Samoan Churches

The rapid growth of various Samoan churches had several unanticipated consequences for the survival of the language and culture. Many Samoans who had worshiped in mixed congregations in which other groups, usually of European heritage, dominated were uncomfortable with the ways in which activities were organized and were unable to take an active role in these activities because they were unfamiliar with practices and the language in which they were conducted.

Some leaders argued early on for the formation of Samoan parishes in which they could exercise control over such elements as the style and language of worship and the organization of parish affairs. Perhaps the most significant of these religious movements occurred when a small group of people left the Pacific Islands Congregational Church and formed a branch of the largest denomination in Samoa, the Congregational Christian Church of Samoa, in New Zealand. Over time, from the mid-1970s, Samoan migrants established their own Seventh-Day Adventist, Latter-Day Saints, Methodist, Roman Catholic, and Assembly of God parishes.

These congregations provided sites where Samoans could use their language and culture as the basis of activity without challenge. Within these entities they could call their own ministers, appoint their own officeholders, teach their own children, and organize and administer their activities in ways, and in a language, with which they were familiar.

The Church as "Village"

Many congregations became, for their members, like the villages that they had left in that the churches became the centers of social life, sites where the social divisions and relations of the village could be recreated, where Samoan norms and values were reaffirmed and became a source of both identity and support. Many congregations raised funds and built new, often large churches and multipurpose halls and, in the process, generated a sense of community solidarity among members. These buildings were, for many, more than a venue for Samoan religious and secular activity. These were the evidence of the organizational ability of Samoans, visible symbols of their commitment to their religion and symbols of Samoan identity.

Congregations began to travel as groups to sing at funerals and weddings and to perform at the openings of new churches. Many became involved in the round of competitions that accompanied the openings of new churches. On these occasions they competed with other congregations in such activities as traditional choral music and new musical and dance compositions, for large prizes, usually of food, fine mats ('ie toga), and money, which were redistributed among members. In the process they met other Samoans and created the foundations of a "new history" of Samoan migration and settlement.

Government Policy

In the 1970s the New Zealand government, under growing pressure from European liberals and members of minorities, formally adopted a policy of multiculturalism that acknowledged the rights of minorities to maintain ethnic identities, world views, and life-styles and provided some resources for the promotion of multiculturalism in such areas as administration and education. The most significant changes occurred within formal education.

Education

The renaissance of Maori culture, which was occurring at that time, was a salutary lesson for many Samoans, who saw, in the Maori case, the consequences of long-term loss of language and culture and the difficulty of reclaiming them. Among the many means that the Maori adopted to reclaim their language were preschool language nests, or *kohanga reo*, in which parents and children were engaged together in a total-immersion language program led by fluent native Maori speakers.

The Samoans soon established their own Samoan language preschools, known as *a'oga amata*, or first schools, often associated with church congregations. Pressure was also exerted for the formal teaching of Samoan in secondary school and in universities, and, aside from the practical benefits for the language, its appearance in these areas sent a message about its significance to some Samoans who were reluctant to teach their children their own language for fear that it would impede their progress in formal education.

Primary and Secondary Schools

As schools with large Pacific Island enrollments became more interested in the growing number of Samoan students, the curricula were revised. This shift was made possible, at least in part, by the growing volumes of scholarship that were becoming available from the University of the South Pacific and that challenged the conventional colonial histories.

In an attempt to provide a social space in which Samoan, and other Pacific Island, students could "feel at home," some Auckland schools established an intercollegiate *kilikiti*, or Pacific cricket competition, which, to everyone's surprise, attracted not only Pacific Islanders but Maori and those of European heritage and became very successful. Others formed Samoan culture groups in which children could learn languages and choral and dance performance skills. In the early 1990s, a secondary school Maori and Pacific Island Festival was organized to bring these groups together to perform for one another. The event proved immensely popular and from small beginnings has grown into a huge three-day-long festival for which new music and dances are composed and traditional performances are learned. The best performances from each group are televised nationally.

Universities

As students from Samoa and New Zealand–born Samoans, who were increasingly interested in their parents' cultures, began to enroll in universities, the demand for inclusion of relevant material on the Pacific started to be felt in many disciplines. As well, the teaching of Pacific Island languages, including Samoan, commenced in universities in Auckland and Wellington.

Samoan Students' Associations represent students' interests and provide support networks. These groups still pursue political agendas and provide a range of social and cultural events for their members. Annual meetings, or *tauvaga*, provide the basis of a network of Samoan professionals who are linked to their "cultural roots" and committed to the maintenance of Samoan culture.

Recent Educational Reform

In 1990, a change in national educational policy created a management structure to ensure that trustees of schools had a greater degree of autonomy in their administration. This policy allowed schools' boards of trustees to ensure that the staffing and curriculum of schools reflect more directly the aspirations of the communities that they serve. This has ensured that schools in districts in which there are large numbers of Pacific Islanders may, if they choose, reflect non-European cultures in their organizations' structures, curriculum, and staff.

Similar pressures in the form of Equal Employment Opportunity and Equal Educational Opportunity policies are providing spaces for Samoans, and other Pacific Islanders, to argue for a more prominent role in and greater recognition of their contribution to New Zealand society. This manifests itself as a claim for greater awareness of the needs for the appointment of more Samoan scholars and researchers in science.

Changing Perception of Colonial History

Some of the changes outlined here have been the consequence of an awareness among New Zealanders of European heritage of the biases in much of the written Pacific history. The evidence introduced by Maori pursuing claims before the Waitangi Tribunal has left many fair-minded New Zealanders profoundly concerned about the morality of some of the actions of their forebears. The spotlight of history focused on the performance of New Zealand administrators in the former "New Zealand Territories" in the Pacific has also contributed to a widespread questioning of the moral bases of their dominance and of the conduct of their administration. In other sectors, acceptance of cultural pluralism was far less complete and Pacific Islanders had to push for changed attitudes.

Winning the Space to Be Oneself

Samoans, and other Pacific Islanders, had to win space in which to be themselves in New Zealand society. They did so by demonstrating talents in a number of "mainstream" activities and by showcasing "culture" at sites, and in ways, that persuaded conservative locals to accept their permanent presence.

In the Mainstream

There is a growing awareness of Samoans' contributions to New Zealand society. For example, a Samoan might be Miss New Zealand, a Rhodes Scholar in Oxford, the head of an English Department in New Zealand's largest university, a member of Parliament, a national or international sports champion, or an award-winning artist, writer, or playwright. These successes contribute to a picture of "progress"; some of the greatest achievements have been in sports and music.

Growth of a Samoan Middle Class

An increasingly visible Samoan middle class committed to Samoan language and culture has been part of a more general transformation of the Samoan profile and has led to shifting perceptions of Samoans and Samoan culture. Over time, this Samoan middle class has emerged in New Zealand's main cities. These people, found in both the private and public sectors, have provided advice and leadership and have been instrumental in shaping various political strategies. They have also acted as "culture brokers," providing visible, articulate interpretation of their cultures for non-Samoan society. They have also formed, with support from the government's Ministry for Pacific Island Affairs, associations such as the Samoan Chamber of Commerce, which provides a range of professional services that take account of the sorts of cultural issues that arise in, for instance, small business development and management. Samoans in public service also network and provide career advice and guidance to each other and to new entrants into the work force.

The Media and the Transformation

Samoan culture resurgence was influenced in several ways by the media. Increasing coverage of community and cultural activities on radio; on television, including cable access–type programs; and in community magazines showed community groups enjoying interesting, nonthreatening activities in the midst of New Zealand society. New mainstream and special-interest programs allowed local people, who had formerly been dependent on secondhand reports, to see these activities and to form judgments of their own.

Increasing numbers of Pacific Islanders in plays, films, and soap operas were portrayed in generally sympathetic contexts. Samoan characters in Samoan-written television sitcoms showed Samoans parodying certain Samoan character types and laughing at themselves, a trait that New Zealanders value in others. In widely watched soap operas, many Samoans were portrayed in professional and semiprofessional roles in mainstream situations holding attitudes and values that New Zealanders generally regarded positively. In some of the portrayals, Samoans were shown to have some concerns that were qualitatively different from those of locals but also to face many dilemmas that were similar. Thus, New Zealanders of

European heritage had the opportunity to see what issues migrants face in their new country.

FOOD FOR THOUGHT

Samoans in New Zealand have created a social space in which Samoan culture has been reclaimed to a degree. What has evolved is not simply a replica of traditional culture. Certainly, Samoans, and particularly those born in the islands, continue to use Samoan language, values, and procedures to organize both their daily lives and life crises that punctuate existence. However, even these have changed as a consequence of constraints of life in an urban, industrial-wage economy. Thus, a new Samoan culture is blossoming, at the intersection of old and new. In much the same ways as in Samoa, people are baptized, married, healed, or buried; chiefly titles are conferred; and churches are opened. Although the principles and language are similar, the ceremonies reflect constraints and adjustments imposed by new social and economic circumstances. Funeral rites, for instance, are shorter because of the practical difficulties and the economic costs of taking time off work and activities such as laying out the body, grave digging, preparing food, and dressmaking are now routinely performed by non-family members, specialists whose services are bought.

Family organization of time and relations has significantly changed. Economic tasks that once fell to unmarried adolescents, for instance, no longer exist; extended schooling and extra school activities are full time. Power relationships within families have also changed; women have their own jobs and incomes and are no longer as dependent. Parents are prevented by legislation from exercising certain forms of punishment and discipline; thus traditional respect and compliance are disappearing.

Samoan culture is being "extended" in New Zealand. Such common events as university graduation and twenty-first birthdays have become part of Samoan celebrations. The giving of fine mats, the making of speeches, and feasting—all traditional Samoan activities—are now incorporated into the new parts of urban Samoan life.

Social roles, such as that of the *fa'afafine*, or transsexuals, a group largely marginalized in Samoa, have been expanded in the new setting. Cultural icons such as *siapo*, or tapa printing, and tattooing of armbands (*taulima*) are becoming a part of a new Samoan art and heritage.

The performing arts are generating new representations of Samoan music, drama, and dance. For instance, religious music has been taken from its choral context and transferred into popular music, and even rap, by young Samoan Christians, in a bid to make Samoan culture "relevant" to New Zealand Samoans. Professional Samoan dance groups use the old and new in their performances. Samoan textile and clothing designers are now using Samoan motifs previously inaccessible in creative designs, which are shown to packed houses in parades and in design competitions. Samoan culture exists not in one place or the other but in a space between them where all the different ways of being Samoan are contested and mediated.

Questions

1. Do you believe Samoan migrant society would have developed in the way it has if it had not been for the chain migration process?
2. What impacts do you think intermarriage between Samoans and non-Samoans could have on the survival of a Samoan culture overseas?
3. Can new traditions become a part of a people's culture or must they always be inauthentic?
4. What impact do you think a slowdown of in-migration of migrant Samoans will have on the Samoan culture that is developing in New Zealand?
5. Will tensions between migrant parents and their overseas-born children persist forever?

RESOURCE GUIDE

Published Literature

Macpherson, C. "On the Future of Samoan Ethnicity in New Zealand." In *Tauiwi: Racism and Ethnicity in Aotearoa/New Zealand*, P. Spoonley, and C. Macpherson et al. (eds.). Palmerston North, New Zealand: Dunmore Press, 1984.

Macpherson, C. "The Changing Contours of Samoan Ethnicity." In *Nga Take: Ethnic Relations and Racism in Aotearoa/New Zealand*, P. Spoonley, D. Pearson, and C. Macpherson (eds.). Palmerston North, New Zealand: Dunmore Press, 1991.

Meleisea, M., (ed.) *Lagaga: A Short History of Western Samoa*. Suva: University of the South Pacific, 1987.

Pitts, D., and C. Macpherson. *Emerging Pluralism: The Samoan Migrant Community in Urban New Zealand*. Auckland: Longman Paul, 1974.

Sutter, F. K. *Samoa: A Photographic Essay*. Honolulu: University of Hawai'i Press, 1984.

WWW Sites

Creative New Zealand—Arts Council of New Zealand
http://www.creativenz.govt.nz

Ministry of Pacific Island Affairs' Homepage
http://www.minpac.govt.nz

Statistics New Zealand's Homepage
http://www.stats.govt.nz

Chapter 12

The South Sea Islanders of Mackay, Queensland, Australia

Clive Moore

CULTURAL OVERVIEW

The People

Today approximately fifteen thousand Australians claim descent from Pacific Islanders taken to Queensland as indentured laborers between 1863 and 1904. Sixty-two thousand contracts were issued to around fifty thousand islanders under the terms of the Masters and Servants Act and other legislation enacted to govern their employment.[1] Queensland is huge, two and a half times as big as Texas. Until about 1880 the Islanders could be employed in any pastoral or maritime industry in the colony, but thereafter they were restricted to the sugar industry along the east coast. The majority were from eighty islands in Melanesia, mainly those included in the New Hebrides (present-day Vanuatu) and the Solomon Islands, but also from the Loyalty Islands off New Caledonia and the eastern archipelagoes of Papua New Guinea, plus a few from Tuvalu and Kiribati. Roughly one-third were from the Solomons and two-thirds from Vanuatu.

The Setting

The Pioneer Valley at Mackay, located midway between Brisbane and Cairns on the coast of central Queensland, is the largest sugar-producing area in Australia and has always had the largest Pacific Islander population, although the residual Islander community there is different in that Islanders of Solomons descent predominate. Descendants of nineteenth-century immigrants from the Pacific Islands, who prefer to be known as *South Sea*

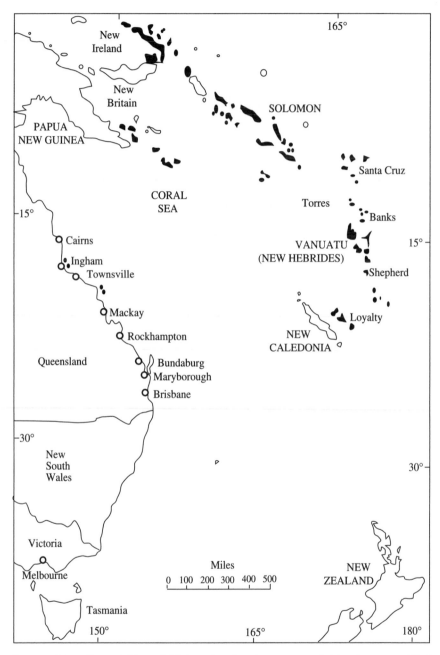

Eastern Australia and Central Melanesia, showing ports and island groups (filled in black) involved in the Queensland labor trade. Courtesy of Nighthawk Design.

Islanders, are very visible around Mackay, making up around twenty-five hundred of the eighty thousand urban population. Including another twenty-five hundred Aborigines and Torres Strait Islanders, there is quite a substantial black component in the district.

Traditional Subsistence Strategies

Subsistence life-styles were replaced in Queensland by work for wages on plantations and farms. The migration was mainly circular: recruits picked up in the islands, working in Queensland, and then returning to the islands. The normal term of indenture was three years; only a minority stayed on, the ancestors of the present South Sea Islanders. Those who opted to reengage in the islands or in Queensland were paid higher wages as experienced laborers. The rerecruiting and "time-expired" laborers (those who entered second or subsequent contracts) made up a considerable proportion of the numbers. They were not subservient in the way first-indenture laborers usually were—European colonists generally considered these long-staying islanders to be noisy and unruly.

Social and Political Organization

The first Islander immigrants were mostly young males aged between fifteen and thirty-five; only 6 percent were women. Historians agree that the initial phase of recruiting in most areas was by kidnapping and deception, but as the trade progressed the next generation followed into the whale boats of the labor trade vessels, lured not so much by outright trickery as by the goods offered by beguiling recruiters and the chance to better themselves when they returned to their home societies after three years. However, the majority of South Sea Islanders prefer to depict themselves as the descendants of kidnapped slaves, not indentured laborers. The method of their recruitment remains debated; what is more certain is the high cost in human lives in the largely circular migration. On average, 50 Melanesians in every 1,000 died each year in Queensland, and at worst, in 1884, the death rate was 147 per 1,000, compared with a death rate of around 9 or 10 per 1,000 among European males of the same age in the colony. The primary cause of the deaths was exposure to bacillary dysentery, pneumonia, and tuberculosis, against which the new recruits had little immunity.[2]

Religion and World View

Although most of the fifty thousand Islander laborers involved worked in Queensland for only a limited number of years, and thus were able to maintain much of their traditional cosmology even while in Australia, those who stayed for longer terms or permanently really altered their world views to become colonists and adapted their beliefs and customs. The first generation of these immigrants retained substantial aspects of their customary religious life, building men's houses and to a limited extent managing to establish ancestral shrines and continue worship. Gradually, though, the large regional differences that marked the diverse origins became blurred, as the community retained substantial aspects of their largely Melanesian cultures, united through and shaped by the colonial experience, pidgin English, literacy, and Christianity. Interisland marriages with the few Melanesian women helped unite the community, as did marriages with Aboriginal and a few European women.

The Pacific Islanders always faced a racist colonial society in Australia, which regarded them as inferior and legislated to control and eventually deport them. In its quest for a "White Australia" the new federal government in 1901 ordered recruiting to cease from 1903 and as many Islanders as possible to be repatriated by 1907. A total of 7,068 Islanders were repatriated back to the islands between 1904 and 1908 and a further 194 departed up to 1914. In 1901, when the deportation order was made, there were around 10,000 Islanders in Queensland and northern New South Wales, one third at Mackay. Eventually, after a 1906 Royal Commission, certain categories, mainly those of more than twenty years' residence and others who could convince the government that they would be in danger if returned home, were allowed to remain. Around 1,500 Islanders were officially allowed to stay and around another 1,000 remained illegally.[3]

During the two final decades of the nineteenth century missions from the Presbyterian and Anglican churches and a nondenominational group converted the Islanders to Christianity. However, when Islander numbers declined in the 1900s, the parent churches withdrew their support, leaving the Islanders floundering as Christians who were not welcome in the white congregations. Then in the 1920s all but a few of the families followed prominent Islanders into the Seventh-Day Adventist and Assembly of God churches. Today their descendants are leading members of these churches. Mission Christianity was always fairly fundamentalist, quite different from the parent churches, which made the transition to the new sects reasonably smooth. The Islanders' churches provided the major networks in their community and church elders their major leaders.

THREATS TO SURVIVAL

Legislation and Policy

The new Australian Federation had as a central part of its rationale the concept of a White Australia. Because Aborigines were thought to be dying out, by halting all further immigration of non-Europeans, Australia would conduct a bold experiment for the world: creation of a nation for white people. This discriminative immigration policy continued until the 1960s and was not formally removed from legislation until 1972, shaping the lives of the remaining South Sea Islanders. Humanitarian concerns had allowed the Islanders to stay in Australia, but within a society that shifted them further to its margins.

Most Islanders who remained in Australia were single men who died in the 1920s and 1930s; very few survived into the 1960s. Among them were the married couples and their families from whom the present-day South Sea Islander community is descended, some now sixth- and seventh-generation Australians. Small South Sea communities, each numbering only a few hundred, remained in all of the cane-growing districts along the coast of Queensland and northern New South Wales, and in one or two pastoral districts in coastal Queensland. Whereas indigenous Australians remained at the back of the collective Australian conscience, on the fringes of rural towns throughout Australia, South Sea Islanders lived in only one region, the tropical east coast, quite invisible to most Australians. Like Aborigines, they were expected to die out, and any remnants to assimilate into the white working class. Public recognition of their survival was minimal until the 1970s.

The confines of geography and a century of legislative discrimination kept the islanders at a semisubsistence level in the first half of the twentieth century and at best employed as field workers in agriculture. Although post 1907 they were no longer governed by the restrictive legislation that had bound them in the nineteenth century, first to tropical agriculture, then to field work, legislative restrictions placed on all nonwhites were tightened in the 1910s and 1920s, particularly in the sugar industry, which government policy, spurred by the Australian Workers' Union (AWU), was to make a totally white industry. In 1903 the federal government introduced a sugar bounty paid to growers who used only white labor to grow and harvest their cane. Ten years later the Queensland government legislated to introduce certificates of exemption that had to be held by any non-Europeans working in the industry. Then between 1919 and 1921 Queensland's Arbitration Court prohibited the employment of "colored" labor except on farms owned by a countryman and gave preference in employment to AWU members. South Sea Islanders were debarred from membership of the AWU until the 1970s, and although all of these legal provisions applied only to the original immigrant generation, not to Australian-born South Sea Islanders, in the early decades of the century because of the strength of Melanesian kinship that bound them to their elders, all Islanders were effectively banned from the only employment available in a district like Mackay where cane was a monoculture.

Political Economy

Elderly Islanders eked out a bare existence on small farms leased from the last plantations, on marginal hill lands not useful for mechanized agriculture. Mackay had 150 of these farms in 1908 but by the 1930s only a handful remained. Mechanization of the farming process, which necessitated greater financial outlays, and refusal of banks to loan money to Islanders, soon meant that in an industry that had undergone a transition from plantation to family farms, none was owned by the Islanders whose labor founded the industry. There were ways around the discrimination, such as putting cane assignments into the names of white friends and cutting cane by lantern light at night, but largely by the 1920s the original Islanders had been totally marginalized to more menial poorly paid itinerant farm work and to a part-subsistence existence. Further mechanization, this time of the cutting process in the 1960s, took away what were major seasonal jobs as cane-cutters, ending a century of association between South Sea Islanders and the sugar industry.

This discrimination and technological change have had long-term results in terms of employment and depressed socioeconomic indicators, leaving the Islanders unwanted on the fringes of prosperous but conservative white farming communities. However, since the 1960s when indigenous Australians were finally recognized as citizens with rights similar to the white population, the South Sea Islanders benefited. Nonetheless, this positive discrimination has also been a threat to their survival as a separate community. Because there were so few Islander women among the first generation, probably around one-third of the Islander families are descended from Aboriginal or Asian mothers. Even up until the 1970s many Islanders denied their indigenous ancestry, partly because of a Melanesian arrogance about Aborigines, to whom they felt superior, but also largely because the wider Australian community saw the Islanders as racially superior to Aborigines. The Islanders were almost at the bottom of society anyway, and there was no advantage to them in stressing their indigenous Australian ancestry. Aboriginality is defined by your identity: whether you acknowledge your indigenous ancestry and whether the indigenous community accepts you. South Sea Islander identity had been achieved at the expense of rejecting any indigenous identity. Then from the mid-1960s onward, after a 1967 referendum that gave the federal government the power to legislate for indigenous Australians, overriding state powers, the Commonwealth began to fund schemes to improve Aboriginal and Torres Strait Islander health, education, housing, legal facilities, employment, and business opportunities.

Mackay district Islanders were in a difficult situation. Between the 1860s and 1890s the original Aboriginal population had been decimated by deliberate extermination and disease, and the remnant Aboriginal community absorbed into the South Sea islander community, which was then the only black community. There are now around twenty-five hundred Aborigines and Torres Strait Islanders in the district, but they are mainly Torres Strait Islanders who are recent immigrants and a few hundred Aborigines who have come from other areas. For some South Sea Islanders there was never a choice: They were proud of their island ancestry and would not claim indigenous status. But many families have altered their primary identity to indigenous so as to receive the special benefits. This has led to a great deal of division in the community and is the major threat to the survival of the South Sea community. There are situations in which one cousin has chosen to identify as indigenous and another as South Sea Islander. And even though the total indigenous funding for the Mackay district is swelled by the South Sea Islanders who have identified as indigenous, there remains resentment among Aborigines and Torres Strait Islanders (who, to complicate matters, also in some cases have South Sea Islander ancestry from early maritime workers in the Torres Strait) that South Sea Islanders are jumping on the indigenous "gravy train" although they have no rights to special assistance.

Education

The immigrant generation were either illiterate or barely literate, taught to read and write as a by-product of mission Christianity. Their children began to attend primary schools from the 1890s, but often for only a few years, and up until the 1940s education remained very limited, with an attempt at segregated education at Mackay in the 1930s. Like low-income rural Queenslanders of all races, South Sea Islanders never went beyond primary school. Equitable access to education and a natural progression through to secondary school did not occur in Queensland generally until the early 1960s. Thus the grandparents and parents of today's Islander children still do not place high value on formal education, provide less learning stimulus at home, and feel that the education system is not geared to the needs of their children. In the 1970s Islander students seldom matriculated, enrolled in commercial and industrial courses terminating at grade ten. Since that time the South Sea Islanders have benefited educationally from financial assistance and programs developed for indigenous Australians. The 1980s and 1990s saw changes for the better: Ten percent of Mackay's high school students are black, presumably about half identifying as South Sea Islanders, with quite high retention rates through to grade twelve and some now continuing to university level. However, high retention rates do not necessarily mean good results, and many black students merely "mark time," staying off the welfare line a few years longer.

Housing

Identifying as indigenous Australians has produced educational benefits for Island children but has had some negative consequences as well. It has also led to the rehousing of many South Sea Islander families, either through indigenous housing schemes or through the Housing Commission. Earlier in the century all of the Islanders lived in rural or semirural areas, usually in traditional leaf-thatch houses or fairly dilapidated European-style houses on flood-prone river banks. The rehousing, although a relief in terms of physical comfort, has been destructive to the Islanders' sense of community. They are now relocated within suburbs, by housing cooperatives that value the quality of their property investment more than the maintenance of any sense of community. Young Islander families who are not able to take advantage of any special assistance, like all Australians at the bottom end of the job market, find it very difficult to make the transition from renting to buying their own house.

Cultural Practice

Another threat to survival is the erosion of their original Melanesian culture. As mentioned, the first major change was the creation of a pan-Melanesian culture, one community formed from an amalgamation of dozens of different island cultures and extensive intermarriages. Indigenous languages died out with the first generation, and only a few words and phrases remained. Even pidgin English, used by the first to third generations, is now no longer spoken, replaced by English with an element of indigenous and Torres Strait (locally referred to as "Broken") Islander creole. Indigenous religious practices finally died out in the 1940s, although the older second- and third-generation Islanders maintain strong belief in a spirit world beyond Christianity. There remains a preference for particular foods—fish and root crops like taro and sweet potato—but these are limited to special occasions. Typically, at a large Islander party all of the meat and root vegetables are cooked in underground stone ovens down by the river. More important for cultural survival, there remains a sense of caring for an extended family, but even this is eroding fast. Until the 1980s there were some members of the Islander community who behaved as classic Melanesian "big men" and "big women," expecting and receiving allegiance from a wide family group. The lack of these leaders is now very evident in Islander politics. Up until the 1970s the elders usually managed to enforce their wishes about marriages, strongly preferring that their children and grandchildren marry their own kind. This practice is now long gone. South Sea Islanders now marry white Australians far more often than they link with Aboriginal or Melanesian Australians.

RESPONSE: STRUGGLES TO SURVIVE CULTURALLY

Demographic Trends

South Sea Islanders could easily have died out, just as authorities expected early this century, but their demographic survival was assured by the 1940s. The first-generation families contained four and five children, then the second and third generations had very large families; families of ten and twelve children were not unusual. There were probably around one hundred first-generation families in Australia; six and seven generations of some very large families have produced a South Sea Islander community numbering about fifteen thousand. This was not a calculated response, but it certainly has worked in their favor.

The community is spread over 1,240 miles of coast, with several major centers, the Mackay district the largest of these. Intermarriage ensures that although there remains a broad division between Solomon Island–identified families and New Hebridean (Vanuatu)–identified families, a web of blood relationships has been created. Although the Australian South Sea Islander community is renowned for its divisions and inability to unite politically and has no geographic center, there is still a real sense of being part of the one big South Sea Island family.

Religion and Sports

Demographic survival was not a calculated response, but it was a necessary component of the community's survival. In similar vein are religion and sport. Until the 1970s sporting activities, and Christian religious beliefs and practices, were two very important strengths that enabled the Islanders to survive as a community.

Worship provided a weekly focus for the original immigrants and later generations to come together. The religious separatism that had characterized the mission churches was carried over into the Adventist and Assembly of God churches for several decades. Islander churches were fairly autonomous until the 1960s and 1970s, after which there was much more incorporation into the parent churches. For the first six or so decades of this century white clergy were not really welcome to interfere in the running of Islander churches—there was a sense of pride in handling their own finances and controlling decision making and authority. The present younger generation are by and large not churchgoers. Religious influences have often been superseded by an interest in sport and gambling, particularly bingo for women.

Sports have been an important leveler in Australian society and remain an all-consuming interest and pastime for many Islanders. Through sports they have readily gained acceptance for several decades, whether it be women in vigoro (a game like cricket) and basketball or men in cricket and soccer. However, in the first half of the century there was a strong degree of separatism, as all-black teams played against white teams. Some soccer players of South Sea Islander descent are household names in Australia (Mal Meninga, Sam Backo, Wendal Sailor), and one Mackay sporting trophy is awarded in the name of a prominent Islander man. National and state politicians called upon to give speeches about the Islanders always mention these sporting heroes as individuals of high status, worthy of community pride. At school, Islanders also excel at sports, which may in some cases cloak less exceptional academic results.

Politics and Identity

Since the 1970s unity has been achieved by directly political means and through reestablishment of links with their islands of origin. Along with this has come further stimulus from media and academic interest, which has provided a clear profile and national legitimacy for the fragmented Islander community. In the 1900s the Islander communities along the northeast Australian coast united to form a Pacific Islanders' Association to protest their deportation. For its time it was the most significant protest organization among Melanesians anywhere, and it did manage to achieve some modification of Australia's callous racist plans to deport all "Kanakas," the name given to the Islander immigrants in the nineteenth century. The 1900s political movement was long forgotten by the 1970s, and unity in the intervening decades was provided only by separatist church congregations. In the 1960s, however, some leading South Sea Islanders became involved in movements to gain rights for indigenous Australians. The benefits gained, alluded to previously, provided necessary special funding for Aborigines and Torres Strait Islanders but inadvertently drove a wedge between South Sea Islanders and their indigenous kin. Although some Islander families had indigenous ancestry, until financial rewards accrued there was little indigenous identification. Since then the next generation of South Sea Islanders has increasingly placed emphasis on their indigenous ancestry, which has alienated Islanders with no indigenous ancestry and produced a degree of ill feeling among "real" indigenous Australians. All of these events brought issues of identity to a head.

The process of campaigning for a remedy to the injustice of their situation took twenty years. Finally in 1994 the Commonwealth government recognized the diverse South Sea Islanders as a disadvantaged ethnic community and announced a package of special grants, programs and funding.

By the 1970s Australian South Sea Islanders lacked any solidarity except that gained through kinship, religion, and a shared past. Just as had occurred in the 1900s, various community leaders recognized the need for a

Noel Fatnowna (1929–91), of Solomon Island descent and an
ambulance officer at Mackay, was Queensland special commissioner for Pacific Islanders (1977–83). For decades he was the
best known South Sea Islander in the Mackay district. Courtesy
of Clive Moore.

political organization to link all communities. The Australian South Sea
Islanders United Council (ASSIUC) was formed in 1974 with branches in
all major centers of Islander settlement and in the east-coast capital cities.
It is significant that at the two recent periods (1974–75 and 1990s) when
the Islanders have been most successful politically, Australia has had a
Labor government in Canberra.

During the intervening years of the 1970s through the 1990s there had
been other changes that aided the Islanders. The Queensland government
announced official recognition of its South Sea Islanders as a distinct ethnic
group and appointed Mackay's leading Islander, Noel Fatnowna, as a special commissioner for Pacific Islanders within an Aboriginal and Torres
Strait Islander Commission (ATSIC). South Sea Islanders managed to reform strong links with their islands of origins, which sparked a cultural
and genealogical resurgence. Radio and television "discovered" the Islanders in a series of programs, which brought them more attention from all

Australians living away from the sugar coast. And at the same time, academic studies, utilizing oral testimony, restored to the community some of its own history, making it possible, for instance, for some of the Australian families to relink with their families in the islands. In the 1990s this renewed Islander search for their ancestors and history resulted in Islander input into a set of government-funded curriculum materials, which now enable teachers to incorporate information on the Islanders into the school system.

ASSIUC and the many other Islander-based organizations that have been created since the 1970s work on a combination of traditional Melanesian values and modern political lobbying skills. In 1990, through Faith Bandler, Australia's most influential South Sea Islander, the Commonwealth government once more recognized the problems of the community. Survey findings revealed a South Sea Islander population of between ten thousand and twenty thousand, many of whom chose to identify as Aborigines and Torres Strait Islanders. Their unemployment rate was two and a half times the national rate, and their home-ownership rate was half the national average. The report concluded that South Sea Islanders were the poorest immigrant ethnic group in Australia. Medical surveys indicated high rates of diabetes, hypertension, heart disease, obesity, and renal disease, comparable with those of indigenous Australians. The final government recommendations in 1994 combined basic assistance for education, housing, health, and culture with a program to increase public awareness of the South Sea Islanders and their role in Australian history. This enabled South Sea Islander identity to survive as separate from indigenous identity.

International Links

The Islanders have through their own initiative created a substantial relinking with their families in Vanuatu, the Solomon Islands, and Papua New Guinea. This has been made possible by improvement in air service between Australia and the islands as well as Islanders' having access to disposable incomes that can be spent on overseas holidays. Since then there has been a cultural renaissance, a strengthening of identity, a sense of assurance of their place in Australia and as Pacific Islanders. It is now commonplace for individual Islanders and whole families to visit relatives in the islands, and for return visits to occur, sometimes on an annual basis. Church groups from the islands and Australia have been making trips back and forth since the 1980s. Honiara, capital of the Solomon Islands, is Mackay's sister city. In 1988 the prime minister of the Solomon Islands stopped off in Mackay to visit his people there, and later that year a group of twenty-two Solomon Islanders led by a cabinet minister took part in a reenactment of the arrival of the first Melanesian laborers brought to the district in 1867. Then in 1990 the Solomon Islands appointed a consul-general for Australia, based in Brisbane, not the natural capital Canberra (although the main consulate was shifted to Canberra a few years later), in recognition of trade and communication links with Queensland and the large number of Australian Solomon Islanders living in the state.

The process of relinking two sides of families separated for sixty years is both exhilarating and bewildering. Australian South Sea Islanders are Australians first and South Sea Islanders second. Depending on how much influence they have had from more traditional older members of their families, they have absorbed some idea of Island customs, some understanding of the cultural powers that remain vibrant in the islands. Often precise details of customary names and village identification back in the islands have been forgotten by Australian Islander families. It is a remarkable experience to return to their ancestral homes, to go back to the villages their grandparents and great-grandparents left so long ago. Instead of being marginal Australians, always obviously black within a white majority, they suddenly find themselves indistinguishable from their kin, except for their broad Australian accents. The impact of discovering that they have close relatives, land, and ceremonial rights in the islands is overwhelming. So too is residual fear of the potency of sorcery and the problem of dealing with false claims of relationship and avaricious relatives who unthinkingly demand reciprocity of wealth. Even the poorest Australian South Sea Islanders seem rich by village standards in the Solomon Islands and Vanuatu. The long-term ramifications of this relinking are probably far more significant than any government assistance, which is intended to be short-term and is fickle, depending on the whims and goodwill of politicians.

FOOD FOR THOUGHT

The South Sea Islander community at Mackay is the largest in Australia, and many of its problems are a mirror of those in other areas, although it does have its own peculiarities, which make it operate differently. One is seemingly unbridgeable political divisions. The government agencies dealing with the approximately fifteen thousand Islanders have never really comprehended the extent of these deep-grained divisions, between individuals, families, and island groups. There are six South Sea Islander community organizations operating in the Mackay district. All of these organizations operate on remnants of the original pan-Melanesianism, new Western values and skills, and newly created supposedly "traditional" values about elders and leadership that owe much to indigenous Australian modern politics and have no real basis in handed-down traditions. Significantly, women have been the most successful political leaders in the Islander community Australia-wide since the 1980s, a phenomenon that has no basis in traditional Melanesian politics.

Although political lobbying and access to government funding are unifying factors, other features of the community are at the same time causing it to disintegrate further. Christianity is losing its force as a unifying and stabilizing factor. Today's churchgoers are really those born in or before the 1960s and 1970s. The 1980s and 1990s generation is not interested and has rebelled, removing one of the long-term foci. There was also once the unity of intermarriage, which created a sense of community. Despite animosities and the enormous geographic spread of the Islander families, the complex web of intermarriage created since the 1920s ensures that each family is in some way related to all the others. Since the 1970s there has been continuing out-marriage, into the Aboriginal and Torres Strait Islander community and into the white community. Now there is immigration of Aborigines and Torres Strait Islanders as well as Polynesians, mainly from Tonga and Samoa. This group of recent nonwhite arrivals for the most part has no respect for tradition and is no longer willing to obey or take the advice of their elders. In the 1990s Mackay developed quite severe problems with youth violence, perpetrated by youths of Islander ancestry who have nothing in common with and cannot relate to their conservative religious elders. Black American influences such as rap music, which give credence to premarital sex and violence, often predominate over older values. This leads to severe problems of cultural identity. Today there is no longer a clear South Sea Islander identity and the younger generation sees themselves as black Australians rather than as South Sea Islander Australians.

Questions

1. Why do some Australian South Sea Islanders depict themselves as the descendants of kidnapped slaves, not indentured laborers?

2. Why did Australian South Sea Islanders oppose government plans for their deportation in the 1900s?

3. Why is the relationship between Australian South Sea Islanders and indigenous Australians difficult?

4. What were the reasons the Australian South Sea Islanders were eventually recognized as a distinct disadvantaged ethnic group?

5. How important is the relinking with their islands of origin to the future of Australian South Sea Islanders?

NOTES

1. Clive Moore, *Kanaka: A History of Melanesian Mackay* (Port Moresby: Institute of Papua New Guinea Studies and the University of Papua New Guinea, 1985), p. 25. The best overall statistical source is Charles Price and Elizabeth Baker,

"Origins of Pacific Island Labourers in Queensland, 1863–1904: A Research Note," *Journal of Pacific History* (11, 1–2): 106–21, 1976.

2. Ralph Shlomowitz, "Morality and the Pacific Labour Trade," in *Mortality and Migration in the Modern World* (Brookfield, VT: Variorum, 1996), pp. 34–55.

3. Patricia Mercer, *White Australia Defied: Pacific Islander Settlement in North Queensland* (Townsville: Department of History and Politics, James Cook University, 1995), pp. 75–110.

RESOURCE GUIDE

Published Literature

Fatnowna, Noel. *Fragments of a Lost Heritage*. Sydney: Angus and Robertson, 1989.

Graves, Adrian. *Cane and Labour: The Political Economy of the Queensland Sugar Industry, 1862–1906*. Edinburgh: Edinburgh University Press, 1993.

Moore, Clive, ed. *The Forgotten People: A History of the Australian South Sea Island Community*. Sydney: Australian Broadcasting Commission, 1979.

Moore, Clive. *Kanaka: A History of Melanesian Mackay*. Port Moresby: Institute of Papua New Guinea Studies and the University of Papua New Guinea, 1985.

Films and Videos

The Islanders, Australian Broadcasting Commission Television ("Peach's Australia"), 1975.

Forgotten People, Australian Broadcasting Commission Television ("Big Country"), 1978.

Kidnapped, Milson's Print: Special Broadcasting Service, July 1989.

Return to Vanuatu, Special Broadcasting Commission Television ("Dateline"), September 1993.

Faith Bandler, Special Broadcasting Commission Television ("Australian Biographies"), 1994.

Sugar Slaves: History of Australia's Slave Trade, Sydney: Film Australia, 1995.

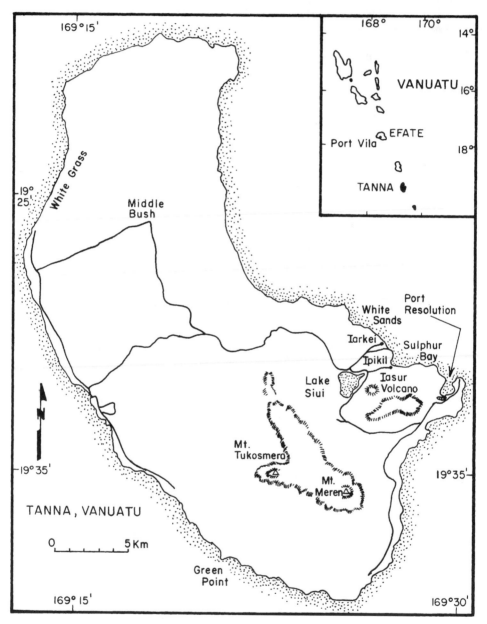

Tanna, Vanuatu. Courtesy of Lamont Lindstrom.

Chapter 13

The Tannese

Lamont Lindstrom

CULTURAL OVERVIEW

A tourist brochure boasts, "Tanna Island is renowned for its active volcano, custom villages, potent kava, cargo cultists, strong traditions, exciting festivals, gigantic banyan trees, magnificent wild horses, long black and white beaches, velvet nights, and much more."[1] This advertisement does not exaggerate. Tanna really is a beautiful and fascinating island—a place that more and more tourists are visiting. People on Tanna—like those of many other small communities affected by global tourism—are both excited and worried about the impact that tourism can have on their lives.

The brochure promises tourists on Tanna will encounter the island's famous "cargo cultists." Anthropologists, journalists, and others since 1945 have used the term *cargo cult* to describe South Pacific social movements. Many of these movements emerged after the end of World War II in the Pacific. In the typical cargo cult, people turned to religious ritual (which may be traditional or innovative) to obtain cargo. Sometimes *cargo* meant money or various sorts of trade goods (vehicles, refrigerators, guns, tools, and the like), and sometimes, metaphorically, it represented the establishment of a moral society, which often included the reassertion of local sovereignty and the withdrawal of colonial rulers.

In the late 1930s, a number of people on Tanna started following the teachings of John Frum, a spiritual guide who appeared during those years and who still today speaks through his prophets. Some of Frum's predictions concerned the impending arrival of the American military, and of its cargo, and the establishment of a more harmonious island society. The John

Frum movement today remains strong on Tanna as both a local church and a political party.

Not many observers have had much good to say of cargo cultists. Up until 1957, many John Frum leaders were arrested, locked up, and deported for years. Government authorities and journalists alike were both troubled and bemused by what they often saw as irrational, even crazy behavior. The official response usually hoped that better education would eventually disabuse people's misguided ritualistic attempts to obtain wealth. But today, tourists are urged to visit Tanna so they can watch cargo cultists in action. An important island organization has become an international tourist attraction. Some tourists expect to see strange, curious, and even primitive ritual. It is a tricky business when one's culture goes on sale in the global tourism marketplace for being primitive and peculiar.

The People

Ocean-going Melanesians first landed on Tanna some thirty-five hundred years ago. About twenty-four thousand people live on the island today. The population is growing at a rate of 3.2 percent per year. The Tannese speak five related languages and most also speak Bislama (Vanuatu's Pidgin English national language). Some are schooled in English and French as well.

The Setting

Tanna is an island in southern Vanuatu (which was called the New Hebrides before its independence in 1980). Tanna is approximately 25 miles long by 17 miles wide at its broadest point, with a total area of 217 square miles. In the south, a well-populated central plateau (Middle Bush) rises to mountains more than 3,281 miles high. The island is mostly forested, except for a grassy plain in the northwest that lies in a rain shadow. In the east, Iasur—a small but constantly erupting volcano—spits up lava bombs and spreads volcanic ash across the landscape. Iasur is a major tourist attraction that draws several thousand outsiders to the island every year.

James Cook, the first European explorer to visit Tanna, gave the island its name in 1774. *Tanna*, in the language spoken around Port Resolution, where Cook had anchored, means "ground" or "land." From the 1860s through 1900, labor recruiters moved more than five thousand Tannese men to work on plantations in Queensland, Australia, and Fiji. During these years, too, Presbyterian missionaries opened coastal stations. Tanna was famous for its resistance to Christianity, but by 1910 the missionaries succeeded in converting two-thirds of the population. Mission success correlated with the establishment of joint British and French colonial rule over the archipelago in 1906. During the next three decades, a few European planters and traders were periodically resident on Tanna and developed small coconut plantations. Many Tannese, too, planted coconuts as a cash crop during these years.

Between 1942 and 1946, the U.S. military established large bases in the New Hebrides to launch counterattacks on Japanese positions in the Solomon Islands. Many Tannese men joined labor corps and worked for the American military on the nearby islands of Efate and Espiritu Santo. After the war, the Condominium government (British and French) reasserted itself until the 1970s, when independence movements gained momentum. Although many Tannese opposed the first national government that took power in 1980, and tried to secede from Vanuatu, others supported the new nation's independence.

Traditional Subsistence Strategies

The Tannese are swidden (slash-and-burn) horticulturists. Using hand tools, they clear and burn off plots in the forest to plant yams and taro—the two traditionally important root crops. They also grow manioc (tapioca), sweet potatoes, bananas, and a range of other fruits and vegetables. Fertilizing ash falls from the Iasur volcano, making the garden plot fallow time quite short. Domestic animals include pigs, dogs, fowl, and also introduced cattle and horses. Coastal villagers fish and gather shellfish to exchange with people from the interior. The Tannese remain engaged primarily in subsistence production, although they also plant cash crops, especially coconuts, coffee, some vegetables, and kava (*Piper methysticum*—a ceremonial beverage containing a narcotic) they sell to kava bars in the national capital, Port Vila. The average family's annual cash income is less than U.S. $500. Because of this, many people are open to new opportunities to earn money, including attracting more tourists to visit Tanna.

Social and Political Organization

Nuclear families are the most important kin groups. People have a notion of patrilineal descent, and families group into something like patrilineages. These larger groups, however, are perhaps better called *name sets* inasmuch as new members are recruited by receiving personal names rather than by being born into a lineage. A man only becomes a member of his father's lineage if he receives one of its names. Two or more lineage/name sets claim rights to drink kava at, and live near, numerous circular clearings that dot Tanna's landscape. The men of several of these "kava-drinking grounds" together belong to larger regional groups, of which there are about 115. Kava-drinking grounds across Tanna are also linked by a complex system of traditional "roads" along which men exchange messages and goods and find spouses.

Some men have rights to claim one of two chiefly positions at various kava-drinking grounds—that of "ruler" or that of "spokesman of the canoe/group." These chiefly titles today have only occasional ritual importance. A principle of egalitarianism governs relations among adult men. Some, however, enjoy more influence and prestige than others. These *nema asori*, or "big men," owe their political status to age, ritual knowledge and skills, and the size of their families and name sets.

Islanders practice "sister-exchange" marriage. The ideal marriage partner is a child of one's mother's brother, or father's sister. If a man marries a woman, her brother obtains the right to marry one of his new brother-in-law's sisters (real or classificatory—classificatory kinship systems expand relationships outward to include more individuals within a specific category). This requirement for balance governs marriage as it does all other forms of exchange.

Religion

Somewhat more than half the people belong to Christian churches (e.g., Presbyterian, Roman Catholic, Seventh-Day Adventist, Apostolic) or to Baha'i. The rest maintain allegiance to religious traditions or to John Frum. There are several John Frum associations on the island. The largest is headquartered at Sulphur Bay on the east coast. Another group combines worship of John Frum with symbolic allegiance to Prince Philip of Great Britain, the husband of Queen Elizabeth II. Christianity has merged with—not replaced—a traditional concern with the ancestors. All are in contact with their ancestors. Kava drinkers, spitting out their last mouthful of the drug, utter prayers to the surrounding dead buried nearby. Islanders also recognize various spirits associated with particular places, such as reefs and mountain peaks.

The Tannese celebrate important life-cycle events, such as birth, naming, a boy's circumcision, marriage, and death, with exchanges of pigs, cooked food, kava, baskets, and mats. After an exchange of such goods between the families involved, people often dance through the night. Larger exchange ceremonies unite people from across the island. The *nakwiari* (sometimes called *toka*), which may involve several thousand participants, is Tanna's most spectacular ceremony. People from two regions exchange pigs and kava after a night and a day of colorful song and dance. These periodic exchanges and dances have become popular tourist spectacles.

Today, many tourists visit John Frum villages to witness and take part in movement rituals. John Frum supporters gather every Friday to dance until daybreak. Celebration of the founding of the movement takes place in Ipikil (Sulphur Bay) each year on February 15. Movement leaders appear in antique U.S. military dress or other khaki uniforms they have more recently acquired. They raise up the American and other flags on long poles

To celebrate the founding of the John Frum
movement on February 15, John Frum
guards raise the American flag at Sulphur Bay
as guests and tourists watch. Courtesy of Lamont Lindstrom.

in the center of the village. Groups of John Frum supporters then pray and
leave flower offerings at the foot of several red wooden crosses. Young
men—soldiers in the Tanna Army—perform drill team march steps. Shirt-
less, they paint *U.S.A.* in red on their chests and backs. Movement
supporters next exchange gifts of food, kava, and local trade goods with
guests. Finally, various "string bands" from supporting villages perform
John Frum hymns to entertain the crowds, some of whom dance throughout the night.

THREATS TO SURVIVAL

The Tannese have maintained a strong, vibrant culture despite 150 years
of contact with the outside world. They have also creatively elaborated on
their traditions by developing new institutions such as the John Frum movement. Paradoxically, their remarkable success in preserving their culture is

attracting growing numbers of tourists who want to experience "real" island life. Cultural tourism (sometimes also called *indigenous* or *ethnic tourism*) is increasingly popular nowadays. People on Tanna know that tourists will pay to see their *nakwiari* dances. But islanders dance for reasons more important than money. The dance still functions to bring together people from two regions.

People manage culture both because it now can be sold and because certain aspects of culture have now come to identify *them* and their home within the global community. The relationship between tourism and identity works both ways. The Tannese now view themselves partly in terms of tourist interests in *nakwiari* and John Frum. The cultural differences that tourists focus on have become part of their identity, for good or bad.

If cultural difference is now a global commodity that people package and sell to one another, then Pacific Islanders are well positioned in this marketplace. The tourist industry packages quick experiences of cultural difference—custom dances in hotel bars and airports; tours of villages; suitcase-sized carvings in gift shops; local foods in restaurants, or tame versions of these at least; and so forth. Culture for tourism, in this way, is both real and manufactured, in the sense that people nourish and protect traditions partly because these can be sold to visitors hungry for the sensation of difference. Tourism thus sometimes promotes culture since people are careful to manage their cultural resources, whether these are dance, religious ceremony, art style, or cuisine. The South Pacific enjoys rich, spectacular traditions—in the Bislama language, *Vanuatu i fulap kastom* ("full of tradition"). Cultural diversity, particularly in its most easily packaged forms of dance, carvings and artwork, food, and architecture, is readily available on Tanna and throughout Vanuatu. Islanders are remarkably skilled at creating and managing cultural difference, which, locally, serves to distinguish family from family, village from village, and valley from valley. It takes much energy and talent to produce and maintain through time the fantastic range of language difference, for example, that exists today in Vanuatu. People have brilliant techniques for creating stylistic distinctions for purposes of local identity claims. Such devices include a traditional system of artistic copyright that asserts rights to cultural forms.

Many tourists arrive in the Pacific with evolutionary dogma still haunting their minds. These myths depict two kinds of native—the ignoble and the noble. Since Bougainville and Rousseau, the Pacific has furnished both sorts of savage to the European imagination. Significant numbers of tourists seek the dangerous thrill of the primitive; others are on a pilgrimage to experience the noble wisdom of human ancestors.

Pacific islands in the global tourist marketplace today have difficulty escaping being positioned as either primitive paradises or primitive adventure lands. Each of these poses has benefits and drawbacks. In the first case, tourists approach a culture as a form of natural and ancient wisdom, but cultural products such as Tanna's may have to pretend to be antique custom and environmentally friendly and some visitors may be upset by any signs of the real world (such as the plastic and tinsel decoration that some dancers wear during a *nakwiari* ceremony). In the second case, people have to put up with tourists who are fascinated by exotic primitiveness but who refuse to accept that island beliefs and rituals, such as the John Frum holiday on February 15, are no more savage than is, say, Christmas.

Tanna for Tourists

The tourist industry is advertising Tanna's cultural and natural attractions in both these terms: Tanna is a natural paradise and an exotic adventure. A New Zealand tourist brochure advertising Vanuatu's attractions calls Tanna "one of the most remarkable islands in the Pacific Ocean" and "an attractive add-on" to a Vanuatu holiday.[2] It promises tourists an experience of Tanna's entertaining volcano and its "mysterious cargo cults," concluding

The most significant attraction on Tanna Island is the Tannese people who live a traditional life style and still practice the ancient customs of their ancestors. . . . overnight stay or longer gives you the opportunity of seeing the splendor of Yasur Volcano at night, and to experience the primitive nature of Tanna.[3]

Tanna is packaged here as primitive experience—a place where tourists might enjoy the spectacle of ancient customs. Tanna possesses "the world's most accessible volcano"[4] and also the world's most accessible cargo cult. Tourist advertisements use the volcano to frame John Frum, and John Frum to frame the volcano. Each magnifies the spectacle of the other. Iasur is thrilling because it is the home of the mysterious John Frum; cargo-cult mystery is heightened by eruptions of black volcanic plumes of ash lowering over the red crosses and flagpoles of Sulphur Bay.

Vanuatu tourist guidebooks all include John Frum as a tourist attraction. They mention in particular the movement's holiday celebrations on February 15 held at Sulphur Bay and its sacred red crosses. Tourists also learn an abbreviated version of the cargo cult story. The Tannese, supposedly, await the return of John Frum and the American military with its cargo ships. Guidebooks provide helpful hints for tourists such as "Wait at the entrance of Sulphur Bay village. Someone will invite you in and show you around."[5] This village "is the center of the John Frum cult . . . To one side is a John From church. This houses the movement's most sacred red cross, which you may photograph but not touch. . . . Every Friday evening, John Frum supporters come from the nearby villages to dance. . . . Grass skirts sell here for about 400 VT [vatu, about U.S. $3.50]."[6] Touristic Tanna here combines tropical relaxation with primitive adventure (not to mention bargain-basement exotic shopping opportunities).

In the global tourist marketplace, thus, Tanna is now the "Island of John Frum Myth." A few visitors come seeking cargo cultists. Most learn about John Frum after they arrive. Planes land daily from Port Vila, Vanuatu's capital town, located on Efate Island in the center of the archipelago. Air service also occasionally links Tanna with New Caledonia. Many tourists fly down from cosmopolitan Port Vila in the morning, take a tour of the volcano and perhaps a village or two, and then fly back up to Vila that evening. Some, however, stay longer in one of several small bungalow resorts.

There are few opportunities to earn cash on the island and some families and entrepreneurs have invested in tourism. A number of men work as taxi drivers and tour guides, driving visitors from the airfield in the west across the central mountains to Iasur volcano and Sulphur Bay on Tanna's east coast. Several of these guides have arrangements to take their passengers to a John Frum or a *kastom* (traditional) village. Several *Kastom*/John Frum villages located in southwest Tanna have made a point of their faithfulness to custom by wearing bark skirts and penis wrappers. Guides also drive visitors across the grassy plains of northwest Tanna to see herds of so-called wild horses. A few entrepreneurs have opened small restaurants, and some people have built guest houses or bungalows that they rent out. Most of these lack piped water or electricity, however, and they attract only the most adventuresome visitors. Some women also earn cash by selling food and handicrafts such as baskets, bark skirts, and mats, in roadside marketplaces.

Tourists, and their cash, are unevenly distributed, and this can produce new sorts of inequality. People around the island have tried to develop tourist attractions with variable success. A number of visitors make their way to Port Resolution on the east coast, where they may stay in local guest houses and swim with tame dugongs. Nearer the volcano, however, a lava tube and bat cave failed to attract tourists. On the southeastern coast, one entrepreneur erected a sign offering to show unique rock formations to the very occasional tourist who might pass by. The sign, written in irregular Bislama and decorated with pictures of an axe and a footprint and the words *Advertise here!*, proclaimed:

Stori mo History belong Matiktiki mo plante samting mo we you save askem long owna blong hem i soem you! You save lookem mak blong lek blong hem, haf pig we i tan, mo ax blong hem mo fenis blong hem mo nalnal. (The story and history of [Tanna's culture hero] Matiktiki and a lot more than you can ask its owner to show you! You can see his footprint, half a cooked pig, and his axe and his courtyard and his club.)

Not many visitors paid the 200 vatu (U.S. $1.75) requested to see these remarkable stones as few venture much beyond the roads that link the airport and government center in the west with the volcano, Sulphur Bay, and Port Resolution in the east.

Tourism draws people, money, goods, ideas, and sometimes disease into the region. Some families benefit if they manage to capture revenue from passing tourists. Tourism can empower certain artists over others if one particular art style comes to be known as characteristic of a place. It can empower the more cosmopolitan young over their elders, who then may complain bitterly about cultural erosion. It may empower men over women, or sometimes women over men, depending on the access of each gender to the tourist economy.

Tourism has sparked sharp conflict over money between competing families and villages. John Frum supporters and their rivals have fought several times over rights to income from Iasur volcano. Visitors pay a fee to ascend the volcano and often also hire local guides. People from villages near Iasur have argued about how this revenue should be shared, who should guide, and also which families and name sets actually own the volcano. Several times since the 1980s these disputes have turned violent and rival villagers have attacked one another. Village leaders have periodically ordered the volcano closed to tourists until tempers cool enough so that the division of volcano income can be renegotiated. The Tannese have also argued about the propriety of charging tourists to attend *nakwiari* festivals. Tourists who attended a *nakwiari* in 1995 paid 3,000 vatu (U.S. $26.25) just to attend—and 5,000 vatu (U.S. $43.75) if they wanted to photograph the dancers. Some people insist that *kastom* (Pacific term for "custom") demands that all be admitted free to these feasts. Others claim that tourist payments are a needed source of income for the development of the island's economy.

Tourism demands constant decisions about where visitors are welcome, about the packaging of local culture, and about the distribution of new revenue. As tourist numbers increase, so do political dispute and argument. Tourist purchasing power may unbalance a local economy so that, for example, the slipper lobster catch once enjoyed by everyone now all goes into tourist bellies. But fishermen profit. Social relations are threatened by tourists in search of sexual encounters. But young men and women may profit, experientially if not also monetarily. Tourist demands may unsettle the timing and staging of local festivals and ceremonies. But local hotels, guest houses, and tour guides profit from these rearrangements, however troublesome.

RESPONSE: STRUGGLES TO SURVIVE CULTURALLY

People on Tanna perceive the increasing numbers of tourists visiting their island as both an economic opportunity and a growing social problem.

They welcome tourists but demand to preserve the cultural and social space in which they might live their lives away from tourist eyes. Fortunately, *kastom* itself includes mechanisms that the Tannese utilize partly to defuse the hazards of tourism. One of these traditional mechanisms is the concept of "road," or controlled mobility. Others are the concept of *tapu* (taboo), and a traditional political structure of dualistic opposition.

Roads

Pacific Islanders are mobile people. In many societies, there are forms of "*kastom* tourism," particularly for younger men. The Tannese, too, are easy travelers and gracious hosts. *Kastom*, however, regulates island mobility. People commonly inherit a number of "roads" that they should follow when they tour. A person is a proper visitor if he or she stays on the *correct* road. People who travel off their customary roads may be fined if they trespass on the important places of others. It is possible to make new roads, but this entails negotiation and the creation of new social relations. If negotiations fail, tourism then becomes a form of trespass when unwelcome visitors arrive without an invitation.

Leaders on Tanna have attempted to insist that all tourists follow proper roads—that tourists only visit the places where they are made welcome. They thus draw on *kastom* to manage tourism. The Lonely Planet guide for Vanuatu (1991) warns that "camping is banned in Tanna. However, there are some leaf houses used by villagers at Sulphur Bay and Ireupuow (Port Resolution) where local people may let you stay."[7] It goes on to note that "there's a fair amount of rivalry between different villages as to who gets the tourist dollar. Accordingly, 'unescorted' tours by foreign visitors are strictly prohibited by the Tafea [local government] Council. So you may need to be rather discreet on Tanna, if independent travel is more your style."[8] These restrictions are local attempts to control tourist mobility by insisting that visitors stay only in local guest houses, rather than camping out in places where they might invade people's privacy. Similarly, attempts to require tourists to hire local guides also aim to force tourists to remain on appropriate "roads" during their visit.

Tapu

Even when people keep to proper tourist roads, certain places remain out of bounds for them because they do not have the right to visit. Customarily, the notion of *tapu* (taboo) protects a variety of sacred places and other culturally important sites. Taboos restrain the impact of visitors on sacred places or in areas where increased tourist presence worsens local conflicts and antagonisms. Tourists may visit Iasur volcano, although taboos have been placed on the volcano when fights over revenue have erupted. Not many tourists, however, visit other sacred places such as Ifekir waterfall or Iankahi because only a few Tannese themselves have the right to follow the roads that lead here.

Dualistic Opposition

Tannese society, ultimately, is egalitarian. One feature ensuring this is an underlying pattern of dualistic political opposition. If one leader, or village, or group increases its power, other people on the island are motivated to join together in opposition. There are overlapping oppositions of this sort in traditional social structure. Most people claim membership in one or the other island social moieties, or "halves." And, at the village level, one name set opposes another. In contemporary politics, too, people support and vote for two main opposed party blocs.

Where some people on Tanna promote tourism, this dualistic political structure often ensures that others will oppose these plans. In the 1970s, when some islanders wanted to increase tourist visitors to Iasur, others stood in opposition and blocked access to the volcano for months. Similarly, although some local entrepreneurs have developed tourist bungalows and tour guide businesses, their neighbors often refuse to cooperate with these efforts. If some *nakwiari* dancers wish to invite tourists to the feast, other participants protest their presence.

The Tannese say that one reason that John Frum first appeared to them in the late 1930s was the overweening power of the Presbyterian mission and its adherents. John Frum requested that people leave the church and return to their traditions, and many did. The Tannese, thus, have sustained their culture's survival once before by reviving *kastom* in order to undermine Presbyterian leaders and chiefs.

FOOD FOR THOUGHT

John Frum's first appearance on Tanna sparked a long-lived movement of cultural revitalization. Now, several decades later, John Frum ceremony attracts growing numbers of tourists whose presence threatens cultural survival. But tourism can also *promote* culture. It does this directly as people protect and develop their art, dance, and cultural landscape to sell artifacts and spectacle to visiting tourists. And it promotes culture indirectly as people engage in lively debate about the definition, value, and ownership of customary practices in which tourists take interest. The difficulty is to manage tourism so that this empowers cultural pride and creativity yet, in so doing, does not result in increased economic inequality and identity loss.

The Tannese face added difficulties in that their culture and home are on sale in the tourist marketplace as a "cargo cult island," the home of John Frum myth. Some visitors point their cameras at what they see as strange and exotic cultists. Many Tannese, though, interpret tourist interest in John Frum shrines and rituals as proof that John spoke the truth. John Frum foresaw that Tanna someday would have new roads and links to the wider world. He predicted that Americans and other traveling outsiders would one day return to Tanna bringing cargo. And here, at last, they come.

Questions

1. Are tourists on Tanna a new sort of "cargo"?
2. How can tourism harm a culture?
3. How might tourism help sustain culture survival?
4. If tourists began visiting your neighborhood or town because they found you strange and exotic, how would this make you feel?
5. Would you vacation on Tanna? Why or why not?

NOTES

1. *Tanna Island: Republic of Vanuatu* (brochure) (Tanna: Tanna Beach Resort, n.d.), p. 1.
2. *Go Vanuatu* (brochure) (Auckland: Go Pacific Holidays), p. 9.
3. Ibid.
4. Ibid.
5. David Harcombe, *Vanuatu: A Travel Survival Guide* (Hawthorne, Victoria: Lonely Planet Publications, 1991), p. 142.
6. Ibid.
7. Ibid.
8. Ibid.

RESOURCE GUIDE

Published Literature

Bonnemaison, Joël. *The Tree and the Canoe: History and Ethnogeography of Tanna.* Honolulu: University of Hawai'i Press, 1994.

Butler, Richard, and Thomas Hinch, eds. *Tourism and Indigenous Peoples.* London: International Thomson Business Press, 1996.

Douglas, Ngaire. *They Came for Savages: 100 Years of Tourism in Melanesia.* Australia: Southern Cross University Press, 1966.

Lindstrom, Lamont. *Cargo Cult: Strange Stories of Desire from Melanesia and Beyond.* Honolulu: University of Hawai'i Press, 1993.

Lindstrom, Lamont, and Geoffery M. White, eds. *Culture, Kastom, Tradition: Developing Cultural Policy in Melanesia.* Suva: Institute of Pacific Studies, University of South Pacific, 1994.

Film

O'Rourke, Dennis, *Cannibal Tours*, Los Angeles, O'Rourke & Associates, Direct Cinema Ltd., 1987.

WWW Sites

The John Frum Homepage
http://www.enzo.gen.nz/jonfrum/

General Vanuatu Information
http://www.vanuatu.net.vu/

Tourist Information
http://www.magna.com.au/~hideaway/vli.html

Vanuatu Cultural Center Homepage
http://artalpha.anu.edu.au/web/arc/vks/vks.htm

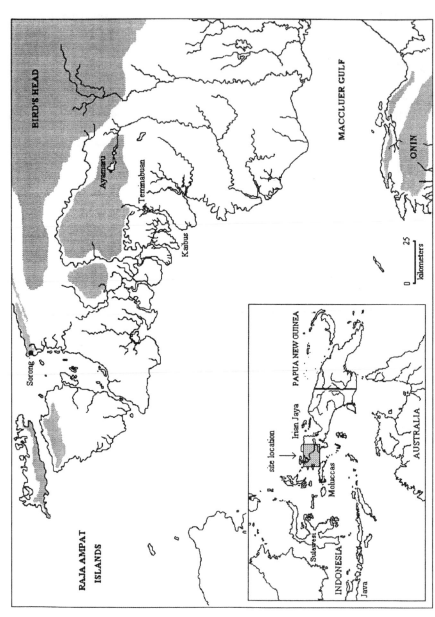

Irian Jaya, Indonesia. Courtesy of Jaap Timmer.

Chapter 14

The Tehit of Irian Jaya, Indonesia
Jaap Timmer and Leontine Visser

CULTURAL OVERVIEW

Traveling by boat to Tehit country (located in the southwestern section of Bird's Head Peninsula, Irian Jaya), one enters the Kaibus estuary, which cuts through vast swamplands. The water is muddy, the sky is blue, and the air is hot and humid. Palm cockatoos and lorikeets scream overhead and hornbills swoop down tall trees that tower above the nipa palms and mangrove. The river is walled on both sides by the mangrove and palms. Beyond the river's edges is a vast estuarine swampland with seemingly endless stretches of mangrove and sago palm forest. This almost impenetrable wilderness is home to a variety of fish, shrimps, crocodiles, and birds. Only with a dugout canoe can one enter the mazes of creeks that cut through this mangrove. The creeks lead to patches of tidal land where cultivated sago and a variety of other trees grow. There are also large sandbanks where Tehit dwell in houses built on stilts. Temporary sheds are also built in the sago groves.

To the north, lush green hills loom above the town of Teminabuan with its 65-foot-high mast of the National Indonesian Television Corporation. In the hilly forests beautiful orchids, marsupials such as tree kangaroos and the cuscus, and a large variety of birds and reptiles have led biologists to classify these forests as some of the richest and most diverse in Irian Jaya. Sailing northward one can hear the humming sounds of motors and boats, and the loading and unloading of goods and people arriving or departing from the city of Sorong. When entering the harbor the pleasant sound of a picturesque waterfall drowns the bustle of commerce. Here, Tehit live in modern brick houses with concrete foundations and roofs of corrugated iron sheets. Buginese and Butonese storekeepers from Celebes (Sulawesi) sell a variety of goods: rice, flour, soap, clothing, gasoline, and kerosene. At a separate marketplace, Tehit village women trade vegetables, fish, honey, sago, medicinal leaves, and pork. Teminabuan town is the main commercial center of the area and the seat of the government for the subdistrict. The town has the only hospital of the subdistrict. Just outside town, alongside the road to the northern subdistrict of Ayamaru, there are a grass airstrip, a police station, and a small army headquarters.

The People

The population of the Teminabuan subdistrict numbers about nine thousand.[1] In addition, there are about fifteen hundred immigrants, mainly from Sulawesi, and about two hundred people from Java. The indigenous Tehit-speaking population is socioculturally Melanesian. They call themselves Tehit people (*na Tehit*) in the local language or the Teminabuan people (*orang Teminabuan*) in the national Indonesian language. They speak one or more of the dialects of the Tehit language and most speak at least some Indonesian. Indonesians from elsewhere generally refer to the indigenous people from Irian Jaya as *Irianese*. Many Tehit live in the town of Teminabuan, but most reside in villages of about two hundred to five hundred inhabitants. These villages are situated in the swampy sago and nipa palm forests or the valleys of the hill range to the north. Villagers must do without good roads, medical facilities, electricity, and telephones. They benefit, however, from an abundance of food and fresh water.

The traditional Tehit world is not isolated. On the contrary, the indigenous people have been connected to the world economy for centuries. At least three centuries ago Tehit had relations with the eastern Indonesian sultanate of Tidore in the northern Moluccas. The sultans claimed authority over large parts of western New Guinea. Local leaders along the coast of western New Guinea dominated trade and sent tribute to the sultan of Tidore. These local trade representatives were called *raja*. They grew wealthy and powerful when world demand for bird of paradise feathers and other forest products made the island of New Guinea an important trade destination. Bird of paradise feathers were especially valuable to European and Asian merchants, who sold them worldwide as decorations for royal headdresses. Teminabuan became an increasingly important post of *raja* who were instrumental in the collection and transportation of local products and manpower. The local *raja* presented these goods as tribute to the representatives of the sultan of Tidore on the Onin Peninsula and in the Raja Ampat Islands.

In return for the local products, the *raja* in Teminabuan provided the indigenous people with eastern Indonesian woven cloths called *kain timur*, copper and bronze products, glass beads, Chinese porcelain dishes and jars, and Portuguese ceramics. The indigenous people associated these products with the Moluccan centers of wealth and power. As a result these items were ascribed magical powers, which remain potent even today. *Kain timur* cloths possess special powers to summon sky deities and the spirits of ancestors, and to ensure the prosperity and fertility of the soil and the people. The less valuable cloths are used in bride-wealth payments.

Despite some isolated expeditions since the sixteenth century, western New Guinea has attracted the interest of missionaries, prospectors, and the colonial government of the Dutch East Indies based in Batavia (present-day Jakarta) only from the midnineteenth century onward. The Dutch formally claimed possession of the western half of the island of New Guinea in 1828 and began to rule West New Guinea indirectly from 1855 through the administrative unit of the Residency of Ternate and Its Dependencies. Dutch colonial rule in Teminabuan began in the late 1920s. The colonial authorities and missionaries wanted to abolish "pagan" practices by introducing Christianity, churches, and schools. At the administrative center, Sorong, established in 1925, the assistant-resident of Sorong governed the whole of the Bird's Head district, including the Raja Ampat islands and the Onin Peninsula, between 1933 and 1945. Until then economic development had been rather slow and West New Guinea remained a backwater in the vast Dutch colony of the East Indies.

After the Japanese occupation of Indonesia and New Guinea during World War II, Indonesia gained independence; West New Guinea remained a Dutch colony. To increase economic development, postwar Dutch governments rapidly extended their authority to more remote areas. Serious efforts were made in social development, education, health, and community organization to prepare the country for eventual independence. Newly independent Indonesia, however, never accepted Dutch rule in New Guinea. After several years of political conflict and minor military clashes between Indonesia and the Netherlands, the General Assembly of the United Nations in 1962 required the Dutch to hand over West New Guinea to Indonesia. It was agreed, however, that the area would be ruled by the United Nations Temporary Executive Administration for some years, after which a plebiscite would be held to decide whether the people wanted independence or union with Indonesia. This so-called Act of Free Choice was held in 1969. During the plebiscite, indigenous people were not allowed to vote. They were instead represented by a select group who supported the unification platform of the Indonesian state. To this day this event causes much discontent among Irianese. The Indonesian government called its new easternmost province *Irian Jaya*. Moreover, after 1963 the Indonesian army suppressed any form of protest or political opposition. The West New Guinea national flag became a symbol of opposition.

By the mid-1960s the Indonesian government moved toward "development" and Westernization. With the gradual expansion of communications and transportation technology during the Dutch period and current Indonesian efforts to develop Irian Jaya, the isolation of once remote villages has diminished and the standard of living of most Tehit has significantly increased. In spite of these developments, the Teminabuan subdistrict has remained one of the world's poorest backwaters. This is not only caused by the geographic remoteness of towns and villages, but also by Indonesian indifference and exploitation. Because of Indonesian nationalism, ethnic discrimination, economic exploitation, and environmental devastation, Tehit, together with most other indigenous peoples of Irian Jaya, increasingly feel neglected and ignored. Irian Jaya has become a land of opportunity for the Indonesian state and foreign mining companies at the expense of largely voiceless Irianese. Moreover, increasing numbers of Indonesians migrate from other Indonesian islands (e.g., Java) to Irian Jaya seeking to make their fortune in the economic frontier. This reduces the labor opportunities for the indigenous people of Irian Jaya. These devastating circumstances have seriously affected how people see their lives, futures, and relationships with outsiders.

The Setting

About a fifth of the population of the subdistrict lives in the spacious green gown of Teminabuan. There is no industrial development to attract many people and there are no slums. Most of the town's houses are built with concrete and iron sheet roofs and are neatly arranged on both sides of the road, following the former colonial layout. Many houses are connected to a diesel generator that produces electricity from late in the afternoon until the next morning. Electricity allows people to have a radio or a television, and sometimes a telephone. In contrast, most of the villages of the Teminabuan subdistrict houses are still on stilts and consist of barely more than a simple plank construction covered with a roof of sago leaves. The traditional layout of a village is a concentric cluster of houses bordered by secondary forest or a riverbank. The Christian missionaries in the 1950s, followed by the Indonesian government in the 1970s, have forced the people to rearrange their houses according to the image of a "civilized" human society. A main road now passes through many of the villages, lined with typical Indonesian village houses with iron sheet roofs and plank walls. In the center of the oblong-shaped modern village most typically are a church, a primary school, and a small administrative office or a village health post.

Traditional Subsistence Strategies

The economic activities of villagers are largely confined to obtaining life's necessities. Any surplus is sold for cash to pay for children's schooling.

Tehit village layout conforming to "civilized" plan. Courtesy of Jaap Timmer.

Tehit usually work as an economic unit within a household, sometimes assisted by other relatives. Depending on obligations and social needs, relatively small quantities of food are bartered with relatives, friends, and neighbors. In the coastal villages, sago palm is the staple. Sago flour is obtained from the pith of mature palms, which is pounded with a blunt tool. The fibrous starch is then washed in fresh water and squeezed. After a few days, sediments of starch are placed in containers made of sago leaves from the same tree. The containers are taken back to the village in a dugout canoe or carried on a woman's back. A full-sized sago palm can supply sago flour for an ordinary family for a month or more. Every day a portion of this sago supply is used to make sago paste, a rather bland, and to outsiders, tasteless dish. The taste and its limited nutritional value are usually improved by adding leaves, fish, and sometimes a bit of pork.

The northern uplands are covered by rain forest. Here the people cultivate small gardens by slashing and burning small patches of forest land. They grow a large variety of tubers, such as sweet potatoes, cassava, taro, and yam, as well as bananas and peppers. After one or two years the plot is deserted and activities shift to an adjacent plot of land. The former garden is left to regenerate (lie fallow) and becomes secondary forest. This agricultural practice is called *shifting cultivation*. When population numbers are very low, as in the Teminabuan area, shifting cultivation does not pose an immediate threat to the forest environment.

Social and Political Organization

A typical Tehit household includes members of three generations (grandparents, parents, and children) who share one house. Other relatives, such as a widowed brother, a sister-in-law, or an adopted child, may also live under this roof. These relatives together constitute one household, as they "eat from one hearth." The hearth stones and cooking fire are the practical and symbolic representation of the household unit. Tehit men may marry more than one wife. If a man marries two wives, he temporarily lives with one wife and children in one house, while his second wife and children live in a nearby house.

The social composition of villages is largely determined by kinship and marriage rules. Kinship is reckoned through both the male and female lines; therefore, a person may have the right of access to and use of land or sago palms owned by the families of his father and mother. However, inheritance of land and valuables, such as cloths, is only calculated through the father's side. Land rights may also change hands during a marriage. The girl's parents give the right of access to and use of a particular plot of land of forest to their son-in-law's parents in exchange for a valuable item like cloth. Generally, it is rare to find someone living in a house or a village who is not somehow related to his neighbors or other villagers. Friendship ties between two unrelated people are not common. Close friendship usually implies mutual obligations governed by kinship rules. Of course, the closely knit kin ties can also generate conflict.

The people of the Bird's Head Peninsula are often characterized as "people on the move." Two factors explain this mobility. First, kinship and marriage relationships are never restricted to one settlement. In fact, people's relatives are scattered over many villages, Teminabuan town, and a Tehit neighborhood in the city of Sorong. Marriage relationships and land transactions among these settlements do not confine economic activities to one place. Economic cooperation in agriculture, fisheries, and trade often includes people from different villages and even subdistricts. During marriage or sickness, entire families or individuals may travel to another village or the city of Sorong, occasionally for long periods. As a result, Tehit resident in Sorong, Teminabuan town, and the villages feel quite close, despite the distances between them. Second, people travel because their sago trees or gardens are located far from the villages. Physical distance presents a special problem in sago production. To obtain enough sago for several months, a family may have to paddle downstream to their sago stand without returning to their village for a couple of days or weeks. Meanwhile, they must live in their canoe sheltered by a small roof or in a temporary forest shelter. One can imagine that village leadership, concerted action of villagers, education, and health care are difficult in such conditions.

Before the first missionaries arrived and promoted village formation, people lived in small unstable settlements. The families and clans lived and moved within a vast territory of forested land and sago marshes along the rivers and estuaries to which they claimed ancestral rights. These groups varied greatly in size. They chose their own leaders, usually an older knowledgeable and powerful man. There were different types of leaders that are still recognized today. Although these leadership positions have different sources of authority, they are often held by the same person. The most important position in society was held by the *na tmak*. He was the ritual leader or initiator of the *wuon* cult. As teachers *na tmak* performed a role that is quite different from that of the teacher in the West. In contrast to a Western schoolteacher, the initiator conveyed his knowledge about the world during initiation through symbolic language, communicating many secret stories about the origin of the world and the workings of magic. Even though the *wuon* cult is abolished, the former initiator still holds a meaningful position in society as a guardian of traditional knowledge, which is considered very important for the future of Tehit.

A more political position was held by the *raja*. During Dutch colonial rule the *raja* continued to play a political role as the preferred representative of the local people. The *na tmak* did not qualify for this position because he was too closely associated with "primitive" customs. During the 1950s some *raja* became government officials; each received a uniform and a salary, and children received elementary education in the mission schools. Some of these children entered a vocational school; often they became the religious leaders and schoolteachers of today. Often the *raja* is also an economic entrepreneur or indigenous "rich man" (*na kohok*). Through the accumulation of family wealth, especially valuable cloth, this entrepreneur is able to maintain a powerful position in society. Consequently, these men, and their families, continue to form the indigenous elite today. The *raja* are often seen as local heroes. Tehit associate the *raja* with the power and wealth of the sultanate of Tidore, which is now seen as opposed to the Indonesian center of power in Jakarta.

Religion and World View

In precolonial times, Tehit performed a vast range of religious practices and rituals to propitiate spirits and ancestors. These former beliefs and practices are referred to as *traditional religion*. This traditional religion centered around spirits that dwell in the forests and waters or take the form of stones. The most important deities live in the sky. The secret knowledge needed to communicate with these sky beings belonged to initiated men and was taught during male initiation called *wuon*. *Wuon* initiation played an essential role in society, and those who organized it were men of prominence. Their knowledge, practices, beliefs, and imagery explain the origin and spread of humankind, including the origin and control of fertility and the reproduction of nature and man. Noninitiated young men, and women, had only partial access to this knowledge.

From the beginning of their work in 1927, Protestant missionaries denounced the initiation rituals as pagan. Many older Tehit recount the violent actions of missionaries patrolling the area, who burned initiation houses and beat the Tehit participants to prepare them for conversion to Christianity. Tehit, however, have adapted and shaped relatively quickly the Christian teachings to their own cultural forms and values. As a result, the last initiation was performed in the mid-1960s. Other major rituals have also disappeared within the last three decades. Today, dependence on the Christian God and belief in the efficacy of church rituals have largely replaced spirit and ancestor worship. Tehit in general want to become good Christians, but they do not deny the past and present importance of traditional knowledge and religious practices.

Many Tehit still remember the old rituals and ceremonies, including the location of gods and supernatural power. Although some names and concepts of former deities have been adapted to Christian beliefs, misfortune is often believed to be caused by evil ancestor spirits, ghosts, and witchcraft. Despite Christian teachings, supernatural power is never discounted.

Tehit religious belief is a creative combination of traditional ideas and practices, and Christianity. The most striking aspect of this mixed religion is the Tehit belief that in the past they possessed a great written story, the Bible. The Bible was the core of Tehit traditional knowledge. Tehit mythology explains how the Bible was taken away to the West, leaving those who stayed behind ignorant, poor, and illiterate. When the first white missionaries and patrol officers arrived in the 1920s, Tehit expected them to return the lost secrets. They believed that these whites were wealthy and powerful because they possessed the Tehit ancestral powers. The association of the missionaries with European wealth and modern medicine largely contributed to an early enthusiasm for Christian teachings. To the present day, many Tehit believe that the white Europeans and Americans still benefit from the knowledge that was taken from Irian Jaya. Tehit blame their current poverty and backwardness on this depletion of their ancestral knowledge.

THREATS TO SURVIVAL

Demographic and Social Trends

When the Indonesian province of Irian Jaya is compared with the eastern half of the island, the independent nation state of Papua New Guinea, political differences are the most apparent. Irian Jaya has been part of Indonesia since the 1970s. The state ideology of Indonesia asserts the unity of all islands of the nation state. In this ideology, national unity and security take priority over political decentralization and cultural diversity. Consequently, the developments that have taken place in Irian Jaya since the 1970s have only one purpose: the political, economic, cultural, and social incorporation of Irian Jaya as a province of Indonesia.

The incorporation of Sorong and Teminabuan into the national administrative structure of Indonesia started in 1967. It has resulted in a never-ending story of village formation and demographic change. In 1974–76, and again after 1979, the implementation of national and provincial laws and regulations on Teminabuan village administration resulted in the creation of five administrative villages, later restructured into ten. This national village model never worked as intended. For example, the Indonesian government arranged for the election of a village head without an existing village. The plan called for the inhabitants of two separate settlements, many of whom worked in dispersed garden plots, to come together to select one leader who would have authority over both settlements. No provisions were made for where the new village head should live, let alone how he should organize the village cooperation needed for the implementation of development projects.

In the 1980s it became evident to the provincial government of Irian Jaya that the national village model did not fit Irianese practice. The sparse population density, the geographic conditions, the lack of infrastructure, different notions of leadership, and a highly mobile people provided little support for the successful implementation of an Indonesian model of village formation. The foreign notion of leadership was rejected and land disputes arose because people's loyalties often reached beyond the artificial territorial boundary of the new settlement. Therefore, in 1992 the governor of Irian Jaya acknowledged the discrepancy between national administrative rules and local practice and issued another reorganization of administrative villages that reflected the ethnolinguistic and historical development of Irian Jaya. In the subdistrict of Teminabuan the previous ten villages were subdivided further into a total of thirty villages and one urban center.

These administrative units are now recognized by the national government as formal villages (*desa*) in the 1994–97 World Bank–supported Indonesian development program for "isolated" or "backward" villages (the so-called IDT program). This three-year development program provides the district government in Sorong with a substantial subsidy sent directly from Jakarta through the national banking system. The district administration distributes these annual funds to the villages. The aim of the program is to encourage the cultivation of peanuts and mungbeans as cash crops. Despite the enormous money flows generated by the IDT program for the people of Teminabuan, they hardly begin to solve the region's problems. The program's implementation has largely failed through a lack of connection between indigenous people's understandings and practices and those of the responsible outside development workers, a lack of cooperation among villagers, administrative inefficiency, and misappropriation of funds at all the levels of the distributive system.

Development and Marginalization

The two main social and economic threats to survival of the Tehit are the paradox of development and the resulting process of marginalization. In an era of increased incorporation in a global market economy, many Tehit perceive development as an exchange of goods and commodities. In exchange for forest land, they expect the direct return of another "good," such as a road, a school, or a medical post. But the development problem is more complex. Tehit see their trees cut down by a private foreign forestry company, with the active support of the district government, in order to build a road or extract more highly valued trees. They receive little compensation for the loss of their trees and no compensation at all for the loss of access to the land. Yet Tehit have no political or socioeconomic power to protect their land and property. They are threatened by the wholescale destruction of their natural environment.

Not every threat, however, originates from outside Tehit society. Some are local, such as the financial corruption of the IDT program and the problems with the implementation of the program. A majority of the IDT funds is siphoned off during the transfer between district and subdistrict bureaus. Public opinion is that apparently this money finances improvement in the houses of some officials and the education of their children. At the village level the leader should distribute the cash, but he sometimes spends portions of the village subsidy during long stays in the city of Sorong. Meanwhile villagers not used to cooperating with nonkin beyond the household level have difficulty cultivating mungbeans or peanuts in a cooperative effort for the market. The implementation of IDT projects in the villages suffers from lack of attention to the local people's social organization and ways of doing things.

Even though the Indonesian government is indeed spending much money on development in Irian Jaya, the results are often the opposite of what is expected, both by central government and by Irianese themselves. This discrepancy creates a paradox. Thus, despite the developmental goal of assisting Irianese, mainly non-Irianese entrepreneurs and government officials are benefiting from the economic opportunities. A high percentage of all government positions is formally allotted to Irianese, but the education and training gaps with non-Irianese are too large to reach this target. Irianese represent only about 15 percent of the province's civil service in the lower ranks. The lack of access to formal jobs creates a feeling of increased frustration and despair.

The world "development" triggers different reactions in Teminabuan. In 1995, the head of the district planning bureau in Sorong, for instance, mentioned two issues that deserved priority in the development of the Bird's Head: improvement of the infrastructure (inland roads) and human resource development. The lack of infrastructure indeed frustrates economic activity because villagers have minimal access to markets. From Sorong light aircraft only fly weekly to Teminabuan, and the hilly northern parts are served at irregular intervals by small missionary-owned planes. Regular heavy rainfall damage to the grass airstrips and airline mismanagement often mean that Teminabuan has no flights for periods exceeding two months. Recurring economic crises in Indonesia have stopped all air flights to Teminabuan.

Poor roads seriously impede the transport of agricultural produce to the market by villagers. Most of the villages in the marshlands in the southern part of the subdistrict are only accessible by canoe or a small motorized boat. This means that men, women, and children must walk eight to twelve hours carrying heavy loads through the forest to deliver their harvest to the market or the nearest waterway. Likewise, because schoolteachers do not receive their monthly salaries in convenient bank accounts, they must walk or pedal down to Teminabuan to fetch it at the post office or the government office.

Human resource development is the second development priority mentioned by a Tehit planning officer. In the context of Irian Jaya there are several interpretations of this concept. First, it refers to the government's view that development requires better economic participation by Irianese. Tehit also share this definition of development. But the gap between Tehit skills and educational level and those of the immigrant Indonesians is still too large. Consequently, labor relationships are marked by stark social differences. For example, the director of a sawmill in Teminabuan town is a Buginese. His foremen are also men from Sulawesi or other eastern Indonesian islands. The lowest-paying jobs are taken by men from Sumba, Flores, or Aru, and Tehit must take the most menial jobs when they are offered. Not surprisingly, they resent their social and economic inferiority. They also resent their own trees' being processed in a foreign mill and feel frustration that foreigners grow wealthy while abusing Tehit workers. Thus national and provincial policy makers have begun to regard the development of Irianese manpower as the best solution to this increasingly unsettling situation.

Ironically, the development of human resources is sometimes equated with personal corruption, as in the case of the local elite's improving their houses with money from the village subsidy. What is at stake here is not that these individuals do not acknowledge the difference between public and private, but that they draw different boundaries between the two. Indeed, to them, their increased status through material welfare is in the public interest.

This perception invokes a third interpretation of human resource development: good governance. Government officials of Irianese descent often stress this point. Because Irianese rarely get white-collar jobs, Irianese government officials often provide jobs for their relatives whether or not they have the required knowledge or skills. Employing relatives benefits the social and economic position of the family involved, but it is uncertain whether it will improve the quality of the institution. Such behavior is called *nepotism* if it occurs in a Western bureaucracy, but with highly turbulent socioeconomic conditions prevailing in places like Teminabuan, the distinction between "public" and "private" is different.

Finally, a major threat affecting Irianese is the national migration program. Its goal is to move thousands of families from Indonesia's overpopulated islands, mainly Java and Bali, to less populated and underdeveloped areas. The "colonization" of Irian Jaya by Indonesian migrants is viewed as a solution to the demographic problems of the Indonesian state and the development problems of Irian Jaya. According to the government, Irianese need the assistance of more clever and better-educated people from other Indonesian islands. Not surprisingly, this state ideology causes many Irianese to feel undervalued and unappreciated. Furthermore, the migration program ignores cultural traditions and decreases the potential livelihood of Irianese. It also damages the natural environment where forests are cut for immigrant settlements. The immigrants also suffer from poor facilities and an inability to meet the government expectations. The following case illustrates how ethnic tensions have worsened between Javanese and Tehit in the Teminabuan settlement established largely for Javanese immigrants in the early 1990s. In 1995, four months of heavy rains destroyed a major road, but local rumor blamed ethnic tensions. As a government official explained: "The rains were caused by local Tehit. They want to take a minibus to the marketplace in town, but the Javanese drivers think that they are dirty and refuse. Angry, the Tehit spit over their left shoulder to invoke the ancestor spirits. Moreover, when this road to Teminabuan town was built, they lost much of their land to the road builders. Now they are so angry that they cause the bridge to break down, and brought the rains to ruin everyting."[2]

Apart from the government-sponsored immigration, there is an increase in voluntary immigration of families from the island of Sulawesi, who go to the towns and rural areas of Irian Jaya as private merchants seeking to make their fortune in an economic frontier. These migrants follow the forestry and migration projects into the hinterland of Teminabuan, further reducing labor opportunities for Tehit. Furthermore, most of these migrants are Muslim, and the growing influx of these people significantly contributes to the ascent of Islam in Irian Jaya. This is of much concern to the Christian Irianese, who view the increasing number of immigrants and the national religion, Islam, as part and parcel of Indonesian imperialism and feel that they are increasingly becoming strangers in their own land.

RESPONSE: STRUGGLES TO SURVIVE CULTURALLY

Until recently, Tehit knew nothing of cash, manufactured goods, employment, wage labor, national government, schools, churches, and modern time measurement. Before World War II, the Tehit economy was based on bartered labor and goods and the exchange of valuables such as cloths. Modernization followed after the war ended. Tehit tried to accommodate to this new world by invoking their traditional institutions. These traditions offer explanations for the arrival of colonial administrators and missionaries and the current Tehit status as second-class citizens of the Indonesian nation state.

In their response to modernization, Tehit do not reject all changes. Most are eager to change. Men and women, old and young, favor in varying degrees such new elements as Christian teachings, modern schooling, health care, and commoditization of land. Many are happy that boys and girls, in greater numbers than ever before, have access to secondary education in town and prospects for a job. Increasing numbers of Tehit men, both young and old, express frustration with the burden of traditional reciprocity which includes the exchange of cloth at life crisis events such as marriages and funerals. These obligations reduce the chances for an individual to become wealthy. Some Tehit resist this burden of tradition by welcoming the immigration of Javanese settlers. One frustrated man sold land to the government to allow immigrants to settle close to his village. He wanted his children to meet non-Irianese children with prosperous future and marry without the traditional cloth exchange obligation, thus increasing family wealth. Many Tehit find the temptation to become "modern" irresistible. They want to live in cement houses, wear shiny shoes, own fancy clothes, earn a good salary, and shop in supermarkets.

It is difficult for Tehit to know how to attain such a life-style because of a growing disparity between the promises of development since the 1950s and reality, in particular for those living in remote villages. They are materially better off than several decades ago, but the world around them is changing even faster, developing even more, and Tehit increasingly have the feeling of falling behind, of being betrayed. They perceive a history of injustice that prevents them from bridging the gap between their expectations and the real world. Discouraged economically, the Tehit take refuge in Christian ideas, and their enthusiasm for Christianity provides an identity in opposition to the Islamic majority of Indonesia.

Many Tehit shape their expectations of a better future in terms of their belief in God and, particularly, in the second coming of the Jesus Christ, who they believe has the power to better their world by returning their lost ancestral powers. Protestant Tehit men and women regularly listen to biblical interpretations by local teachers. The Bible has become a source of "true" knowledge that opposes the lies and deceit of former colonial officers, missionaries, and current Indonesian government officials. The Book of Revelation plays an especially important role as the source of favorable predictions about the future.

In fact, Revelation describes for the Tehit their concept about the landscapes drying up. Many people talk about the drying up of lakes and the poor quality of crops and fish catches. Stories are told about olden days, when tubers, fish, cuscus, and humans were bigger and stronger. Furthermore, many see that youths do not show respect for their elders, that the health of people is deteriorating, and that witchcraft is escalating. Many Tehit consider the Buginese, Butonese, and Javanese immigrants the source of disease and witchcraft. Moreover, they believe that the ascent of Islam brought about by the increasing numbers of Muslim migrants will bring about a religious war, the end of the world, the return of Jesus Christ, and the independence of Irian Jaya from Indonesia.

FOOD FOR THOUGHT

The notions of development and change are crucial in this discussion of the transforming conditions of Tehit lives. The living conditions of Tehit are simultaneously shifting but at different speeds. For instance, the cultivation of mungbeans for market with the financial support of the IDT development program has promoted alternative ideas about development and village cooperation. In this context, the paradox of development is apparent because of its unintended and often negative impact on the conditions of local Tehit. How can this paradox of development be resolved?

The institutional formation of villages, on the other hand, involves more complex and long-term changes in indigenous notions of leadership, the reallocation of people, and traditional rules for access to land and water resources. The administrative interventions of both colonial and Indonesian governments affected local leadership and settlement patterns. The modern Indonesian village (*desa*) concept contrasts with indigenous notions of leadership. In these modern villages, leaders are no longer selected according to their status and descent group affiliation, but on the basis of modern education, fluency in the Indonesian language, and an acceptance of state ideologies. How does this influence the relationship between generations and between men and women?

One major factor that makes developmental change among Tehit rather complex is the fact that Irian Jaya is not an autonomous state, unlike Papua New Guinea. It is a province of a nation state, Indonesia, and as such subordinate to the centralist ideology of the dominant cultural group, the Javanese, who have different historical, ethnic, and cultural backgrounds.

The Tehit case is not unique in contemporary Irian Jaya. They share with other Irianese a history of rapid changes. Over the last few decades Irian

Jaya is increasingly drawn into the larger world at the expense of Irianese people's political and cultural autonomy. Their marginal status in the world, in particular within the nation state of Indonesia, triggers increasing concern with their identity and autonomy. With the fall of the Suharto regime in May 1998, their concerns are expressed much more openly. Regularly, reports of protest and political meetings appear in the newspapers and on the Internet. Less known are indigenous forms of protest that are often less concrete or outspokenly political. An example is Tehit enthusiasm for Christian teachings.

The Bible has a particular role and importance as a source of "true" knowledge, and as a symbolic weapon against the political and military supremacy of Indonesia. In what respect is this kind of symbolic resistance different from armed protest? Do Tehit have a choice? It is important to realize that modernization incites different forms of protest. In Irian Jaya armed protest is known by the name of the Free Papua Movement (*Operasi Papua Merdeka* [OPM]), which has frustrated colonial and Indonesian governments over the last few decades. The OPM fights for an Irianese identity and independence from Indonesia through guerrilla warfare and invocation of ancestral and spiritual power. The OPM began as a reaction against government oppression, but disorganization has hurt the movement. Tehit support the goals of the OPM, but without openly participating in armed protest because they fear reprisal from the Indonesian military. Their only option is to expect the return of Jesus Christ. Until that day arrives, Tehit patiently wait for the tide to turn.

Questions

1. Indigenous people, like Tehit, are often considered to be isolated. But the definition of isolation depends on the social position of the speaker. We have shown that Tehit are not isolated except geographically. Why not?

2. Traditional knowledge, unlike modern school education, is not passed on to everybody in Tehit society. Therefore, knowledge is not "free." What consequences does this have, for example, for the position of women?

3. Friendship and trust mainly are characteristic of kinship relationships. What impact will development, through schooling, the church, or supravillage administrative organization, have on the traditional relationships?

4. The benefits of the IDT program for the indigenous people are few because of corruption, inefficient administration, and poor infrastructure. In the villages the implementation of the development projects suffers from lack of attention to the indigenous people's social organization, perceptions, and ways of doing things. What would be an alternative to the IDT program?

NOTES

1. Demographic materials were collected and analyzed by H. Lautenback in "Population Dynamics in Teminabuan Subdistrict, Irian Jaya, Indonesia," Ph.D. thesis, University of Groningen, the Netherlands, 1999.

2. Interview with John Wanane, Sorong, June 1995.

RESOURCE GUIDE

Published Literature

Ballard, Chris. "Melanesia in Review: Issues and Events, 1996—Irian Jaya." *The Contemporary Pacific* 9(2): 468–74, 1997.

Ballard, Chris. "Melanesia in Review: Issues and Events, 1997 Irian Jaya." *The Contemporary Pacific* 10(2): 433–41, 1998.

Miedema, Jelle, Cecilia Odé, and Rien A. C. Dams, eds. *Perspectives on the Bird's Head of Irian Jaya, Indonesia: Proceedings of the Conference*, Leiden, October 13–17, 1997. Amsterdam: Rodopi, 1998.

Osborne, Robin. *Indonesia's Secret War: The Guerrilla Struggle in Irian Jaya.* Sydney: Allen and Unwin, 1985.

Osborne, Robin. *West Papua: The Obliteration of a People.* London: Tapol, 1983.

Sands, Susan. "West Papua: Forgotten War, Unwanted People." *Cultural Survival* 15(2): 40–44, 1991.

Start, Daniel. *The Open Cage: The Ordeal of the Irian Jaya Hostages.* London: HarperCollins, 1997.

Films and Videos

Bob Burns and Gil Scrine, *One People, One Soul*, Australian Film Commission, 1987.

Tracey Groome, *Arrows against the Wind*, Land Beyond Productions, Australia, 1992.

Wiek Lenssen, *Rufus Saati: The Spirits Have Gone*, Harfst, the Netherlands, 1996.

WWW Sites

Irian Jaya Homepage
http://w.irja.org/index2.shtml

West Papua Information Kit
http://ww.cs.utexas.edu/users/cline/papua

Chapter 15

The Torres Strait Islanders of Australia

Judith M. Fitzpatrick

CULTURAL OVERVIEW

The People

For the contemporary indigenous population of Torres Strait, the seascape is prominent in the formation of cultural identity. Protection of the marine environment with its multiple layers of cultural meaning—symbolic, economic, environmental, and political—is the challenge that faces them today. Political autonomy and cultural identity are on the line as changes to local life-style accelerate and numerous interest groups scheme to expand access to the rich marine resources and strategic passageways of Torres Strait.

The early population in the Torres Strait numbered between three thousand and four thousand residing across the islands and coastal fringes of present-day Papua New Guinea and northern Australia. Prehistorians believe that the early people lived in small groups of twenty-five to forty individuals with social relations defined by kinship. Communal food sharing was routine within these groups, and a patrilineal emphasis on recruitment of the residential groups. Alliances between groups and island populations were formed through marriage and trade, and occasionally these groups joined in warfare against other, more distant peoples in the region.

The culture history of the region represented symbolically in contemporary myths and stories extends back centuries and includes accounts not only of warfare, but of vast trade networks between Torres Strait Islanders and peoples of New Guinea and Australia. The indigenous inhabitants of

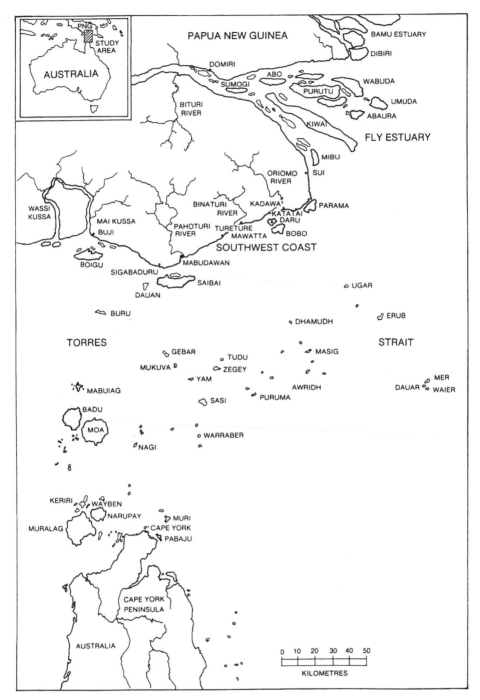

Torres Strait region. Courtesy of Lawrence and Cansfield-Smith, 1991.

the larger Torres Strait region are differentiated by phenotype (physical characteristics) language (Austronesian and non-Austronesian), and culture traits. Nonetheless, they have common culture heroes from the mythical past. This strongly suggests some complementary cultural tradition among the coastal and marine-based island peoples of the Torres Strait region.

The Setting

The Torres Strait is a shallow shelf stretching about ninety-five miles between the island of New Guinea and continental Australia. Separating the Arafura and Coral seas, this narrow passageway has tremendous tidal ranges and strong currents. There are hundreds of islands, extensive coral reefs, submerged rocks, and shifting sandbars between the two landmasses in this archipelago located close to the equator in the southern hemisphere. Many ecological habitats are represented on the land: wet mangrove islands, sandy cays, large high islands with granite outcroppings, and others with ancient rich volcanic soils. Since as long ago as the Pleistocene (Ice Age), when it is hypothesized that humans first had a permanent settlement in this archipelago, there have been a range of subsistence activities practiced. The primary focus and dependency have always been upon the marine habitat.

Traditional Subsistence Strategies

The Torres Strait is dominated by major wet and dry seasons typical of a monsoon climate. The early human inhabitants were highly mobile in their canoes, hunting turtle and dugong and fishing and harvesting many different species from the waters, reefs, and foreshores. Depending upon the local land base, varying greatly between the different types of islands, the people cultivated or collected vegetable foods. The relative location of these different activities varied, depending upon the availability of fresh water sources. Year round, however, human proficiency in extracting from the rich marine base provided adequate protein resources. Little archaeological research has been conducted in the region, but recent findings indicate that middens (accumulation of refuse around a dwelling place) with evidence of marine species are located in rock shelters on some small islands with dates of at least two thousand years and still earlier horticultural sites exist on some of the larger, more fertile islands.

Early visitors and colonizers supply selective snapshots of the recent past. These glimpses vary with the particular perspective of the observer—explorer, entrepreneur, missionary, government official, or researcher. Early newspaper accounts of cannibals and headhunters yielded vivid images of the treacherous water route from the South Pacific through the Torres Strait to Asia. Indeed, numerous shipwrecks, the result of shallow, reef-strewn waterways, provided local inhabitants with new knowledge and commodities, such as iron, which became a major trade item.

By the mid-1800s traders and laborers arrived in Torres Strait to collect from the rich beds of pearl shell, a highly valuable commodity, used for buttons, jewelry, and furniture inlays. Such valuable resources as sandalwood and pearl shell already had been depleted in the South Pacific, where the boom and bust cycle was in a downturn. The Torres Strait offered a new rich marine base as the frontier for expansion in resource extraction. Over the next hundred years the local indigenous people provided labor, and, more significantly, they entrusted local knowledge previously used in subsistence activities to outsiders for the exploitation of more and more marine products from Torres Strait waters.

The various groups within the Torres Strait, whether an entire island, a large extended family group, or a defined community, possess a specialized knowledge explicit to a subsistence zone. These areas are generally acknowledged as belonging to specified individual groups and people know exactly where certain species are located at specific times of the year, moon cycle, and tidal sequence. This type of information applies to subsistence species and commercial ones. Thus, when a hunter goes out to free dive from his aluminum dinghy for *kiar* (tropical rock lobster), he uses time-honored information about the tides and location of a shallow coral outgrowth, an ideal habitat for this valuable species. As well, Torres Strait Islanders distinguish what areas of the marine environment belong to whom among their neighbors. So, a hunter eager to capture dugong for a feast will mention plans to visit a distant reef, recognized as a favorite spot for this particular species, to fellow Islanders, some of whom may be the owners of that particular area. These domains have sustained many intrusions during colonialization. Unaccountably the local management practices and declaration of territorial boundaries in the sea have been tenaciously maintained.

Social and Political Organization

In the 1870s Torres Strait was annexed by Queensland and in 1901 became part of Australia when the Australian states formed a federation. During this thirty-year period many laborers from Asia (Philippines, Malaysia, Indonesia, Japan) and other parts of the Pacific, especially Melanesia (present-day Vanuatu and Solomon Islands), worked out of Thursday Island (Wayben) in the prospering marine industry of Torres Strait. New international labor laws by the British resulted in a repatriation scheme demanding that all South Pacific Islanders return after 1901 to their home islands. Regardless, some chose to remain and primarily through marriage ties were allowed to settle in parts of Queensland and the Torres Strait, where new communities were established. All of the immigrants exerted a significant and long-lasting influence on local politics.

The colonial experience in the Torres Strait was not as traumatic as it was on the mainland for Aboriginal groups. Torres Strait Islanders, for the most part, were not dispossessed of their land or decimated in attacks by settlers. As a result of geographic isolation and an unusual localized paternalistic colonial policy, the Islanders existed within a type of social separatism that had an emphasis on protection not repression. Even so, government agencies defined where the people were allowed to travel, controlled access to their earnings, and restricted whom they could marry. Marriage to non-Islanders was discouraged and church weddings became mandatory. Unlike the Aboriginal people on the mainland of Australia, the Torres Strait Islanders were able to maintain local control and practice ideals of production and exchange in their subsistence activities. Still, similarly to the contemporary situation, commercial fishing was tightly controlled by government and associated business operations dominated by non-Islanders.

Religion and World View

In the prehistory of Torres Strait Islanders, an elaborate totemic classification system prevailed, and body scarification of women using totemic images was practiced. The totems included animals such as the dugong, the mating green turtle, the dog, the snake, the shovel-nosed shark, and the saltwater crocodile. Ritual life was abundant, and within each region groups joined together to perform ceremonies for male initiation and to honor deceased ancestors. Ancestor worship is an important feature of Melanesian cosmology, and the peoples of the Torres Strait used the skulls of deceased relatives for divination.

The arrival of the first recorded missionaries in 1871, now celebrated annually as the "Coming of the Light," marked the establishment of Christianity in the Torres Strait. This introduction to a new moral order by the London Missionary Society (LMS) demanded many changes in the Torres Strait social world. Most of the preachers were from Polynesia (eastern and western Samoa and Niue), where Christianity had already been introduced. They encouraged the small, scattered groups of Torres Strait Islanders to move close to good anchorages, to reside in permanent villages, and to build churches and permanent houses. An array of Pacific culture traits— new crops and gardening techniques, cooking styles, and dances and songs—were also introduced, and for a few decades some traditional ceremonies and dances were forbidden. However, in 1914, the Church of England (Anglican church) took over from the first missionaries; they relaxed the constraints on practicing local customs and trained local islanders to be priests. Then, much later in the 1980s, various evangelical denominations began to proselytize throughout the Torres Strait region. Contemporary world view is a mixture of Christian dogma with traditional cosmology and belief kept active through rituals and interaction with culturally significant sites and story places spread across the vast marine environment.

THREAT TO SURVIVAL

Demographic Trends

The ratio of Torres Strait Islanders resident on the mainland to those resident on the home island in Torres Strait is six to one. Most people who identified themselves in 1997 as Torres Strait Islander (thirty thousand) reside in cities, primarily in the state of Queensland. Among those on the mainland and under thirty years of age, more than 50 percent have never visited the Torres Strait.[1] Many return to the home islands for funerals and the subsequent Tombstone Openings (secondary funeral ceremonies). Earlier rituals involving ancestor worship have been modified and today are part of elaborate celebrations that take place at least one year after the death of a relative. Family members spend large sums of money to purchase an intricately decorated headstone that is ceremoniously unveiled at the grave side and to entertain the many guests. Culturally prescribed dancing and food exchanges are practiced. Those visiting from the mainland may decide to remain for a few months in the islands in order to become acquainted with local traditions. Return migration overall, however, does not account for much population increase in Torres Strait. In the late 1990s, even with the increase in living standards and provision of services on the islands, there were just not enough houses or jobs to encourage large numbers of young people or families to return. Out-migration does, however, continue to serve as an important option, especially for young people and those with major health problems. There is no reason to believe the pattern will significantly change in the future, primarily because increases in the development of infrastructure are limited by the size of home islands, sustainable economic ventures, education, health care, and employment opportunities.

Health

Indigenous Australians, who represent only 2 percent of the total Australian population (19.5 million), have the shortest life expectancy of all citizens. After Aboriginal women, Torres Strait Islanders are the youngest mothers and have the shortest intervals between births of all child-bearing-age women in Australia. Together, these factors lead to high rates of morbidity, or sickness, among younger Torres Strait women. Diabetes, locally considered to be an epidemic, is the most common disease in the population; residents of the outer Torres Strait Islands have more complications of the disease than any other group in Australia. Respiratory infections and accidents are also a major cause of sickness and hospitalization among islanders. The greatest causes of mortality are coronary heart disease, stroke, and carcinomas of the lung and cervix.

A minimal health service became available in Torres Strait after the establishment of a government station in the late 1800s on Thursday Island. Over the next one hundred years there emerged a substandard health service with occasional public health campaigns against malaria and smallpox. A commonly accepted practice was for the wives of teachers, preachers, and other public servants to provide unskilled nursing care in communities where they were resident. Today, the Torres Strait region still suffers from problems inherent to providing services to small population groups in isolated areas. For instance, women may not give birth in their home communities because of the assumed potential risks of childbirth outside a hospital. Local midwives stopped practicing during the 1960s. Also, individuals with severe, chronic ailments and elderly adults without family support are forced to move closer to available health care services. Even common preventative procedures like mammograms, Pap smears, eye examinations, and dental care require travel to Thursday Island or to the mainland. This travel is a contributing factor in the disruption of family life and steady employment for residents of the outer islands.

Citizenship, Migration and International Border

During World War II, Torres Strait Islanders served in a specially created unit of the Australian armed forces, based on Horn Island in Torres Strait. They observed the interactions between black and white soldiers of the U.S. Armed Forces and formed friendships with white soldiers of the Allied Forces, including Australians. After the war, Islanders began to campaign for equality with white Australians and started migrating, although technically illegally, to the mainland, where work opportunities on the railroad and in agriculture, especially sugarcane cultivation, promised better wages. Postwar employment needs increased on the mainland, and the paternalistic government control, at least for Islanders, was not enforced. Then in 1967, a national referendum redefined civil rights for black Australians. This granted all indigenous Australians (Aboriginals and Torres Strait Islanders) full citizenship rights, including the right to vote. It is generally asserted, however, that the federal government failed to force state governments, and in particular that of Queensland, to reform discriminatory policies and practices in indigenous affairs. Therefore, life in the islands remained the same as before the war, economically and politically constrained. Emigration by Torres Strait Islanders to the mainland escalated, and entire families in search of better jobs, health care, and education joined the exodus to southern cities, especially Cairns, Townsville, and Rockhampton, and later Brisbane.

Political representation in the Torres Strait evolved from a nineteenth-century hybrid model combining local, South Pacific, and colonial bureaucratic notions. On the islands councilors were elected in each community and periodically met together with government officials. Such a system was not transferable to the mainland communities, where Torres Strait Islanders were viewed as a Melanesian minority in Australia.

In 1976 when Papua New Guinea (PNG) became independent of Australia, foreign relations between Australia and its former colony took on a new aspect. Immediately, a dispute erupted over the placement of an international maritime border and resulting control of the vast marine resource base in the Torres Strait. Torres Strait Islanders living very near the PNG coastline demanded Australian sovereignty and, indeed, the islands had been considered part of a Torres Strait political region for the preceding hundred years. The PNG government claimed, however, that the border should be at the 10th parallel. Ultimately, when the Torres Strait Treaty was signed in 1985, the border was established within an incredible one and a quarter mile marine corridor along the PNG coastline. It must be kept in mind that the internationally recognized maritime sea rights zone around all sovereign nations is 124 miles. Thus, this new frontier with PNG represents Australia's only close border with another nation. At the time, many of the coastal PNG groups were very upset with this symbolic division between two historically and culturally related populations.

The treaty is fundamentally about resources—fisheries and rights to the seabed. But a special area, the Torres Strait Protected Zone (TSPZ), was created to be jointly managed by the two countries. This vast expanse of rich marine habitat is north of the 10th parallel and includes many Torres Strait Islands and culturally significant places. The TSPZ maintains jurisdiction over all commercial fisheries and *allows for* traditional fishing rights (defined by local legislation in each country). Marine species such as green turtle and dugong, endangered species elsewhere in the world, are hunted only for consumption by indigenous inhabitants and are not to be sold. On the other hand, all commercial fishing is controlled through licensing. Catch limits are established for all species by various scientific advisory groups to the TSPZ management group. Control over these valuable resources, such as the spiny tropical lobster (crayfish), prawns, and trochus (a shell used in similar products to pearl shell), continues to be dominated by nonindigenous fishers, even though some Islanders do fish for these species. Consequently most profits from the Torres Strait marine realm are still retained by outsiders, and the early contact arrangement between local and outsider has been maintained.

Notably, the TSPZ also tightly regulates the movement of all people and goods and restricts the exchange of traditional trade items across the international border, especially goods traveling south from PNG into Australia. Raw materials such as pigs, garden produce (sweet potato, taro, banana), and forest products (feathers for dance costumes and nuts for musical instruments) from PNG present a risk for the spread of disease and pests—they are considered a major quarantine threat. Modern cash crops such as marijuana present other risks and demand a new customs surveillance operation.

A repercussion of the new international border is an alarming economic disparity between old trading partners, the coastal indigenous peoples of Western Province in PNG and the residents of fifteen inhabited islands of Torres Strait in Australia. The social and political structures of the two groups are becoming increasingly alienated. The people of PNG are poor and unable to obtain services or infrastructure support from their own provincial or national governments. They make every effort to travel south across the border for needed manufactured goods, wage labor, and medical services from their Torres Strait neighbors and relatives in Australia.

Until very recently life was hard in the Torres Strait. Access to commercial activities for individual Islanders was barred by the languishing paternalistic government controls. There were substandard water supply, transport, and store goods on the outer islands and minimal education and health services. But, as a result of the new border and creation of the TSPZ, Torres Strait Islanders acquired an improved life-style. A permanent power supply, satellite communications, running water, reliable and varied store supplies, and scheduled air transport from outer islands to Thursday Island, where federal and state government offices have proliferated, and general services and commerce have greatly improved. The Torres Strait as a strategic outpost of Australia entered a new phase in the last decade of the century.

Sociocultural Crises

Economic self-sufficiency in the Torres Strait, similarly to that in other parts of the Pacific, disappeared with the introduction of wage labor. As early as the 1880s, government reports indicate that island communities were unable to produce adequate food supplies. In fact, all able-bodied men from these islands had been recruited to work aboard fishing boats operating long distances away from their home communities. The men were unable to provide the customary subsistence dugong and turtle meats. Instead, in exchange for their labor, they received goods, including tobacco and liquor. The colonial authorities also started to supply outside food goods to the dependents of the laborers. Even later, when the men received minimal wages for their labor, subsidies, in the form of bulk foods, were provided to the families. After World War II, this pattern of wage labor was supplemented with transfer payments (welfare monies) by government social services in order to augment the unreliable employment situation. This ultimately reduced reliance on subsistence and encouraged a welfare dependency that has become the norm. What jobs are available on the islands, as teachers, teacher's aide, nurse's aide, office clerk, store manager, and mechanic, are government service positions. A relatively new scheme, locally referred to as "working for the dole," exists whereby the government provides subsidies to local councils, who in turn pay wages to community members who perform labor on community defined projects. These jobs provide a basic wage but are not perceived by locals to have much status or employment security.

Today subsistence activities, primarily fishing by both men and women, still supply culturally and nutritionally valuable foods—fish, dugong, and turtle. But the diet is mostly foodstuff produced outside the region and purchased in a government owned store. Obesity is common because of a change in activity (less walking in gathering and fishing pursuits) and consumption of a diet high in sugars, fats, and simple carbohydrates. Ideas about nutrition have been formed by a restrictive and an unenlightened market supply system. Until the past few years, there was a lack of culturally appropriate public health messages. Newly trained primary health care workers have begun to focus on antismoking, exercise, and healthy diet programs.

The reciprocal food exchange system from the precontact days has been forever changed. In 1976 the sharing of prestige foods from the sea was the only remnant of the earlier exchange system whereby groups traded items they produced more readily and in return received those items they did not have access to in their local environment. Twenty-five years later, in most communities, close relatives from different households still exchanged needed items, but there exists a clear distinction between store-bought and subsistence goods. Significantly, communal sharing of the prestigious dugong and turtle has become constrained because of the availability of freezers, residence of hunters not socially connected in the community, and competition with commercial fishing activities for hunting time.

Work at sea furnishes more than economic return and sustenance. Travel in the marine environment provides continuity with time-honored cultural domains of the seascape—affinity with places and sites named centuries ago in the stories from ancestors. These locales need customary visits and routinely are checked for natural occurrences or species movement and weather patterns. The information is then integrated into existing models, accumulated over generations of experience, and ultimately dictates behavior of hunters and fishers. Such information traditionally was passed from uncle to nephew and more recently father to son and mother to child, but always within the context of interaction in the marine environment while hunting, fishing or gathering. This cultural immersion in the seascape is not easily passed on to the present-day generation.

Those who grow up on the mainland are deprived of the firsthand experiences in the seascape and therefore of the knowledge and customs of their cultural homeland. On the home islands, a threat to transference of knowledge is the requirement for young people to depart their home island in order to obtain education in grades eight to twelve. While young, children hear myths, folk stories, and legends about cultural heroes, but generally they do not receive specialized knowledge about places and sites. Ideally, a boy's first hunting trip takes place at around fourteen years of age. Teenage girls learn by fishing with aunties and older siblings, but younger girls are customarily restricted to casting a line off the beach in front of their community, and often they are not provided with important knowledge about cultural places until they become adults.

Oral transmission of cultural knowledge has been the means for humans to pass on information for centuries, and only recently have all the new communication forms become available throughout the world. At the close of the twentieth century on the outer islands, Torres Strait school children learned how to read and use computers in Standard Australian English and were able to watch American and British programming on Australian television transmitted through satellite. Outside school children talked together in a local English-based Creole (a local language resulting from acquisition of a subordinate group of languages by a dominant language). While at home many still conversed in a local native language. Education in local schools does not accommodate the local language names for places, or customary patterns of the transference of culturally important information. Once the local language is lost, the accumulated knowledge associated with the places in the seascape could easily disappear.

Environmental Crisis

There are numerous potential environmental threats to the Torres Strait region, and most are related to the marine realm. The Torres Strait seabed is currently protected from development by the PNG Australia Treaty arrangement, which stipulates a moratorium on all mining. The agreement is renegotiated periodically, and many developers believe that rich petroleum reserves on the seabed will be discovered. The use of the sea floor for other purposes is under consideration, in particular with regard to laying a pipeline to transport natural gas. Another potential threat concerns the major international shipping lanes that pass through the Torres Strait, commencing at Bramble Cay in the northeast and terminating near Booby Island in the southwest. Portions of the route for these enormous transoceanic freighters run through rich local fishing areas and narrow passages located between heretofore undefiled coral reefs. A third major environmental threat to the archipelago is pollution from the Trans Fly region in PNG. Baseline monitoring to ascertain levels of dangerous chemicals (e.g., mercury, cadmium) is currently being undertaken on selected species that are locally consumed. Earlier research proposes that chemicals polluting the Fly River had not, as yet, moved south, out of the Fly River delta area into the waters and food chain of the rich fisheries in Torres Strait.

The indigenous residents of the home islands in Torres Strait are concerned about these potential threats to their seascape. The three threats described are each highly contingent upon an array of political jockeying. Indeed, both the PNG and Australian governments want to maintain the current moratorium but are also realistic about future development and the need for economic growth. As well, international laws of the sea and free passage for shipping are critical factors that cannot be ignored when considering any closure of the existing shipping lanes in Torres Strait. There seems little that can be done regarding the Fly River delta environmental crisis except to learn from the mistakes of the past, and, if necessary, provide protection through public health warnings to local consumers of seafood, and, when necessary, restrict commercial production and marketing of seafood.

Current Events

Chevron, a multinational petroleum company, has been prospecting and operating in various PNG projects since the 1980s. Australian and PNG joint ventures including Chevron interests are presently operating on both sides of the international border. A plan has evolved to market natural gas, a side product of petroleum, from fields near Kutubu in Gulf Province, PNG. In years past, elsewhere around the world, this residue from petroleum extraction was burned off, hence the long lasting fires observed around oil drilling sites. Today, environmental standards prohibit this burning and the previous dregs are now a commodity.

The Australian joint venture eager to sell the product has already spent millions of dollars on the planning phase, which includes environmental protection approval along the entire route of the pipeline. Thousands of miles of pipeline will carry natural gas to supply energy for an aluminum smelter. The proposed route includes above-ground and underwater segments from the source at Kutubu in PNG through Torres Strait along the sea bed and from Cape York to Gladstone in the state of Queensland on the mainland of Australia. Whether this particular project succeeds is not really the predominant issue. Instead, it is critical to reflect on how development plans override the interests of local people and to consider what avenues people like the Torres Strait Islanders have when intrusions such as an underwater pipeline are proposed.

RESPONSE: STRUGGLES TO SURVIVE CULTURALLY

There are a variety of responses to the cultural and environmental threats to Torres Strait Islanders' way of life: policy, legislation, and local community initiatives.

Marine Strategy

In 1992 the Marine Strategy for Torres Strait (MaSTS) was designed to complement environmental management provisions set out in the Torres Strait Treaty. It was intended to promote community participation and responsibility for managing their own resources. Ultimately, it aspires to be a vehicle for advancing aims for self-government and greater autonomy for Torres Strait Islanders. MaSTS obtains funding from the Commonwealth government and is the first indigenous community–led marine conservation effort in Australia. By 1999 this strategy served primarily as a mechanism for regional development and conservation planning, in particular linking outer island communities with a range of government assistance and extension programs.

Native Title Claims

In June of 1992, the federal court of Australia ruled in favor of a claim for native title over Murray Island, located in the eastern Torres Strait. This was the first successful native title claim in Australia and marked the abolition of the concept of *terra nullius* ("empty land") whereby the colonists were originally able to claim land in Australia under British law. A group of Torres Strait Islanders, including Eddie Mabo, fought the case (referred to popularly as the "Mabo decision") for over ten years in a struggle to have customary law recognized in the ownership of their land. The resulting legislation provides indigenous people with the right to claim lands, in many cases acquired earlier by pastoralists and developers. As might be expected, there is great debate over the issue, and in the future there will be many contentious political battles about this highly significant legislation.

Furthermore, of major concern are claims to the sea. A regional Torres Strait Sea claim is being developed, to be lodged with the Native Title Tribunal, a federal government agency. The gravity of this issue is reflected in the words of Aven Noah, a Torres Strait Islander media specialist: "These islands have been home for my ancestors, and my people, for thousands of years. And the sea is our home too. It's the sea, more than anything else, that makes us Torres Strait Islanders different."[2]

Torres Strait Regional Authority

From the early colonial period there have been government agencies charged with the care of the indigenous inhabitants of Australia. Until very recently the paternalistic apparatus for social welfare ignored any differentiation between Aboriginal and Torres Strait Islander peoples—they all were under an umbrella of "Aboriginal." Legislation amalgamated many of the services for indigenous people into one federal government agency and established the Aboriginal Torres Strait Islander Commission (ATSIC). Elected commissioners from specified geographic regions are in charge of allocating funds for a range of services and activities to indigenous communities countrywide. Torres Strait Islanders, eager for more local autonomy, were able to secure a separate agency, the Torres Strait Regional Authority (TSRA), in 1994 which represents only residents of Torres Strait and has a budget allocation specified by government. Locally, this is considered a significant step toward autonomy for Torres Strait as it provides a federal bureaucratic structure mandated specifically with local issues. It is physically located in Torres Strait on Thursday Island, not in Brisbane, the capital of Queensland, or Canberra, the national capital of Australia. Torres Strait Islanders resident on the mainland, however, are still represented by ATSIC.

Cultural Festival

One way we can keep our traditions is through song and dance. We islanders are very good at this. Through song and dance we can remember our warrior days, our stories, our religion, historic events and daily life.

Ephraim Bani[3]

For more than a decade an annual festival promoting dance and song has been taking place on Thursday Island. Inspired by participation in a Pacific Arts Festival during the 1980s, Torres Strait Islanders decided to organize a festival of their own. The Cultural Festival is held either during the July or September school break, and dance teams from the various outer island elementary schools participate, as well as adult dance teams. Over the years participants from PNG and other South Pacific islands and Aboriginal groups from other parts of Queensland have performed. Stalls are built from traditional materials, and food and crafts are sold during the three-day event. The Cultural Festival provides a venue for artistic expression and helps maintain continuity with past traditions.

Cultural Heritage

The high school on Thursday Island holds some artifacts in a small museum and local cultural history is often the focus of senior projects. Students

Torres Strait Islander, Brian Whap, assisting in the documentation of ceremonial sites as a team member in a project on community-based management and protection of cultural heritage, 1998, Pulu Island. Courtesy of Judith Fitzpatrick.

might collect oral histories about World War II or the pearl shell industry from their elders. On many of the outer islands community groups sponsor various activities to promote cultural heritage issues. Some have small collections of material culture items on display, very often in the library of the elementary school. Included are artifacts such as war clubs and stone axes, and contemporary wood and shell carvings, drums, paintings, and articles used in dancing.

On one island, a group has formed a nonprofit organization to work on the documentation of culture sites located in their home island land and sea territory. Their island was the site of research conducted more than one hundred years ago, published in *Cambridge Anthropological Expedition to Torres Strait, 1989* (Alfred C. Haddon, editor, 1901–35). The famous expedition has provided the present-day people with photographs and written descriptions of important cultural sites, including rock art, sacred caves, ceremonial dance grounds, middens, and story places. An example of a site of great importance is the grave of Kuiam, a warrior known throughout the region whose death at the hands of his enemies took place near a six-foot-long pile of rocks referred to as his grave. Shells that are considered sacred are placed on top of the rocks. This site, located on a high lookout on Mabuiag Island, has numerous other physical features in the nearby environment associated with stories of Kuiam, the culture hero. The stories are retold to children each generation, and visits to the places are an important part of tradition and custom. Active interaction with the place helps maintain the cultural association. Fewer people are making visits to the sites as a result of changing patterns in schooling for children, employment for adults, and subsistence activities around the island. Thus local cultural heritage management provides some opportunities to maintain connections with the past in addition to protection.

The local grass roots organization is hiring anthropologists to work with them on managing culturally significant places such as those around Kuiam's grave. Some sites, however, are located far from the community. The motivation behind all of the work is to develop a management plan to preserve the culture sites for the future.

FOOD FOR THOUGHT

> If we are to be respected as traditional owners, we need to have ownership of the knowledge that relates to our islands and waters. As Torres Strait Islanders our children need to learn and understand the environment, natural resources and traditions of the region that is our home.
>
> Torres Strait Islands Regional Education Committee, 1989[4]

Protection and management of the marine environment inclusive of culture sites are goals of today's Torres Strait Islanders. The Torres Strait is a place defined primarily by the marine environment, and the Islanders' cultural identity is connected with interaction in the domain of the sea—manifested in stories and symbolic actions; hunting, fishing, and gathering of valuable resources; and traveling to and visiting culturally significant places.

Questions

1. Consider the role of environment in the notion of cultural identity using examples from the Torres Strait. Can you think of other examples from your own society?

2. Looking into the future in Torres Strait, what are some possible effects of the implementation of the pipeline project? Discuss both positive and negative outcomes for the indigenous inhabitants of the outer islands of Torres Strait and the people in PNG. It might be useful to consider the following options with regard to the gas pipeline in your discussion: Instead of exporting the natural gas to Australia in order to use it for a manufacturing scheme, why not utilize the gas in PNG, where most people cut down trees for cooking? Or, why not build a manufacturing plant fueled by natural gas in PNG and process local raw

materials, thereby creating jobs in a country with widespread youth unemployment and violence?

3. Great changes have been made to the traditional way of life of Torres Strait Islanders since the coming of the Europeans. Discuss some of the recent benefits of the European influence.

4. Why is modern education a threat to indigenous people? Discuss how Torres Strait Islanders may overcome some of the risks to their threatened culture.

5. Discuss factors that affect the lives of local people with regard to quarantine and customs issues in an international border such as that between PNG and Australia in the Torres Strait.

NOTES

1. House of Representatives Standing Committee on Aboriginal Torres Strait Islander Affairs, *Torres Strait Islanders: A New Deal—a Report on Greater Autonomy for Torres Strait Islanders* (Canberra: Parliament of the Commonwealth of Australia, 1997), p. xv.

2. Aven Noah, *The Torres Strait Islanders: Teacher's Manual and Student Study Guide*, Australian Today Series, compiled by Joann Schmider and Ian Pattie (Lismore, New South Wales, Australia: Northern Star Press, 1991) p. 21.

3. Ephraim Bani, *Our Culture: Maintenance and Preservation of Torres Strait Culture*, Workshop, January 22–24, 1992, Island Coordinating Council (ICC), Thursday Island, Queensland, Australia (author attended workshop and took notes).

4. Torres Strait Islands Regional Education Committee (TSIREC), *The Torres Strait Islanders: Teacher's Manual and Student Study Guide*, Australian Today Series, compiled by Joann Schmider and Ian Pattie (Lismore, New South Wales, Australia: Northern Star Press, 1991), p. 3.

RESOURCE GUIDE

Published Literature

Beckett, Jeremy. "The Murray Island Case," Special Issue on Western Oceania: Caring for the Ancestral Domain. *CS Quarterly* 15(2): 16–17, 1991.

Beckett, Jeremy. *Torres Strait Islanders: Custom and Colonialism*. Cambridge: Cambridge University Press, 1987.

Cordell, John and Judith Fitzpatrick. "Cultural Identity and the Sea." *CS Quarterly* 11(2): 15–17, 1987.

Fitzpatrick, Judith. "Home Reef Fisheries Development: A Report from Torres Strait," Special Issue on Western Oceania: Caring for the Ancestral Domain. *CS Quarterly* 15(2): 18–20, 1991.

Fitzpatrick, Judith. "Obstetric Health Services in Far North Queensland." *Australian Journal of Public Health* 19(6): 580–588, 1995.

Haddon, Alfred C. *Reports of the Cambridge Anthropological Expedition to Torres Strait (1901–1935)*, 6 vols. Cambridge: Cambridge University Press, 1935.

Lawrence, D. and T. Cansfield-Smith, *Sustainable Development for Traditional Inhabitants of the Torres Strait Region.* Proceedings of the Torres Strait Baseline Study Conference, Cairns, 1990. Townsville: Great Barrier Reef Marine Park Authority, 1991.

Films and Videos

Cracks in the Mask, Talking Pictures, Frances Calvert, 1997. Videocassette (VHS) (55 minutes), sd., color ½ inch, 35mm, color (55 minutes). Writer and director: Frances Calvert. Producers: Lindsey Merrison and Frances Calvert for WDR Germany, SF DRS. Subjects: Protection of cultural property, in Australia, anthropology of Queensland and the Torres Strait Islands.

Mabo, Film Australia, 1997. 16 mm (87 minutes), sd., color. Coproducer/director: Trevor Graham. Coproducer/editor: Denise Haslem. Executive producer: Sharon Connolly, Sydney, Australia. Subjects: Torres Strait Islanders, Native Title Act claim, Queensland, Eddie Koiki Mabo.

Land Blong Islanders, Australian Broadcasting Corporation, 1993. Videocassette (VHS) (52 minutes), sd., color, ½ inch. Writer/director: Trevor Graham. Producer: Sharon Connolly, Sydney, Australia. Subjects: Torres Strait Islanders, land tenure, law and legislation, Queensland.

WWW Sites

Cambridge Museum of Archaeology and Anthropology homepage, Cambridge, United Kingdom, Torres Strait Islanders exhibition
http://cumaa.archanth.cam.ac.uk

Island Coordinating Council (representative for Torres Strait Islander; manages research, conservation, and cultural affairs), Thursday Island, Queensland 4875, Australia
IslandCoordCouncil@bigpound.com.au

Torres Strait Regional Authority (federal body representing all communities in Torres Strait; manages funding for infrastructure and development in region), Thursday Island, Queensland 4875, Australia
TSRA@atsic.gov.au

Organization

Torres Strait Islander Media Association (TSIMA)
Thursday Island
Queensland 4875
Australia

Newspaper

Torres News Weekly News Bulletin
Torres News Pty. Ltd.
P.O. Box 436
Thursday Island
Queensland 4875
Australia
Fax: 61–740691561

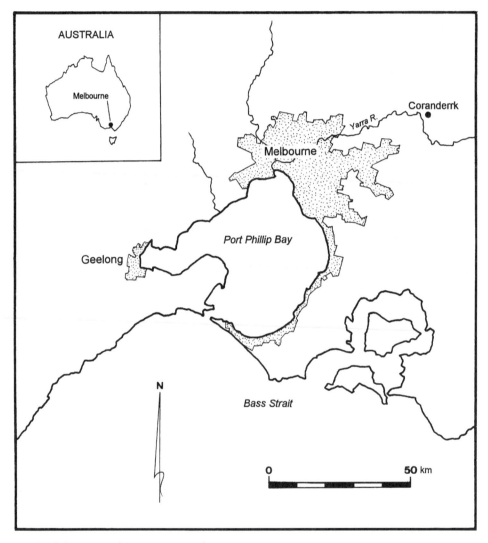

Lands of the Wurundjeri. Courtesy of Ian J. McNiven.

Chapter 16

The Wurundjeri of Melbourne, Australia

Lynette Russell and Ian J. McNiven

CULTURAL OVERVIEW

The People

The Wurundjeri are the Aboriginal people of the lands that surround Port Phillip Bay on the southeast corner of Australia. Much of this land is now taken up by Melbourne, the capital of the State of Victoria and the second largest city in Australia (after Sydney). *Wurundjeri* is the clan name used by speakers of the Woiwurrung language of the Melbourne region; *Koorie* is the popular, generic name for contemporary Aboriginal people of southeastern Australia. Over the last 160 years, the Wurundjeri have had to contend with colonial dispossession and the covering of their lands by concrete and asphalt. Despite this, the Wurundjeri maintain spiritual and cultural ties to their lands and continue to reassert their role as the traditional owners of the region. Indeed, the Wurundjeri have maintained one of the longest-running struggles by any indigenous group in Australia against colonial dispossession and oppression.

The tenacity of Wurundjeri in their struggle to survive is matched by archaeological evidence for long-term Aboriginal occupation of the region back to forty thousand years ago. During these early times, lowered sea levels placed the coastline some 124 miles from its present position, and the ancestors of the Wurundjeri shared their then-cooler and -drier landscape with a number of now-extinct marsupials such as giant kangaroos and the hippopotamus-sized Diprotodon. Remarkably, the subsequent rising of sea levels and the creation of Port Phillip Bay some six thousand years ago are recalled in local stories:

Murray, an Aborigine, assured me that the passage up the bay, through which the ships came, is the Yarra River, and that the river once went out at the heads, but that the sea broke in, and that Hobson's Bay [baylet within Port Phillip Bay] which was once hunting ground, became what it is. (William Hull, 1858)[1]

The world of the Wurundjeri was shattered in 1835 when British colonists sailed into Port Phillip Bay and settled the region. The focus of activity was Melbourne, and as it grew so did pastoral expansion into surrounding river valleys. Unaccustomed to European diseases such as the common cold, many Wurundjeri died within the first decade of European occupation. Other Wurundjeri were murdered. The destruction of forests also destroyed traditional food resources, and the remaining Wurundjeri found themselves dependent upon the newcomers for food, shelter, and work. In the 1860s, the government established Coranderrk Mission Station as a refuge for the Wurundjeri. The station became a new social, political, and cultural focus for the people, a position it holds to this day. Although the Wurundjeri lived a quiet existence on the margins of European society for the next one hundred years, in recent decades their economic and political profile has been elevated considerably through a wide range of community initiatives. These initiatives are explored further in this chapter.

The Setting

Wurundjeri lands take in Port Phillip Bay and the Yarra River drainage basin to the north. Their region experiences a temperate climate with warm, dry summers and cool, wet winters. The mean monthly temperatures for Melbourne range from 55°F in winter to 79°F during summer. The swamps and marshes that were a feature of the lower Yarra River plains have been replaced mostly by Melbourne's streetscape. Farmland interspersed with remaining areas of eucalypt forest can be seen across the hills and mountains behind Melbourne. Although all Wurundjeri mourn the loss of native plants and animals from their traditional territory, the land itself remains, as does their deep spiritual attachment to it.

Traditional Subsistence Strategies

The Wurundjeri were a hunting and gathering people who moved their campsites in response to the seasonal availability of resources. Wetlands of the lower Yarra were a rich source of water birds, fish, and plant foods, particularly in summer. Emus and kangaroos were hunted on surrounding plains and grasslands by men using wooden spears and boomerangs. From these plains, tubers of *murnong* (a local staple) along with a wide range of other plant foods were collected by women using digging sticks and woven baskets. From the northern forested valleys, possums could be cut from hollow trees with stone axes or simply knocked out of trees with throwing clubs. Possum skins were sewn together to form the distinctive large cloaks of the Wurundjeri. Wallabies, kangaroos, wombats, and koalas were also hunted within the forests during winter. The Yarra River was an important source of fish, particularly the short-finned eel, which was caught using stone dams. Port Phillip Bay supplied fish and seals, and a wide range of shellfish were collected from tidal flats and rocky platforms.

Social and Political Organization

The basic unit of Woiwurrung society was a clan based upon families who traced descent through the father's side. Clans belonged to one of two groups (or moieties), either *bunjil* (eaglehawk) or *waa* (crow), and clan members obtained spouses from an opposite moiety. Clan heads gained their position by demonstrating competence to other clan members. The Wurundjeri, along with other groups of central western Victoria, belonged to a confederacy of tribes known as *Kulin*. At certain times of the year various Kulin groups would meet to perform ceremonial dances (corroborees), exchange goods, arrange marriages, and discuss various social and political issues.

Today, the extended family forms the core of Wurundjeri social life. As in the past, community leaders gain their position through life experience and through respect earned from other members of their community. The two main political organizations of the Wurundjeri are the Wurundjeri Tribe Land Compensation and Cultural Heritage Council Incorporated and the Halesville and District Aboriginal Cooperative. Most official government and commercial dealings with the Wurundjeri are conducted through these two organizations.

Religion and World View

Very little is known of the religious and spiritual life of the Wurundjeri, because of the devastating impact of European settlement and the secrecy with which it was often surrounded. It seems clear that the formation of the world was attributed largely to *Bunjil*, an ancestral being. Today, the Wurundjeri cosmological view also attributes to other creator beings of the Dreaming (time of creation) the formation of the landscape, plants, animals, and people. Such beliefs imbue the landscape with structure and deep spiritual meaning. Following tradition, senior Wurundjeri know it is their responsibility to take care of their lands and culture sites out of respect for their ancestors and for the benefit of future generations.

Group of Aboriginal men at Coranderrk, 1858. From the Daintree/Fauchery collection, circa 1858. Courtesy of the La Trobe Picture Collection, State Library of Victoria, Australia.

THREATS TO SURVIVAL

Demographic Trends in the Last Two Hundred Years

[I] visited the Black's Camp South of the Yarra this morning—several of them are suffering from syphilis, dysentery, etc. Five or six have recently died.

James Dredge, Aboriginal Protector, 1839[2]

Estimating the number of Wurundjeri before European contact in the early 1800s is difficult because of the unknown impacts of sealers and whalers who frequented the region prior to official colonization in 1835. Thus, whereas the number of Wurundjeri within five years of European settlement was put at three hundred to four hundred, it is likely this figure is very conservative as smallpox and other diseases, not to mention murder and massacres by the newcomers, had already taken a devastating toll. The government was unable to control the murderous activities of some colonists in the early years of settlement as a result of a conspiracy of silence on the frontier and the simple fact that Aboriginal evidence was not accepted in courts. A high mortality rate plus a high sterility rate from venereal diseases transmitted by European men caused the Aboriginal population of Victoria to plummet from an estimated fifteen thousand in 1835 to only nineteen hundred in 1863 and a mere eleven hundred in 1877. In major settlements such as Melbourne, Aboriginal people became reduced to living on the edges of urban development, where they became known as "fringe-dwellers." Many Wurundjeri fell prey to alcoholism, prostitution, and petty crime. In 1863, a government census recorded thirty-three Aboriginal people for the Melbourne district. In 1877, five Aboriginal people remained in the Melbourne district.

Between 1876 and 1912, the main cause of death for Victorian Aboriginal people living on government stations was respiratory diseases, followed by "senile decay." The single largest killer was tuberculosis, which accounted for 38 percent of adult deaths. Between 1850 and 1960, the infant mortality rate decreased dramatically from around 50 percent to less than 5 percent of all births.[3] These high mortality rates, plus a desire for more children and early marriages, may help account for the fact that in Victoria today, Aboriginal people often have much larger families than the rest of the community. However, large families have not translated into major population increases as Aboriginal people continue to have the poorest health, highest infant mortality rates, and lowest life expectancy of any ethnic/racial group in Australia. The current Koorie population of Victoria is around seventeen thousand, of whom nine thousand live in the Melbourne metropolitan region.

Dispossession

Blackfellows all about say that no good have them pickaninneys [babies] now, no country for blackfellows like long time ago.

Billi-bellari, Woiwurrung leader, 1843[4]

In 1835, John Batman and his party of colonists from Tasmania were some of the first Europeans to settle in the Port Phillip district. Upon arriving, Batman entered into an agreement with Wurundjeri leaders whereby he believed that he obtained the rights to some 600,000 acres of land in exchange for a yearly tribute of blankets, flour, tools, and beads. This so-called treaty has been called a farce as Aboriginal Australians had no concept of clan lands as a salable commodity. Furthermore, Australia represented the only major British colony where native title rights were not acknowledged and treaties were not made with indigenous groups.

By 1840, thousands of Europeans occupied Wurundjeri territory, and essentially all of their lands had some form of European occupancy. The Wurundjeri did what they could to resist the invasion including the destruction of valuable sheep flocks and the killing of at least fifty-nine Europeans in the greater Port Phillip District by 1850. European frustration with these activities resulted in the establishment of a native police force in 1842, and the local Aboriginal population paid dearly with their lives. By 1851, the colony of Victoria was inhabited by 77,000 Europeans, 391,000 cattle and 6,590,000 sheep. By 1861, the number of Europeans had risen to 540,000 and the lands of the Wurundjeri, like those of their neighbors, had been overrun by colonists and their grazing animals.

Environmental Destruction

I could not but feel for the poor blacks. They had till this visit an undisturbed range among lagoons and supplied themselves for a month or 5 weeks, now one side of the Yarra is forever closed to them.

William Thomas, Aboriginal Protector, 1841[5]

Dispossession of the Wurundjeri also went hand in hand with major destruction of their cultural setting. Forested areas to the north of Melbourne were cleared extensively in the nineteenth century to supply timber for Melbourne and to allow the establishment of agricultural fields. In the new settlement of Melbourne, trees were cleared, swamps were drained, creek channels were altered, and the habitats for most of the traditional resources used by the Wurundjeri were destroyed. Thus, the complex mosaic of resource zones that had been used by hundreds of generations of Wurundjeri was replaced by an ever-expanding maze of cobblestone streets lined with factories, shops, and houses. In 1840 the population of Melbourne was 4,000. The city grew rapidly to nearly 30,000 people in 1851, and by 1900 it crossed the 500,000 mark. Today, the city's population stands at 3,300,000 with some suburbs supporting over 8,000 people/square mile.

Destruction of Cultural Heritage Sites

A potent force in any process of dispossession is the destruction of cultural heritage sites. Among the trees and along many creek banks now subsumed by Melbourne was a complex array of campsites, resource extraction sites, ceremonial sites, sacred sites, and a wide range of other places imbued with deep spiritual meaning to the Wurundjeri. Today the Wurundjeri manage and preserve their culture sites. Site preservation extends to known historical sites (e.g., Coranderrk Mission Station) and to sites revealed by archaeological research, particularly those uncovered by development. Indeed, archaeological research since the 1980s has revealed hundreds of old campsites in the form of scatters of stone tools along creek banks and piles of shells (middens) along the shores of Port Phillip Bay. These sites represent a tangible link with their ancestors and an acknowledgment of their past, present, and future ties to the land.

Sociocultural Crisis

The sociocultural threats of disease, dispossession, premature death, death in custody, and unemployment remain significant issues for contemporary Aboriginal people throughout Australia. The forced removal of Aboriginal children from their families has had a devastating impact on the Wurundjeri, as well as other Aboriginal groups. The separation of families began in the nineteenth century and continued until recent times.

In May 1997 a Human Rights Commission report, *Bringing Them Home*, examined the social impacts of the removal of Aboriginal children from their families. These children, known as the "stolen generation," were taken from their parents in the belief that they could be raised as white people and assimilated into the broader community. The motives for these actions were the paternalistic belief that Aboriginal people could not adequately care for their children and the widely held opinion that Aborigines were a dying race. The impact of the separation of children from their families has been horrific. The incidence of stress-related psychological trauma is high, and many of the commission's informants have been deeply and permanently scarred by their experiences.

Australia has a shocking record of Aboriginal people's dying in either police or institutional custody. In 1988, the Royal Commission into Aboriginal Deaths in Custody released its findings. During the period 1980–88, ninety-nine Aboriginal people died while held in the custody of the police or judicial system. The commission looked at not only the individual circumstances of each death, but also the economic, social, and political reasons that led to the high rate of Aboriginal involvement in the criminal justice system. The recommendations of the commission were adopted by the Victorian government, and numerous centers were set up around the state to deal with Koories in crisis. Legislative changes were put in place to ensure the police contact the Victorian Aboriginal Legal Service whenever they deal with Koories. Many of the commission's recommendations are yet to be implemented. Despite the commission and the changes outlined, Aboriginal people continue to die in custody: A further fifty-nine Aboriginal people, across Australia, died in police custody in the period 1990–95. The legal and criminal justice system continues to present a major sociocultural crisis for Aboriginal Australians.

Generations of government oppression and lack of opportunity have meant that Aboriginal Australians suffer some of the worst health in the country. In response to this crisis, the Aboriginal people of Melbourne have successfully pushed for the establishment of Koorie health and medical services. These services are run and staffed by Koories and people sensitive to the needs of the indigenous population.

Koorie communities witness extremely high rates of unemployment, particularly among the younger generations. Education and training, which are vital for employment, have been one of the focuses of the Wurundjeri. Many young Koories now receive university education and training that will allow access equity and enable them to compete for jobs.

RESPONSE: STRUGGLES TO SURVIVE CULTURALLY

The arrival of white settlers on the banks of the Yarra River in 1835 was the beginning of the destruction of the traditional life of the Wurundjeri. The initial contact was with John Batman and his party, who attempted to negotiate a treaty with the Wurundjeri. For the next twenty years they were dispersed, rounded up, and placed in forced settlements. In 1859 a group of elders and important men from the Kulin nation approached William Thomas, the protector of the aborigines in the state of Victoria, and requested that they be allowed to establish a community of their own on a property reserved for this purpose and selected by the headmen themselves. Acheron Station, located approximately 50 miles northwest of Melbourne, was set aside for this purpose. Soon after, the colonial government moved the reserve to Mohican Station and appointed a white trustee as an administrator. Both stations were a failure. Discontented with the interference of white people, both government and nongovernment, the Wurundjeri leaders, Simon Wonga and William Barak, led their people south in 1863 to the newly gazetted Coranderrk Aboriginal Mission Station. Within four months of settling, the community had constructed nine of their own houses, and later they built a school and other buildings.

Money was raised through the sale of vegetables, animal fur cloaks, rugs, baskets, and other artifacts. The community was self-sufficient and was held up as a model for future station ventures. Crops were planted and cattle supplied both meat and milk. Hunting continued and the diet was supplemented by traditional means. Work on the station was communal and families exchanged labor for supplies such as sugar, tea, and flour. The Koories who settled here had a sense of achievement, as this was a community that had chosen the spot for their settlement, constructed their own homes, and believed that their future was theirs to control.

John Green, the government-appointed superintendent of Coranderrk, was supportive of the Aborigines' desire to be self-sufficient and self-governing. Green was also concerned by the constant threats to move the station and relocate the community elsewhere. Unfortunately his view did not win him popularity with government, and in 1875 he was dismissed and the Board for the Protection of Aborigines closed the station. A well-publicized deputation of Aboriginal people from Coranderrk, led by William Barak, approached the government and argued their case to stay on at Coranderrk. A number of sympathetic locals were also supportive of the community's desire to stay where they chose. An eventual victory was had, and the Aboriginal community was allowed to stay. This struggle for land and self-determination has been described as the first organized protest movement by an Australian Aboriginal group in the postfrontier period.

Unfortunately, interference in the community's affairs continued. An appendix to the 1882 report by the board to "Enquire into, and Report Upon, the Condition and Management of the Coranderrk Station" stated that the opinions of the Aboriginal people should be disregarded as they must be, from the nature of the case, the least capable of all persons to decide how or by whom the station should be managed. These views were held despite the acknowledgment that the Aboriginal community of Coranderrk believed the station to legally belong to them.

The Aborigines Protection Act, often referred to as the *Half-Caste Act*, was passed in 1886, and all Aboriginal people of mixed descent, and over thirty-four years of age, were removed from the station environment and merged into the wider community. The removal of many of the able-bodied young men and women from Coranderrk meant that the work force was dramatically reduced, the station community became considerably less able to sustain themselves, and farming was abandoned. In 1893 half of the lands at Coranderrk were sold to outsiders. By the early years of the twentieth century the board began to reduce drastically the number of Aboriginal stations across Victoria. Many of the communities were so attached to their land, which in most cases they had been led to believe belonged to them, that their removal was only enforceable by the stopping of rations.

In 1903 the leader of Coranderrk, William Barak, died and was buried at his beloved Coranderrk. In 1917 the state government determined to close all Aboriginal stations except Lake Tyers Station in far eastern Victoria, to which all Victoria Aboriginal people, living on reserves, would be moved. Coranderrk had 150 Aboriginal residents, although this number varied because of the transient population. On closure, Aboriginal people were moved to a range of places including Lake Tyers. It took until 1923 for the board to hold a clearing sale at Coranderrk in the belief that the Aboriginal people associated with the station were to move on. In 1924 the board officially agreed to allow six Aboriginal people to remain living on the site of the old Station. Unofficially many more Wurundjeri remained at Coranderrk. The local police officer was made a nominated local guardian of Aborigines, and he issued rations to those who refused to move to Lake Tyers. Even though the government had removed the Wurundjeri and other Aboriginal people from Coranderrk, in their unseemly eagerness to obtain land they initially failed to revoke the grant of land in accordance with legal requirements. Thus, to sell off the last 1,432 acres of reservation land for a World War II soldier settlement program, the government had to introduce legislation in 1948 to remedy the situation (Coranderrk Lands Act 1948). Up until this time it was arguable that post-1863 grants of Coranderrk lands to non-Aboriginal people were invalid. All that remained of the station by the 1970s were the cemetery and residence of the former managers.

In spite of the government land grab, the connection the Wurundjeri had with Coranderrk remained strong and many Wurundjeri continued to reside near it or visit whenever possible. In particular the cemetery was the site of many visits. After the 1967 referendum that enfranchised Aboriginal Australians and allowed the federal government to legislate on Aboriginal issues, many more Wurundjeri returned to their homelands. Today, the Wurundjeri maintain their attachment to their land, and especially to the Coranderrk site, by relaying its importance to their children and taking an active part in the community surrounding the area. In 1988 the cemetery was handed over to the Wurundjeri community, an action designed to coincide with Australia's European bicentenary celebrations.

Native Title

On June 3, 1992, the High Court of Australia ruled on what became known widely as the Mabo decision. This decision, for the first time in the history of Australia, recognized that Aboriginal Australians had native title rights over the country they maintained they owned. Up until this point, the acquisition of Australia by European settlers had rested on an assumption of *terra nullius*, which means literally "empty land." The High Court decision had implications for all of indigenous Australians as it meant that British possession and sovereignty exerted in 1770 did not automatically extinguish native title. All Crown land that had not been alienated was in theory available for native title claims. Unfortunately for those Aboriginal communities whose traditional lands were now cities and other populated areas, native title claims would be difficult to uphold. In 1993 the federal government developed the Native Title Act, which established a native title office of the federal court whose sole responsibility would be to legislate on land claims. The act also provided access to compensation for those groups whose land was lost to the native title process, with the establishment of the Indigenous Land Council. In March 1998 the Indigenous Land Council purchased the mission house and 200 acres at Coranderrk; thus, the Wurundjeri people now own a small portion of their traditional territory.

Reconciliation

Reconciliation between Australia's Aboriginal and immigrant communities is considered to be a vital component of Australia's aspirations for the future. In 1991, with unanimous support of Parliament, the Council for Aboriginal Reconciliation was established. In the Melbourne area the Wurundjeri have played an important role in the process of reconciliation, working with local, state, and federal governments to implement the aims of reconciliation. Justice and equality have been the aims of this work, with cross-cultural education and awareness the main mechanisms. Cross-cultural programs have been established by Aboriginal education officers attached to the Department of Education. Similar programs have also been developed for local government officers across the state.

The road to reconciliation is not easy, but the Wurundjeri have shown a commitment that will in time ensure Aboriginal heritage issues are given standing. Any agreement will need to strike a balance of non-Aboriginal law, the High Court's recognition of native title, and Aboriginal law. In the past there has often been a reluctance to acknowledge Aboriginal law and knowledge. The Wurundjeri, through their commitment to reconciliation, are committed to reaching that balance.

Cultural Centers

Over the past decade many Aboriginal people have begun education projects aimed at informing the wider community on Aboriginal issues. Two cultural interpretation centers operate within the Wurundjeri homelands, providing venues for Koorie artists and exhibitions. *Galeena beek* ("To love the earth") is a cultural center in Healesville near Coranderrk. In metropolitan Melbourne, the Koorie Heritage Trust acts as a focus for the repatriation of cultural materials and often negotiates and acts as liaison between museums and other institutions and the Aboriginal community. The Koorie Heritage Trust has as its motto "*Gnokan Danna Murra Kor-*

Ki," which means, "Give me your hand my friend and bridge the cultural gap."

Reclaiming the Cultural Landscape

In the 1990s the Wurundjeri instigated a program of identifying Aboriginal culture sites throughout their homelands, with a focus on Melbourne. Many of these places are now highlighted by signs that proclaim the Aboriginal identity of the Melbourne landscape. This enables tourists and non-Aboriginal inhabitants to see Melbourne and the surrounding districts as an Aboriginal cultural landscape. Past ceremonial sites, corroboree (group meeting) sites, and hunting grounds are all identified even if they are now beneath layers of asphalt and concrete. At the Victoria Market a plaque commemorates the Koories buried at the first Melbourne General Cemetery during the first years of European settlement. This colonial cemetery became the site of the market, and although many bodies were relocated, the Aboriginal section of the cemetery was not touched. The Wurundjeri considered it an act of desecration to touch these graves, and agreement was reached between the Wurundjeri elders and the Melbourne City Council. This agreement is considered to herald a new phase in race relations in Victoria. At Kings Domain, near the National Gallery of Victoria, thirty-eight Aboriginal people were finally laid to rest in 1985; these remains had been held at the Museum of Victoria for decades. The Wurundjeri were committed to the reburial of these people and a plaque with the following words marks this site:

> Rise from this Grave
> Release your anger and pain
> As you soar with the winds
> Back to our homelands
> There find peace with our
> Spiritual Mother The Land
> Before drifting off into the
> Dreamtime.

Other sites reclaimed by the Wurundjeri include a walking trail, a "bush foods" trail, and the site of the infamous and false Batman treaty, an unjust agreement. The Koorie walking trail was designed by the Wurundjeri, in close cooperation with the Melbourne City Council. It is targeted at tourists and identifies eight significant sites within the city of Melbourne. The most recent and perhaps the most powerful action of reclamation for the Wurundjeri was the purchase of Coranderrk Station for the Wurundjeri. An official handing-back ceremony is to be held in 2000.

FOOD FOR THOUGHT

Questions

1. Why would the Wurundjeri wish to influence development across Melbourne when most of this area is now a concrete jungle covered with houses, shops, factories, and asphalt roads?

2. How do fencing off and sign posting selected archaeological sites within Melbourne help enhance non-Aboriginal people's appreciation of Wurundjeri spiritual ties to their land?

3. Should the Wurundjeri be given greater powers to influence town planning in Melbourne?

4. What approach should a Wurundjeri cultural center/museum within Melbourne take to promote contemporary Aboriginal views as opposed to merely memorializing the past?

5. As required in Native Title claims, should contemporary Wurundjeri people be asked to document their family ties back to the time of European settlement in order to demonstrate cultural authenticity?

NOTES

1. W. Hull, Evidence in "Report of the Select Committee of the Legislative Council on the Aborigines, 1858–59." *Victorian Legislative Council Votes and Proceedings* (Melbourne: Government Printer, 1858).

2. J. Dredge, Diary, MS Collection, La Trobe Library, Melbourne, 1837–39.

3. Diane E. Barwick, "Changes in the Aboriginal Population of Victoria, 1863–1966," in *Aboriginal Man and Environment in Australia*, D. J. Mulvaney and J. Golson (eds.) (Canberra: Australian National University Press, 1971), pp. 288–315.

4. Cited in S. W. Wiencke, *When the Wattles Bloom Again: The Life and Times of William Barak, Last Chief of the Yarra Yarra Tribe* (Woori Yallock: Shirley W. Wiencke, 1984).

5. W. Thomas, Private Papers, 16 volumes and 8 boxes of papers, journals, letterbooks, reports, etc., uncatalogued manuscripts, set 214, items 1–24, Mitchell Library, Sydney, n.d.

RESOURCE GUIDE

Published Literature

Eidelson, M. *The Melbourne Dreaming: A Guide to the Aboriginal Places of Melbourne.* Canberra: Aboriginal Studies Press/Aboriginal Affairs Victoria, 1997.

Horton, D., ed. *The Encyclopaedia of Aboriginal Australia*. Canberra: Aboriginal Studies Press, 1997.

Presland, G. *The Land of the Kulin: Discovering the Lost Landscape and the First People of Port Phillip*. Fitzroy: McPhee/Gribble, 1985.

Wiencke, S. W. *When the Wattles Bloom Again: The Life and Times of William Barak, Last Chief of the Yarra Yarra Tribe*. Woori Yallock: Shirley W. Wiencke, 1984.

Films and Videos

Living Aboriginal History, Bendigo, Victoria, Video Education Australasia, 1991. The program "Koorie culture, Koorie control" is entirely spoken by Koories, who give their account of the changes and history of their culture since white settlement began. People of the lake look at the culture of the Kerupjmara people, the impact of European settlement, the resistance and the submission of the Kerupjmara to life on Lake Condah Mission. Format: VHS, color. Rating: G.

Victoria's First Settlers, Ministry of Education, Victoria, 1986. The state historian of Victoria, Mr. Bernard Barrett, talks to Trevor Lunn about Victoria's Aboriginal past, the first British visitors, sealers and whalers, and the settlements at Portland and Melbourne. Format: VHS, color. Rating: G, Adolescents (thirteen to fifteen years of age).

Voices in the Wind, Shepparton, Victoria, Pronesti Productions & Merle Publications, 1991 "Voices in the Wind" is an Aboriginal multidisciplinary cultural education kit. The video of the play depicts a Koori family's twenty-seven-year struggle in the Goulburn area, northeast Victoria. Format: VHS, color. Rating: G.

When Dreaming Paths Meet, Golden Seahorse Productions for Dept. of Health & Community Services, 1994. This program aims to promote cross-cultural awareness and explores situations in which the actions of Aboriginal people have been misinterpreted by non-Aboriginal people in a work environment. Three scenarios highlight body language differences in a youth custody situation, bereavement issues, and community relations. At the conclusion of each scene, Richard Frankland summarizes and discusses proactive measures that can be implemented to prevent such cross-cultural problems in the future. Designed to be used by non-Aboriginal professionals to promote an understanding of cultural issues. Format: VHS, color. Rating: G, Adolescents (thirteen to fifteen years of age).

WWW Site

The Australian Painting Collection at the National Gallery of Victoria on Russell
www.ngv.vic.gov.au/landscap/barak.html

Organizations

Galeena beek
Living Cultural Centre and Keeping Place
P.O. Box 242
Healesville, Victoria 3777
Australia

Healesville and District Aboriginal Cooperative
P.O. Box 457
Healesville, Victoria 3777
Australia

Koorie Heritage Trust
328 Swanston Street
Melbourne, Victoria 3000
Australia

Wurundjeri Tribe Land Compensation and Cultural Heritage Council Incorporated
P.O. Box 26
Boolara, Victoria 3870
Australia

Glossary

Affines—relatives through marriage (in Anglo-American kinship, these affinal relatives are known as *in-laws*)

Atoll—coral reef appearing above the sea as a low ring-shaped coral island or a chain of closely spaced coral islets around a shallow lagoon that may vary in diameter from less than a mile to eighty miles or more (e.g., Morovo, Rangiroa)

Breadfruit—large round seedless fleshy tropical fruit that grows on a very tall tree (when baked, it resembles "bread" in color and texture)

Copra—dried coconut meat processed through a sun or oven drying technique (used primarily as a cash crop and sold for use in the production of soap and cosmetics, margarine, and explosives)

Corroboree—a social gathering of Australian Aboriginals, often with songs and symbolic dance

Custom—synonym in Pacific is *Kastom*

Endogamy—rule or preference that individuals marry only within their particular kinship group, social group, or other defined category (locality, class, religion, and so on)

Exogamy—prohibition of marriage between members of specific groups

Gerontocratic—form of government in which old men of the community are rulers because of their powers, wisdom, and prestige

Lineage—a group of persons tracing descent from a common ancestor who is regarded as its founder

Manioc—(also known as cassava, tapioca plant) any of several plants cultivated throughout the tropics having fleshy rootstocks yielding a starchy food staple

249

Glossary

Pandanus—nut tree of the tropics; nuts are a source of food and the large leaves are used as roofing, temporary raincoats, and woven baskets

Patrilateral—kinship system whereby descent is only traced through the males (Note: patrilineal descent [or agnatic descent] in which inheritance passes from a father to his children)

Pidgin—a form of speech with a limited often mixed vocabulary and is used principally for intergroup communication

Poi—food made of taro root that is cooked and pounded and kneaded into a smooth starchy paste traditionally eaten with the fingers (a food source in Samoa and Hawaii)

Sorcery—the use of power gained from the assistance or control of magic

Swidden (slash-and-burn or shifting agriculture)—form of cultivation characterized by the clearing and burning of existing vegetation (typically tropical forest) in order to plant; the technique improves the quality of the soil and destroys weeds and is generally associated with low population density and regions of low soil fertility

Tiki—embodiment of the male principle in Polynesian (Maori and Marquesan) mythology often depicted as the first man or superhuman creator of mankind

General Bibliography

Aoki, Diane, and Norman Douglas. *Moving Images of the Pacific Islands: A Guide to Films and Videos*, 3d ed. Honolulu: Center for Pacific Islands Studies, University of Hawaii, 1994.

Bodley, J., ed. *Tribal Peoples and Development Issues: A Global Overview*. Mountain View, CA: Mayfield Publishing Company, 1988.

Connell, J., and R. Howitt, eds. *Mining and Indigenous Peoples in the Pacific Rim*. Sydney: Oxford University Press, 1991.

Cordell, John, ed. "Western Oceania: Caring for the Ancestral Domain." *CS Quarterly* 15(2): 2–76, 1991.

Figiel, Sia. *Where We Once Belonged*. Honolulu: University of Hawaii Press, 1997.

Hau'ofa, Epeli. "The Ocean in Us." *The Contemporary Pacific* 10(2): 392–410, 1998.

Hau'ofa, Epeli. "Our Sea of Islands." *The Contemporary Pacific* 6(1): 147–161, 1994.

Hays, Terence, ed. *Encyclopedia of World Cultures*. Vol. II. *Oceania*. Boston: G. K. Hall & Co., 1991.

Hobart, Mark, ed. *An Anthropological Critique of Development: The Growth of Ignorance*. London: Routledge, 1993.

Howe, K. R., Robert C. Kiste, and Brij V. Lal. *Tides of History: The Pacific Islands in the Twentieth Century*. Honolulu: University of Hawaii Press, 1994.

Keesing, Roger. *Custom and Confrontation: The Kwaio Struggle for Cultural Autonomy*. Chicago: University of Chicago Press, 1992.

Linnekin, Jocelyn, and Lin Poyer. *Cultural Identity and Ethnicity in the Pacific*. Honolulu: University of Hawaii Press, 1990.

Marshall, Leslie, ed. *Infant Care and Feeding in the South Pacific*. New York: Gordon & Breach, 1985.

Miller, Mark, ed. *State of the Peoples: A Global Human Rights Report on Societies in Danger*. Cultural Survival, Boston: Beacon Press, 1993.

Oliver, Douglas. *Oceania: The Native Cultures of Australia and the Pacific Islands*, 2 vols. Honolulu: University of Hawaii Press, 1989.

Reyes, Luis I. *Made in Paradise: Hollywood's Films of Hawai'i and the South Seas*. Honolulu: Mutual Publishing, 1995.

Trask, Haunani-Kay. *From a Native Daughter: Colonialism and Sovereignty in Hawai'i*. Monroe, ME: Common Courage Press, 1993.

Watson, Virginia Drew. *Anyan's Story: A New Guinea Woman in Two Worlds*. Seattle: University of Washington Press, 1997.

JOURNALS

The Contemporary Pacific: A Journal of Island Affairs
Journal of Pacific History
Journal of the Polynesian Society
Mankind
Manoa: A Pacific Journal of International Writing
Oceania
Pacific Studies

FILM

Cannibal Tours. O'Rourke & Associates, 1987. Producer, Director and Writer: Denis O'Rourke.

WWW SITES

Cultural Survival
http://www.cs.org

Mookini Library—Oceania and Pacific Links
http://www.uhh.hawaii.edu/~mookini/oceanialinks.htm

National Geographic Magazine
http://www.nationalgeographic.com/index.html

Pacific Islands Information
http://www.pacificislands.com/countries

Pacific Islands Internet Resources Homepage
http://nic2.hawaii.net/~ogden/piir/index.html

University of Hawaii Press
http://www2.hawaii.edu/uhpress/UHPHome.html

Index

Index

About the Editor and Contributors

DAVID J. BOYD is an associate professor of anthropology at the University of California, Davis.

RICHARD FEINBERG is a professor of anthropology in the Department of Anthropology at Kent State University, Kent, Ohio.

JUDITH M. FITZPATRICK is a consultant anthropologist in Berkeley, California and conducts research with the Tropical Health Program, University of Queensland, Brisbane, Australia.

DAVID HYNDMAN is a reader in anthropology in the Department of Anthropology and Sociology at the University of Queensland, Brisbane, Queensland, Australia.

BRIJ V. LAL is professor of history and head of the Centre for the Contemporary Pacific in the Research School of Pacific and Asian Studies at the Australian National University, Canberra, Australia.

LAMONT LINDSTROM is a professor of anthropology at the University of Tulsa, Tulsa, Oklahoma.

CLUNY MACPHERSON is an associate professor in the Department of Sociology, University of Auckland, Auckland, New Zealand.

DAVID F. MARTIN is a research fellow at the Centre for Aboriginal Economic and Policy Research at the Australian National University, Canberra, Australia.

IAN J. MCNIVEN is a lecturer in the School of Fine Arts, Classical Studies and Archaeology at the University of Melbourne, Melbourne, Australia.

CLIVE MOORE is an associate professor of history at the University of Queensland, Brisbane, Australia.

JANE FREEMAN MOULIN is a professor of ethnomusicology in the Department of Music at the University of Hawaii at Manoa, Honolulu, Hawaii.

KAREN L. NERO is a senior lecturer in the Department of Anthropology, University of Auckland, New Zealand.

EUGENE OGAN is a professor emeritus of anthropology at the University of Minnesota, Minneapolis, and conducts Pacific Island research from Honolulu, Hawaii.

GLENN PETERSEN is a professor of anthropology and international affairs in the Department of Sociology and Anthropology at Baruch College, City University of New York, New York.

NANCY J. POLLOCK is a senior lecturer in anthropology and a member of the Masters in Development, Board of Studies at Victoria University, Wellington, New Zealand.

LYNETTE RUSSELL is a research fellow in the School of History and Gender Studies at Monash University, Melbourne, Australia.

JAAP TIMMER is a doctoral student with the Irian Jaya Studies Project at the University of Leiden, Leiden, the Netherlands.

LEONTINE VISSER teaches in the Department of Anthropology at the University of Amsterdam, the Netherlands.